Race Relations in the United States, 1900–1920

Race Relations in the United States
Ronald H. Bayor, General Editor

Race Relations in the United States, 1900–1920
John F. McClymer

Race Relations in the United States, 1920–1940
Leslie V. Tischauser

Race Relations in the United States, 1940–1960
Thomas J. Davis

Race Relations in the United States, 1960–1980
Thomas Upchurch

Race Relations in the United States, 1980–2000
Timothy Messer-Kruse

Race Relations in the United States, 1900–1920

John F. McClymer

Race Relations in the United States
Ronald H. Bayor, General Editor

GREENWOOD PRESS
Westport, Connecticut • London

Library of Congress Cataloging-in-Publication Data

McClymer, John F.
  Race relations in the United States, 1900–1920 / John F. McClymer.
      p. cm. — (Race relations in the United States)
  Includes bibliographical references and index.
  ISBN 978-0-313-33717-8 (set: alk. paper)
  ISBN 978-0-313-33935-6 (vol.: alk. paper)
    1. United States—Race relations—History—20th century. 2. United States—
  Ethnic relations—History—20th century. 3. Racism—United States—History—20th
  century. 4. Minorities—United States—Social conditions—20th century. I. Title.
    E184.A1M148 2009
    305.800973—dc22   2008031362

British Library Cataloguing in Publication Data is available.

Copyright © 2009 by John F. McClymer

All rights reserved. No portion of this book may be
reproduced, by any process or technique, without the
express written consent of the publisher.

Library of Congress Catalog Card Number: 2008031362
ISBN: 978-0-313-33935-6 (vol.)
        978-0-313-33717-8 (set)

First published in 2009

Greenwood Press, 88 Post Road West, Westport, CT 06881
An imprint of Greenwood Publishing Group, Inc.
www.greenwood.com

Printed in the United States of America

The paper used in this book complies with the
Permanent Paper Standard issued by the National
Information Standards Organization (Z39.48–1984).

10 9 8 7 6 5 4 3 2 1

Contents

Series Foreword *by Ronald H. Bayor*   vii
Introduction   ix

1900s   1
   Timeline   1
   Overview   7
   Key Events   11
   Voices of the Decade   23
   Race Relations by Group   42
   Law and Government   56
   Media and Mass Communications   60
   Cultural Scene   62
   Influential Theories and Views of Race Relations   66
   Resource Guide   69

1910s   75
   Timeline   75
   Overview   81
   Key Events   87
   Voices of the Decade   115
   Race Relations by Group   132
   Law and Government   144
   Cultural Scene   148
   Media and Mass Communications   152

Influential Theories and Views of Race Relations	153
Resource Guide	155
Selected Bibliography	165
Index	171

Series Foreword

W.E.B. Du Bois, an influential African American civil rights activist, educator, and scholar, wrote in 1903 that "the problem of the twentieth century is the problem of the color line." Although Du Bois spoke only of the situation affecting African Americans, we now know that the twentieth century brought issues to the fore that affected all of America's racial and ethnic groups. It was a century that started with vicious attacks on blacks and other minority Americans as evident in the 1906 Atlanta race riot and included within its years substantial civil rights gains in legislation and public attitudes as revealed by the Civil Rights Act of 1964 and the Voting Rights Act of 1965. Everything that occurred took place during the time of two world wars, the Great Depression, the Cold War, the turbulent 1960s, the Civil Rights and Women's movements, the rise of the Conservative movement, and the Persian Gulf and Iraqi wars.

The first volumes in the *Race Relations in the United States* series include coverage of significant events, influential voices, race relations history, legislation, media influences, culture, and theories of inter-group interactions that have been evident in the twentieth century and related to race. Each volume covers two decades and encapsulates the state of race relations by decade. A standard format is followed per decade, allowing comparison of topics through the century. Historians have written the topical essays in an encyclopedic style, to give students and general readers a concise, yet authoritative overview of race relations for the decade studied.

Coverage per decade includes a Timeline, Overview, Key Events, Voices of the Decade, Race Relations by Group, Law and Government, Media and Mass Communications, Cultural Scene, Influential Theories and Views on Race, and a Resource Guide. Furthermore, each volume contains an introduction for the two decades and a selected bibliography and index. Historical photos complement the set.

The volumes not only deal with African Americans, Native Americans, Latinos, and Asian Americans but also with religious entities such as Jewish

Americans. The history is a fascinating story that deals with such personalities as Henry Ford, Marcus Garvey, Martin Luther King, Jr., Cesar Chavez and Dolores Huerta, Russell Means, and George Wallace; defining events such as the imprisonment of Japanese Americans during World War II, the 1943 Zoot suit riots in California against Mexican Americans, the Selma to Montgomery Civil Rights march in 1965, and the American Indian Movement's occupation of Wounded Knee, South Dakota in 1973; and legislation and court cases deciding who could enter the country and who could become a citizen. The 1960s as a decade of new civil rights acts, immigration, laws and cultural changes are covered along with the increase in new immigration that marked the 1980s and 90s. The volumes will familiarize readers with the role of the Ku Klux Klan, the fear of a "Yellow Peril," and the stereotypes that impeded the attainment of equality for many minorities.

The books' focus will enable readers to understand the progress that has been made in the face of relentless persecution and oppression. As the year 2000 approached and passed, the United States was a different country than it had been in 1900. Many problems remained in relation to immigration and civil rights, but the days of lynching, racially discriminatory laws, and culturally negative stereotypes have largely faded. The story is a positive one of growth and change, but one that provides lessons on the present and future role of race relations.

One of the enduring changes that can be seen is on TV where the human landscape has evolved from ugly images of racial and ethnic groups to more multicultural and accepting views. When television first appeared, African Americans, Native Americans, Asian Americans, and Hispanic Americans were portrayed in negative ways. Blacks were often portrayed as ignorant servants and Native Americans as savages. "Stepin Fetchit," Charlie Chan, wild Indians, and the "Frito Bandito" are gone. These negative images evident in the 1950s would not find a place in today's media. By itself, that represents a significant change in attitudes and indicates the progress that has been made in inter-group relations. How this happened is what students and general readers will find in these volumes.

Ronald H. Bayor
Series Editor

Introduction

The opening decades of the twentieth century witnessed worsening white racism—as measured by numbers of lynchings, race riots in which white mobs attacked black neighborhoods, and ever more elaborate segregation laws. At the same time, hostility to immigrants, especially the so-called new immigrants from southern and eastern Europe, grew exponentially. Anti-Catholicism and anti-Semitism grew more virulent. It was an era of "exclusionary nationalism," to use the historian Gary Gerstle's apt phrase.[1] Yet these decades also saw African Americans, immigrants and their children, Catholics and Jews take the lead in shaping a new, diverse, and multiracial culture and society. This book explores this paradox. Why did racism and nativism grow worse? What forms did the "exclusionary nationalism" they fostered take? How did the objects of these hatreds seek to protect themselves? How did blacks and white ethnics come to shape American popular culture in the face of such discrimination? In seeking to answer these questions, we will look closely at several key events for each decade, read the words of influential people, and analyze changes in law and government, media, and culture, as well as the experiences of major ethnic and racial groups. The hope is that this multipronged approach will enable readers to find their own way through the history of the early twentieth century.

In choosing key events, I have tried to tell important stories in fresh ways. Some, such as the story of the Triangle Fire or the "Bread and Roses" strike in Lawrence, Massachusetts, are well known. Others, such as the Philippine Reservation at the St. Louis World's Fair, are not. But each illumines a crucial aspect of the history of race and ethnicity in the United States. Similarly, some of the voices chosen are familiar; others have long been forgotten. All spoke to and for their age, and all have something to say to us as well.

Each decade's story can stand alone. There is a chronology of events and development for each, along with separate listings of recommended resources for further study. Nonetheless, several themes characterize the entire period. W.E.B.

Du Bois, a founder of the National Association for the Advancement of Colored People (NAACP), expressed the most important of these:

> THE problem of the twentieth century is the problem of the color line; the relation of the darker to the lighter races of men in Asia and Africa, in America and the islands of the sea.[2]

Viewed from the perspective of the twenty-first century, it is only too apparent that Du Bois, the most influential civil rights activist of the first half of the twentieth century, was right. As early as 1835, Alexis De Tocqueville, the eminent French traveler and political thinker, predicted in *Democracy in America* that slavery could not long survive. Great Britain and France had abolished it. The newly independent countries of South America, with the exception of Brazil and the remaining Spanish possessions of Cuba and Puerto Rico, had done the same. But racial prejudice would remain. As De Tocqueville wrote,

> slavery recedes, but the prejudice to which it has given birth is immovable. Whoever has inhabited the United States must have perceived that in those parts of the Union in which the Negroes are no longer slaves they have in no wise drawn nearer to the whites. On the contrary, the prejudice of race appears to be stronger in the states that have abolished slavery than in those where it still exists; and nowhere is it so intolerant as in those states where servitude has never been known.[3]

In the North, he observed, blacks might vote in several states, but only at the risk of life and limb. They could sue but would encounter only white judges and jurors. They could not attend the same theaters or schools or churches as whites. They could not seek treatment in the same hospitals or be interred in the same graveyards. The "Negro is free, but he can share neither the rights, nor the pleasures, nor the labor, nor the afflictions, nor the tomb of him whose equal he has been declared to be; and he cannot meet him upon fair terms in life or in death."[4]

Tocqueville doubted that whites in America would ever accept blacks as their equals. Du Bois, too, had doubts but also hopes. The latter rested upon no evidence of improvements in race relations. If anything, relations were deteriorating when he wrote. Instead, his hopes were grounded in necessity. Whites had to overcome their prejudices if only because the domination of Asia, Africa, Latin America, and the Pacific Islands by white Europeans and Americans could not endure over the long term. Closer to home, Du Bois thought that white America could not permanently maintain its regime of segregation and discrimination.

In this, too, Du Bois was right. Things would change for the better. But not at first. During the first two decades of the twentieth century, race relations remained poisonous. The Great Migration, the movement of hundreds of thousands and then millions of African Americans out of the rural South to the urban and industrial North that began in 1915, would in the long run help change the prospects of blacks for the better. They would gain voting rights. They would improve their economic and educational opportunities. But, at first, the Great Migration provoked race riots and other violence as whites sought to drive the newcomers out.

The color line was *the* problem of the new century but hardly the *only* problem. Ethnic and religious hatreds also divided American society. The longest standing of these was anti-Catholicism, which dated back to the founding of the colonies. Until the 1830s, however, America was an almost entirely Protestant country, and anti-Catholicism remained largely rhetorical. That changed abruptly as large numbers of Irish and German Catholics emigrated to the United States in the 1840s and thereafter in response to famine and political turmoil in their homelands. By the mid-1850s, the Know-Nothings exploited distrust of, and disdain for, Catholics to sweep into power in a number of states. The Know-Nothings collapsed, in part because of their leaders' corruption and in part as a result of the rise of the new Republican Party. Secession, war, and Reconstruction of the South dominated people's concerns throughout the 1860s and 1870s. But, by the 1880s, sectarian hatreds again came to the fore.

On March 13, 1887, Henry Bowers, a lawyer from Iowa, launched the American Protective Association in Clinton, Iowa. Like the Know-Nothings, it was a secret anti-Catholic organization pledged to removing Catholic teachers from public schools and banning Catholics from running for elective office. Unlike the Know-Nothings, the Association never succeeded in electing governors or congressmen, even during its peak years, between 1891 and 1896. Nonetheless, its ability to enroll millions of members testified both to the pervasive nature of anti-Catholicism and to Catholic success in claiming important niches in American public life. In many northern and midwestern cities, Irish and German politicians controlled mayor's offices, city councils, and school boards, thereby convincing nativists that they intended to gain control of the Republic.

In the 1880s, the sources of European immigration to the United States shifted south and east from Great Britain, Scandinavia, and Germany to Italy, Poland, Hungary, and Russia. This exacerbated existing sectarian hatreds as millions of Catholics and Jews added to the nation's religious and ethnic diversity.

Anti-Semitism, previously peripheral, became a major issue. Colleges and universities established quotas to limit the number of Jewish students. Resorts, golf and tennis clubs, and hotels refused to admit Jews. Not as pervasive or as virulent as anti-Catholicism, anti-Semitism nonetheless was a disheartening instance of an increasingly intolerant and less inclusive America.

The white Protestants of northern and western European backgrounds who dominated the economy, the universities, and national politics responded to the growing diversity of the population by proclaiming themselves the only real Americans. Everyone else, they decreed, must become like them. Nativism thus combined a sense of entitlement—they were the real Americans, descendants of those who founded the nation—and a sense of endangerment. These alien peoples were threatening to change America, displacing them in the process. As a result, concern over whether various racial, religious, and ethnic communities could assimilate peaked in the 1900s and 1910s.

Assimilation meant learning English, even though there was no official national language. It meant attending public schools, taught by Protestants rather than by second-generation Irish-American spinsters. The existence of Catholic and Orthodox parochial schools and Jewish yeshivas, in contrast, seemed to offer proof of an unwillingness to assimilate. So did foreign-language newspapers, mutual benefit societies (virtually every group founded these to tide members over periods of unemployment or other hardships), and saloons and other businesses that catered to a particular ethnic or racial clientele.

The programs of the Bureau of Indian Affairs provide an example of what the demand that non-WASPs (White Anglo-Saxon Protestants) assimilate meant in practice. Students in its schools not only had to become literate in English; they had to take an English name. They had to wear American-style clothes, cut their hair to white standards, and abandon tribal life.

Many Indians and non-Indians alike refused to conform. They insisted upon their right to their own names, languages, schools, religious beliefs, and cultures. Many others could not conform. African Americans found themselves in this category regardless of their attitudes toward white values. A small minority of fair-skinned blacks could "pass" as whites. The rest could not escape their racial identity or the discrimination that went with it. A somewhat larger number of Hispanics, like the movie star Ramon Navarro, could live as whites. For most, skin color, a Spanish name, and an accent identified them as Mexicans.[5] In much of the Southwest, Hispanics faced the same discrimination as blacks.

For people from Asia, the situation was equally bleak. Congress had excluded immigrants from China in 1882. In the 1900s, white Californians and other westerners successfully campaigned to exclude the Japanese and Koreans, as well. Those already in the country were prohibited by California law from owning property and were barred from occupations, from cutting hair to plumbing, that required a license. They were ineligible for citizenship,[6] and the California Supreme Court ruled in 1852 that they were covered by the provision of the state constitution that prevented blacks from testifying against whites. Paradoxically, their children were all U.S. citizens by birth and thus could own property, testify in court, and hold any occupation. But they were still treated as "Chinks" and "Japs" by hostile whites.

Immigrants from Canada and Europe found that their prospects directly depended upon their country of origin and their religion. English-speaking Protestants from Canada, for example, experienced virtually no discrimination of any kind. French-speaking Catholics from Quebec, in contrast, were "the Chinese of the Eastern States," according to Carroll D. Wright, director of the Massachusetts Bureau of the Statistics of Labor.[7] As a rule of thumb, Protestants were more welcome than Catholics, Jews, or Russian, Greek, and Serbian Orthodox Christians were. Immigrants from Great Britain (excluding Irish Catholics), Scandinavia, and Germany were more welcome than those from Italy, Poland, Hungary, Greece, or the Middle East.

There was a queue, a pecking order.[8] Where one stood on this line that led to jobs, housing, education, and other opportunities was a function of the public repute of one's group. White Anglo-Saxon Protestants stood first in line. Right behind were Protestant immigrants from northern and western Europe and English-speaking Canada. Then came other European groups, each conscious of its own and others' places in the queue and each struggling to elbow the others aside.[9] Last in line were people of color—Indians, Asians, Hispanics, and African Americans.

Different groups adopted different strategies to get ahead. The Irish and the Jews, for example, placed special emphasis upon education. For the Irish, this meant putting more emphasis upon educating girls than boys. For Jews, it meant the reverse.[10] African Americans had significantly more education on average than European immigrants. But, because of discrimination, their higher educational attainments did not translate into economic success. Poles, Italians, and some other European strove to own property, especially houses. Protestant groups, including blacks, tended to ally with the Republican Party, while Catholics and, to a lesser extent, Jews became Democrats.

Virtually all groups emphasized patronizing their own. French-Canadians in Worcester, Massachusetts, for example, insisted upon French-speaking clerks in downtown department stores, even when they were themselves fluent in English. As a consequence, all racial and ethnic groups developed professional and business classes. Each sought out doctors, lawyers, teachers, undertakers, saloonkeepers, and clergy from within its own community. Each bought its drugs, vegetables, baked goods, sausages, and other meats from people with the same roots.

These professionals and businessmen provided leadership for the group. They organized the "days" each group celebrated, such as St. Patrick's Day or *Midsommar* or Mardi Gras. They, especially the journalists and clergy, mounted public defenses of the group when it came under attack. And they encouraged political participation. Rabbis, priests, and ministers routinely organized naturalization clubs among their congregants. As one French-Canadian priest put it, "How long have you been someone? Since you started to vote!"

As first the Irish and then other ethnics began to vote, they pressed the political parties to nominate members of their group for office and to put them on the public payroll. By 1900, Irish policemen and Irish schoolteachers had become commonplace throughout the North and the Midwest. These successes spurred other groups to follow the example of the Irish. The so-called balanced ticket, the slate of candidates that reflected the relative voting strength and reliability of the various groups in a city or state, became normative. Progressive Era reformers, called Goo Goos because of their advocacy of "good government," decried ethnic, religious, and racial politics. The voters should choose the best man for the office. But ethnic, religious, and racial groups continued to insist upon voting for one of their own.

Political success meant a measure of real power. The Irish ran Tammany Hall in New York City from the fall of the Tweed Ring, in the 1870s, through the 1930s.

Tammany politicians, in turn, ran New York City for most of that time. This meant jobs, and not just on the public rolls. Contractors with the city learned to set aside jobs for friends of key politicians. As other groups learned to push for their portion of the spoils, the Irish learned, grudgingly, to share the wealth.

In the South, the opposite was happening. There whites succeeded in disenfranchising African Americans in open defiance of the Fifteenth Amendment. State after state adopted the "grandfather clause," which limited voting eligibility to those whose grandfather had been eligible to vote, or the literacy test, which allowed white registrars to disqualify voters (including many whites) who could not explain the meaning of some obscure portion of the state constitution, or the poll tax, which priced the vote out of the reach of poor blacks and whites alike. As they lost the vote, blacks also lost political jobs. There had been African American postmasters, deputy sheriffs, and other officeholders in the years following the Civil War. With disenfranchisement came the loss of patronage.

Asians also could not follow the Irish example, as they were ineligible for citizenship. Latinos born in the United States were citizens but faced the same disenfranchisement that afflicted African Americans. Lack of political influence did much to keep people of color at the back of the queue.

However much discriminated against, Catholics, Jews, and African Americans began to shape American popular culture in powerful ways. One was music. Prior to the twentieth century, popular American songs had been, for the most part, copies of English music hall ditties and ballads. But, as the Czech composer Antonin Dvorak commented during his tenure from 1892 to 1895 as conductor of what became the New York Philharmonic, there was an original American music waiting to be discovered in the melodies of African Americans:

> I am satisfied that the future music of this country must be founded upon what are called the Negro melodies. These can be the foundation of a serious and original school of composition, to be developed into a settled conviction. These beautiful and varied themes are the product of the soil . . . they are American . . . they are the folksongs of America, and your composers must turn to them. All the great musicians have borrowed from the songs of the common people.[11]

Almost as soon as Dvorak said this, Scott Joplin published the "Maple Leaf Rag," and the ragtime rage began. It lasted through World War I, when it gave way to other forms of black-influenced music such as jazz and the blues. Whites also wrote rags. Joseph Lamb, in particular, was a master of the form. And other whites wrote bouncy, rag-inflected tunes, like Irving Berlin's "Alexander's Ragtime Band." But Dvorak had it right. American music would spring from African American sources.

With ragtime came a new craze, dancing. Suddenly the waltz had competition from the foxtrot, the turkey trot, the bunny hug, and other "animal" dances. Virtually all of the new dances originated in African American communities and then spread among whites. Whites could learn the new steps by paying to see

Vernon and Irene Castle, two of the biggest stars of vaudeville. The Castles, who were white, performed somewhat more decorous versions of the dances than one would find in a black nightspot, but they did insist upon using James Reese Europe's Society Orchestra, since, they maintained, only black musicians could play the new music properly. Going to see the Castles was expensive. Most working-class white ethnics, who eagerly embraced the music and the dances, instead took lessons, at twenty-five cents each, at local dance halls. Their white instructors, in turn, had learned the steps from black entertainers.

European ethnics also began to influence American culture. Minstrel shows in which white and, later, black performers "corked up" and sang songs and told jokes in what was supposed to be "Negro" dialect had dominated popular entertainment from the antebellum years through the late nineteenth century. Then vaudeville came into its own. Vaudeville houses sprang up in every middle-size and large city. Entrepreneurs then linked them into "circuits," that is, theaters in various cities that featured the same acts so that performers would sign up for an entire season traveling one or another circuit. The typical vaudeville bill featured nine acts, with the star performers coming on "next to closing." Acts included jugglers, acrobats, dancers, singers, comedians, trained dogs, plus any novelty that might bring in a crowd. The swimmer Annette Kellerman performed in a glass tank to packed houses. The heavyweight boxer John L. Sullivan cashed in on his fame, as well.

Black entertainers could not perform in whites-only theaters in the South and encountered discrimination in the North, as well. Nonetheless, many made it in vaudeville. Bert Williams, the great comedian, headlined the Ziegfeld Follies. So did the dancer Bill "Bojangles" Robinson. Innumerable white ethnics like Harrigan and Hart, Fannie Brice, George M. Cohan, and Gallagher and Sheen, one of many acts to find comedy in ethnic difference, also made it big in vaudeville.

Show business was much more of a melting pot than the rest of the society. The comedian Ole Olson, whose character was a naïve Swedish lumberjack, was born in the United States and had to learn to speak with a Swedish accent. In one celebrated "bit," he barely escaped being trapped into marrying a middle-aged Irish spinster. Al Jolson, son of Russian Jewish immigrants, sang of his longing for his "Mammy" in the South in blackface. Vaudeville exploited racial, religious, and ethnic stereotypes. But it celebrated talent. Vaudeville brought African Americans and white ethnics, and their comedy and music, to local theaters. Comic strips did the same with local newspapers. The hero of the first strip, the Yellow Kid, was Irish American. The Katzenjammer Kids were German. Perhaps the most influential of the early comics, Krazy Kat, was drawn by George Herriman, an African American.

The most important new medium was film. Its pioneers were first- and second-generation immigrants, most often Jews. At first, movies lasted only a few minutes and were shown in storefronts. Admission was five cents. Within a decade, Cecil B. DeMille, a second-generation Jewish American, produced and directed the first full-length feature, *The Squaw Man*, about an Indian woman who sacrifices her own life for her white husband and their son. Two years later, in 1915, D. W. Griffith made *The Birth of a Nation*, a film that transformed the entire business of movie making. With Griffith came more sophisticated use of the camera, new techniques in editing, and the star system. Lillian Gish, who played the heroine in many Griffith films, was perhaps the first movie star.

The Birth of a Nation glorified the Ku Klux Klan and the doctrine of white supremacy. The National Association for the Advancement of Colored People (NAACP) struggled long and unsuccessfully to prevent it being shown or, at least, to have the most racially derogatory scenes cut out. As the NAACP leaders realized, the new medium would exercise a hypnotic-like hold over the American imagination. And its portrayal of blacks could scarcely have been more prejudicial. They lusted after white women, just as apologists for lynching claimed. They were lazy, ignorant, and stupid—clearly unfit for the vote. Blacks would begin to make their own movies and offer more positive portrayals, but not until the late 1910s.

Griffith did make a feature that condemned prejudice against Asians, *Broken Blossoms* (1919). It was a failure at the box office. So was *Intolerance* (1916), his film that showed the evil effects of racial, religious, and ethnic stereotypes throughout history. Few movies of the period focused upon the European ethnic experience. One that did was Charlie Chaplin's *The Immigrant* (1917). Chaplin himself was an immigrant, as was the biggest female star (Lillian Gish excepted), Mary Pickford. They were among the first of a long stream of immigrants from Europe and Canada who would carve out places for themselves in Hollywood.

Perhaps the strongest influence that blacks and white ethnics exerted was over behavior. At the beginning of the new century, there was a new question: Who would protect the working girl? There had been women in the labor force at least since the building of the textile mills in Lowell, Lawrence, and other New England cities. In Lowell, the companies built special boarding houses, complete with matrons, for their female employees. Such corporate paternalism did not disappear completely, but it soon ceased to characterize the workplace. Instead, more and more young men and women began to live alone or with roommates. By the turn of the twentieth century, reformers like Jane Addams, founder of Hull House, in Chicago, had identified the problem of unsupervised young people adrift in the city as a serious threat to the well-being of the whole society.

Such working girls and boys would fall prey to unscrupulous businessmen who would exploit their desire for excitement and pleasure. So Addams feared. She had in mind operators of dance halls, many located above saloons, as well as of amusement parks and other places that offered entertainment unalloyed with inhibition. There was no end of people who fit her description. Out to make a buck, they offered whatever their customers wanted. But the working girls and boys did not agree with Addams that these "places" were dens of iniquity. Instead, they developed a new ethos and a set of new behaviors that soon became normative for their middle- and upper-class contemporaries.

These black and white ethnic pioneers did not have the dance halls, amusement parks, and movie theaters to themselves for very long. Middle- and upper-class young people shared their love for ragtime and "rough" dancing, for amusement park rides that afforded opportunities for sexual play, and for pleasure. A new consumer culture was in the making, one keyed to gratification, and the new ethos complemented it to a tee.

NOTES

1. Gary Gerstle, *American Crucible: Race and Nationality in Twentieth Century America* (Princeton, NJ: Princeton University Press, 2001).

2. W.E.B. Du Bois, "The Freedman's Bureau," *Atlantic Monthly* 87 (1901): p. 354.

3. Ohio might serve as an example of Tocqueville's claim that racial prejudice was strongest in states where slavery had never existed (*Democracy in America,* vol. 1, p. 373). In 1836, James Birney launched an antislavery paper, *The Philanthropist,* in Cincinnati. On July 30, 1836, a mob destroyed his press, demolished his paper's offices, and attacked the city's free blacks.

4. Alexis de Toqueville, *Democracy in America* (New York: Alfred A. Knopf, 1945), vol. 1, p. 374.

5. Puerto Rico became an American possession as a result of the Spanish-American War. There was very little migration from the island to the mainland in these decades. The same was true of Latin American countries.

6. The first Congress, in 1790, limited naturalization to free white people.

7. See John F. McClymer, "Carroll D. Wright, L'Abbe Jean-Baptiste Primeau, and French-Canadian Families," in *The Human Tradition in the Gilded Age and Progressive Era,* ed. Ballard C. Campbell (Lanham, MD: Rowman & Littlefield, 2000), pp. 2–18.

8. Stanley Lieberson, *A Piece of the Pie: Blacks and White Immigrants since 1880* (Berkeley: University of California Press, 1980).

9. See Charles W. Estus Sr. and John McClymer, "Guest Editors' Introduction," *The Swedish-American Historical Quarterly,* vol. 46 (January 1995), for a discussion of such ethnic "triangulating."

10. See Hasia R. Diner, *Erin's Daughters in America: Irish Immigrant Women in the Nineteenth Century* (Baltimore, MD: Johns Hopkins University Press, 1983) and Irving Howe, *World of Our Fathers: The Journey of the East European Jews to America and the Life They Found and Made,* 30th anniversary edition (New York: New York University Press, 2005).

11. Quoted in "Real Value of Negro Melodies," New York Herald, May 21, 1893.

1900s

Timeline

1900–1910	A total of 8,795,386 immigrants arrive in the United States, primarily from Europe.
	Conditions on Indian reservations remain deplorable; there are very high rates of unemployment, alcoholism, homicide, and suicide. Unknown numbers of Indians leave the reservations and try to assimilate into white culture.
1900	
January 20	Representative George H. White (Rep., N.C.) introduces the first national antilynching measure; it does not pass. Nor would any of the other bills that sought to make lynching a federal crime. Lynchings, meanwhile, continue to claim more than 100 victims a year, most of them African Americans.
March	A bubonic plague outbreak in San Francisco leads to Chinatown being cordoned off and quarantined. This is in keeping with the common, but erroneous, theory that particular races are more likely to carry particular diseases than others.
April 30	The Organic Act makes all U.S. laws applicable to Hawaii, ending contract labor in the islands. Many Japanese, Chinese, and Filipino workers had contracted to work in the pineapple and other harvests in Hawaii while still in their native countries.

	Japanese Hawaiian plantation workers begin migrating to the mainland. This quickly led to calls for the exclusion of Japanese immigrants.
May 7	The first large-scale anti-Japanese protest in California is held; it is organized by various labor groups.
November 6	The presidential election becomes a national referendum on American imperialism, pitting the incumbent, William McKinley, against the Democrat and anti-imperialist William Jennings Bryan. McKinley and his vice presidential running mate, Theodore Roosevelt, win decisively.
1901	A total of 105 black Americans are lynched during the course of the year.
March	Indians in Oklahoma become U.S. citizens by legislative fiat; the objective is to speed up the territory's eligibility for statehood, on the one hand, and to facilitate the transfer of valuable mineral rights, especially petroleum and natural gas, to non-Indians.
March 4	Congressman George H. White gives up his seat. No African American would serve in Congress for the next 28 years.
September 6	President William McKinley is shot by a Polish–American anarchist; he dies on September 14. In response on March 31, 1903 Congress passes the Anarchist Exclusion Act, which prohibits the entry of anarchists into the United States.
October 16	President Theodore Roosevelt invites Booker T. Washington to dinner. Washington is the first black American to be invited to dine at the White House with the president. White supremacists, South and North, protest vigorously. Roosevelt shrugs off their objections but does not repeat his action.
1902	The Chinese Exclusion Act is renewed; the original law (of 1882) had a 20-year expiration date. The new law prohibits Chinese immigration permanently.
	Immigration officials and police raid Boston's Chinatown and arrest almost 250 Chinese who allegedly have no registration certificates on their persons.
	A total of 85 black Americans are lynched during the year.

July 4	Roosevelt proclaims victory in the War in the Philippines, claiming that the main fighting is over. In fact, the Filipino resistance continues for another decade.
	A riot occurs in New York City when a Jewish funeral procession is attacked by Irish-Americans.
1903	Filipino students (*pensionados*) first begin to come to the United States for higher education.
	W.E.B. Du Bois's *The Souls of Black Folk* is published. Du Bois rejects the accommodationism of Booker T. Washington and calls for a more militant campaign for African American rights.
	A total of 84 black Americans are lynched over the course of the year.
January 5	In *Lone Wolf v. Hickcock*, the Supreme Court decides against the Kiowas and Comanches who sued the Secretary of the Interior to prevent the transfer of their lands without the consent of tribal members. According to the 1867 Treaty of Medicine Lodge, tribal consent was required for the transfer. The Court rules that the land is held in trust for the tribe by the U.S. government and that, therefore, Congress can alter the provisions of the treaty. The ruling effectively gives Congress absolute power over tribal holdings.
February 11	A total of 1,500 Japanese and Mexican sugar beet workers go on strike in Oxnard, California.
April 6–7	The Kishinev Massacre, one of a series of pogroms in which Russian soldiers murder and rape Jews and burn their villages, increases the Jewish exodus from Russia. Many Russian Jewish immigrants, aided by American Jews, settle on the Lower East Side of Manhattan.
December	The American Breeders Association creates a Committee on Eugenics to lobby for laws requiring the involuntary sterilization of those deemed mentally defective, unwed mothers, and the offspring of those alleged to be hereditary criminals. David Starr Jordan, president of Stanford University, is a leading supporter, as is Prescott Hall, founder of the Immigration Restriction League.
	First group of 7,000 Korean workers arrives in Hawaii to work as strikebreakers; many Japanese workers are on strike.
1904	The Louisiana Centennial Exposition World's Fair opens in Saint Louis. The Philippine Reservation, a 47-acre re-

creation of parts of Manila and of Filipino villages, becomes the leading attraction.

A total of 76 black Americans are lynched during the year.

1905 For the first time in American history, more than one million immigrants come to the United States in a single year.

Congress creates the Border Patrol to prevent Asian workers from coming to the United States through Mexico.

A total of 57 black Americans are lynched over the course of the year.

February 23 "The Japanese Invasion: The Problem of the Hour" reads the front page of the *San Francisco Chronicle*; this is typical of the escalating antipathy toward the Japanese in the Bay Area.

May 14 The Asiatic Exclusion League is formed in San Francisco. In attendance are labor leaders and European immigrants. This begins the formal organization of the anti-Japanese movement.

California's Civil Code is amended to outlaw marriage between whites and "Mongolians." Included in that category are Chinese, Japanese, and Koreans.

July 11–13 African American intellectuals and activists, led by W.E.B. Du Bois and William Monroe Trotter, begin the Niagara Movement. It explicitly repudiates the leadership of Booker T. Washington and lays the foundation for the modern civil rights movement.

1906 A total of 62 black Americans are lynched over the course of the year.

April 18 The San Francisco earthquake and fire destroy all municipal records, including those concerning immigration, so Chinese immigrants are able to claim they are U.S. citizens and have the right to bring their wives and children to America. This leads to an influx of so-called picture-book brides, women who marry immigrants by proxy while still in China and then come to America.

May	The Burke Act amends the Dawes Severalty Act of 1886, which allocated tribal lands to individual Indian families. It provides that these lands be held in trust. The Burke Act gives the Secretary of the Interior the power to remove allotments from the trust before the time set by the Dawes Act by declaring that the holders have "adopted the habits of civilized life."
June	Congress passes the Antiquities Act, which declares that Indian bones and objects found on federal land are the property of the United States and not of tribes or individual Indians.
	The Naturalization Act of 1906 makes knowledge of English a requirement for citizenship and creates the Bureau of Immigration and Naturalization in the Commerce Department to enforce immigration restrictions and supervise naturalization procedures.
August 13	In Brownsville, Texas, black troops riot against segregation.
September 22–24	In a race riot in Atlanta, 10 blacks and 2 whites are killed.
October 11	The San Francisco Board of Education segregates children of Chinese, Japanese, and Korean ancestry from the majority population.
November	The American Jewish Committee is founded. It is the first national Jewish organization.
November 6	President Theodore Roosevelt discharges three companies of black soldiers involved in the August riot. Blacks had served in the U.S. Army since the Civil War.
December	Oscar Straus is appointed Secretary of Labor and Commerce, the first Jew to hold a cabinet position.
1907	The National Liberal Immigration League is founded, largely under Jewish auspices, to fight against imposition of a literacy test for prospective immigrants.
February	Congress establishes the Dillingham Commission to investigate the impact of immigration on the United States. Its 42-volume report, published in 1911, heightens calls for the restriction of immigration from southern and eastern Europe.

March 2	The Expatriation Act terminates the citizenship of American women who marry citizens of foreign countries.
March 9	Indiana adopts the first involuntary sterilization law, the initial legislative victory for the new eugenics movement.
March 17	President Theodore Roosevelt issues Executive Order 589, which prohibits Japanese with passports for Hawaii, Mexico, or Canada to re-emigrate to the United States.
September 4	White rioters drive Asian Indians out of Bellingham, Washington. The following year, a white mob will do the same in Live Oak, California.
November 16	Congress establishes the State of Oklahoma by merging the Oklahoma and Indian Territories. This opens the former Indian Territory to additional non-Indian settlement.
1907–1908	Under the terms of the "Gentlemen's Agreement," the United States agrees not to prohibit Japanese immigration; in return, Japan agrees not to give passports to Japanese laborers. Japanese women are allowed to immigrate if they are wives of U.S. residents. The United States also agrees to seek to end discrimination against Japanese-Americans. Japan is particularly concerned about California laws such as that which requires the children of Japanese immigrants to attend segregated schools. California retains these laws and passes still other discriminatory statutes.
1908	A total of 89 black Americans are lynched over the course of the year.
January 6	In *Winters v. United States*, the Supreme Court decides in favor of Indians from the Fort Belknap reservation in Montana who had sued to keep a white settler from damming the Milk River and diverting water from their reservation. The Court holds that, when Congress created reservations, it did so with the implicit intention that Indians should have enough water to live.
August 14–19	Many are killed and wounded in a race riot in Abraham Lincoln's hometown of Springfield, Illinois. This event inspires the creation of the National Association for the Advancement of Colored People (NAACP).
October 5	Israel Zangwill's play *The Melting Pot* opens in Washington, DC. It quickly provides a powerful metaphor for those defenders of open immigration by proclaiming that the

	mixture of diverse peoples and cultures will produce a stronger America.
1909–1910	Jewish and Italian shirtwaist workers go on strike in New York City in what becomes known as "The Uprising of the Twenty Thousand." It is the first successful strike by women workers and leads to the creation of the International Ladies Garment Workers Union.
1910	A total of 69 black Americans are lynched over the course of the year.
	Croats, Serbs, and Slovenes in the United States create the Yugoslav Socialist Federation. But distrust among the groups forces the alliance to publish newspapers in the three languages.
October–November	At the New Mexican state constitutional convention, Mexican-American delegates succeed in winning a provision providing that both Spanish and English are to be used for all state business; this is in keeping with the terms of the 1848 Treaty of Guadalupe Hidalgo, which ended the War with Mexico and ceded New Mexico, Arizona, Utah, Nevada, and California to the United States.
November 20	The Mexican Revolution begins. Thousands of refugees come to the United States, beginning a migration flow that will bring more than a million Mexicans to the United States by 1930.

OVERVIEW

The determination of whites to hold blacks back during the years 1900–1910 enjoyed the blessing of the U.S. Supreme Court. In *Plessy v. Ferguson* (1896), Justice Henry Billings Brown, writing for the majority, held:

> The object of the [Fourteenth] Amendment was undoubtedly to enforce the absolute equality of the two races before the law, but in the nature of things it

could not have been intended to abolish distinctions based upon color, or to enforce social, as distinguished from political, equality, or a commingling of the two races upon terms unsatisfactory to either.[1]

Southern laws that prohibited blacks from using the same railroad cars or bathrooms or schools were all constitutional, the Court ruled, provided blacks received "separate but equal" treatment. It was a blank check for racists, and they lost no time cashing it. By the 1900s, Jim Crow laws covered virtually every aspect of daily life. There were even separate Bibles in southern courts, lest whites have to swear on the same one used by black witnesses.

Worse even than segregation was the casual violence blacks endured. Any crossing of a racial line, and whites were the sole judges of where those lines were, provoked an outraged response. This might be a tongue-lashing. It might be economic. "Uppity" African Americans found they could not find jobs, could not get loans. Or the response might involve a beating or, in thousands of cases, a lynching. Lynchings were communal events. They often involved scores or hundreds or even thousands of participants. No one feared any legal consequences. No white was ever convicted in connection with a lynching until the Supreme Court found Sheriff Joseph Shipp in contempt for failing to protect Ed Johnson from a Chattanooga mob in 1907.

Blacks were divided over how best to protect themselves. Booker T. Washington, who was born in slavery and who founded Tuskegee Institute, advised conciliation. In his famous Atlanta Compromise Address (1895), he said that in matters social the two races could be as separate as the fingers, while in economic affairs the two could cooperate as the hand. Cooperation did not mean equal opportunity, Washington continued. African Americans would accept a second-class status until they had educated themselves and could prove their worth to whites. Equality became a far-off goal. This did not satisfy younger and more militant blacks. Their spokesman was W.E.B. Du Bois, the first African American to get a Ph.D. from Harvard.

White America, for the most part, favored Washington's approach. Theodore Roosevelt, for example, invited him to lunch at the White House in 1901. Enough whites, however, saw justice in Du Bois's demand for equality for him to found the National Association for the Advancement of Colored People (NAACP) on a biracial basis in 1909. Actual progress toward equality, however, did not take place.

Most blacks remained in the South in the 1900s. The vast majority of the newcomers who crowded into the cities of the Northeast and the Midwest were white, many of them from southern and eastern Europe. In many cities—Chicago, Buffalo, New York, Pittsburgh, Worcester, Scranton, and Milwaukee are cases in point—two-thirds or more of the population were immigrants and their children. Cities, industrial villages, and farming communities all had foreign-language churches and ethnic lodges. The bigger places had foreign-language newspapers and bilingual schools. And cities had crowded ethnic neighborhoods where

W.E.B. Du Bois. Courtesy of Library of Congress.

residents could get along without using any English. They could shop, sue and be sued, get their teeth fixed, go out for a beer or to a show, get married, have children, grow old, and be buried without having to deal with a self-identified real American.

Such insularity, real and perceived, worried those "real" Americans. Some immigrant groups, they held, would never assimilate, could never assimilate. This was not a new idea. The first federal Congress passed a law in 1790 that limited citizenship to white immigrants. In 1882, Congress excluded Chinese immigration. And, in 1907, President Theodore Roosevelt negotiated the "Gentlemen's Agreement" whereby Japan agreed to prohibit its citizens from emigrating to the United States. All of the excluded were nonwhite. In the first two decades of the twentieth century, however, restrictionists targeted European immigrants.

Some did so on racial grounds. They believed that the various European ethnic groups were actually distinct races or "stocks." At the top of the racial hierarchy were Anglo-Saxons and Aryans or Nordics, that is, people from Great Britain, Germany, and Scandinavia. Next came the Alpine peoples, such as the Swiss.

At the bottom were the Mediterranean, Slavic, and Hebrew stocks—Italians, Greeks, Poles, Hungarians, and Jews. These were peoples who, according to Professor Edward A. Ross of the University of Wisconsin, had been "left behind" by evolution. The Jews aside, they were intellectually dull, lacked artistic talent, and were suited only to simple manual labor. Jews were intelligent, racial theorists conceded. And they also excelled in some of the arts. Their flaws were ones of character. They were clannish, penurious, and prone to radical politics.

Giving these stereotypes credibility was the new science of eugenics. Its central teaching was that it was possible to breed better people by encouraging the "fittest" to have more children and, even more important, by preventing the "unfit" from reproducing at all. Starting in the 1900s, more than 30 states would adopt involuntary sterilization programs. In 1927, the Supreme Court, in *Buck v. Bell*, ruled that the Fourteenth Amendment did not prevent states from sterilizing those it found to be unfit. Justice Oliver Wendell Holmes wrote, in the majority opinion, that:

> We have seen more than once that the public welfare may call upon the best citizens for their lives. It would be strange if it could not call upon those who already sap the strength of the State for these lesser sacrifices . . . in order to prevent our being swamped with incompetence. It is better for all the world, if instead of waiting to execute degenerate offspring for crime, or to let them starve for their imbecility, society can prevent those who are manifestly unfit from continuing their kind. . . . Three generations of imbeciles are enough.[2]

Carrie Buck, the young woman who contested Virginia's sterilization law, came from a family that had lived in America for generations. But eugenicists asserted that disproportionate numbers of the "defective" were new immigrants and their children.

Other restrictionists believed that new immigrants threatened the Protestant character of American civilization. Anti-Catholic feelings had deep roots. The revolutionary generation's outrage at the Quebec Act, a measure that granted religious toleration to Canadian Catholics, helped spur the drive for independence. In the 1850s, the Native American Party (the Know-Nothings) campaigned against Catholics and attracted millions of supporters. In the 1880s, the American Protective Association (APA) renewed the fight against Catholics in public office and Catholic teachers in public schools. At that time, the only major Catholic ethnic groups were the Irish and the south Germans. The new immigrants of the 1880s and thereafter were from eastern and southern Europe and included millions of Italian, Polish, Hungarian, and Lithuanian Catholics. When they voted, restrictionists complained, they did so as their priest or an Irish political boss told them.

Anti-Semitism, like anti-Catholicism, was also becoming more virulent in the new century. Millions of Jews from the Pale of Settlement (the area of the Russian Empire in which Jews had to live) and the rest of eastern Europe came to the United States. Initially, almost all settled in New York's Lower East Side neighborhood. Soon, however, there were rapidly growing Jewish communities throughout the Northeast and the Midwest. Resorts, golf and tennis clubs, and other facilities began to bar Jews. Harvard University's president, Charles W. Eliot, long resisted pressures from the Board of Governors to limit the number of Jews admitted. But, once he retired, in 1909, Harvard joined the other Ivy League schools in establishing a strict quota for Jewish applicants.

Intolerance, in short, was on the march. But so were developments in the popular culture, pioneered by African Americans and white ethnics, many of them Catholics and Jews, that would ultimately shape a new more inclusive America. Ragtime music became the rage, despite its origins in the black community. Irish and Jewish entertainers, along with some blacks, dominated vaudeville. The Harlem Renaissance in literature, music, painting, and theater would not begin until after World War I, but Eugene O'Neill and Theodore Dreiser, to mention only two examples, challenged WASP (white Anglo-Saxon Protestant) domination in the arts. Equally important, perhaps, the German American H. L. Mencken established himself as an important arbiter of literature and the theater as co-editor of *The Smart Set*.

KEY EVENTS

"OUR LITTLE BROWN BROTHERS" AT THE WORLD'S FAIR, ST. LOUIS, 1904

When the United States declared war on Spain, in 1898, the first shots were fired not in Cuba but in the Philippines. On May 1, Commodore (soon to be Admiral) George Dewey destroyed the Spanish fleet in Manila harbor. Philippine nationalists, led by Ernesto Aquinaldo, were already in the field against Spain. They and the United States made common cause and quickly succeeded in forcing the Spanish to surrender. The Filipinos expected independence. The United States had pledged not to interfere with Cuba once Spain was defeated. Aquinaldo and his followers expected that the United States would adopt the same policy in the Philippines. It did not. Instead, under the terms of the Treaty of Madrid, it purchased Spain's claim to the islands for $20 million. When the Filipinos refused to accept this outcome, the United States undertook the conquest of the archipelago. It was an extremely brutal campaign, marred by atrocities in which the Americans burned whole villages suspected of harboring "Insurrectos." An estimated quarter of a million Filipinos, out of a total population of 8 million, died. The total of U.S. dead numbered more than 12,000. By July 4, 1902, the main islands were under American control, and President Theodore Roosevelt declared the war over. Actual fighting, however, continued for another decade.

12 Race Relations in the United States, 1900–1920

In the spring of 1904, the St. Louis World's Fair opened. It officially celebrated the hundredth anniversary of the Louisiana Purchase, but its most popular attraction by far had nothing to do with Thomas Jefferson or the development of the Mississippi Valley. The *New York Times* reported:

> The fame of the Philippine exposition has captured the World's Fair city, and the most constant question which the Jefferson Guards have to answer is, "Which way to the Philippines?" This interest is largely excited by the widespread publicity which Igorot dog-eaters and head-hunters, the cannibal Moro, and the aboriginal Negrito have obtained.[3]

The Filipino "reservation," a word freighted with meaning for Americans, was a 47-acre exhibition on Filipino life and culture. It contained more than 1,100 Filipinos, clad in their native costumes (or lack thereof), housed in villages they

Straw-thatched house of a Moro Village, Philippine section of the World's Fair in St. Louis. Courtesy of Library of Congress.

built themselves using bamboo and nipa (palm), and engaging in an array of exotic dances, ceremonies, and feasts. This reservation abutted another 47-acre exhibition, the Native American reservation.

According to the *Official Guide to the World's Fair*:

> Probably the most interesting single feature of the Exposition is the Igorote[4] Village. This includes three tribes; the Bontoc, the Suyoc and the Tinguanes. The Suyocs are the miners and show their method of extracting the metal from the ore. Some of their work in copper is remarkable. They have their own rice paddies and sweet potato patch. The Bontocs are the head-hunters. Tattooing is considered an art by them, and across the chest of several chiefs in the village is recorded the result of their head-hunting expeditions. These Bontocs are the dog eaters, of whom so much has been written in the newspapers. The Tinguanes are the agriculturists and are of a milder disposition. . . . Their [the Igorotes'] religion is a kind of spirit worship.[5]

Bontoc craving for dog did indeed garner enormous press coverage. So did their dances, which preceded and followed the feasts. To white Americans, this was proof positive of their savagery and thus the need for American assistance in civilizing them.

Evidence of America's efforts at what President McKinley had called the "benevolent assimilation" of "our little brown brothers" was what the visitor to the reservation first encountered. A recreation of a portion of Manila's city wall, built by the Spanish to keep out the Chinese and other potential invaders, enclosed several large exhibits. One was a recreation of Manila's cathedral. It contained an art gallery and several statues. The main government building in Manila had also been re-created. There the fairgoer could find information about the islands' history and a collection of antique weapons.

Perhaps the most popular attraction in this portion of the reservation was a school with a Filipina teacher, a recent graduate of the Manila Normal School, as teacher colleges were then called. The 20 pupils were drawn from the children of the reservation. All lessons were in English, and visitors could observe for themselves the rapid progress the students were making.[6] Journalist Alfred Newell interviewed one:

> One of these pupils is Antaero, an Igorot boy, aged twelve. I had seen him among his own people, wearing only a breech-clout, dancing the joy-dance of his tribe, with the sunlight gleaming on his copper skin. Yet, at school he wore a coat. He is the only one of the Igorots at the Fair who can speak English. He went to an American school in Luzon [for] two years. His face is keen and bright, and his eyes have a merry sparkle. Clad in Western clothes, he would look like a dark American mulatto.
>
> "Did you like to go to school in the Philippines?" I asked him. "Yes."
> "Do you want to go back to school there?" "Yes."

"What are you going to do when you are a man?" The boy hesitated. His people were just then beating their brass instruments, as they whirled around in a dance.

"Would you like to teach school?" I continued. "Yes."

"Would you then wear clothes like these I wear?" With a laugh, Antaero pointed to the breech-clout and said: "I like to wear string-breech." String is what he called his clout.[7]

In this part of the reservation, there was a plaza, Newell pointed out, where you could rest next to a statue of Magellan, the first European to visit the Philippines, and "take in at a view the several stages of Filipino development." "On the wooded hillsides" were "the naked Igorots and Negritos," while "to the north the Moros disport themselves in Arrow Head Lake." In the Cathedral and Government building "are the products of Filipino looms and hand-work; the pictures and sculpture from Filipino studios, and, best of all, compositions, drawings, and handwork from Filipino schools." In the distance "the American Flag floats over the camps of the Filipino scouts and the constabulary."[8]

As Newell noted, the Igorots shared the spotlight with several other tribes. On the shore of Arrow Head Lake was the Visayans' village of thatched bamboo houses. It contained a Catholic church and a theater at which the Visayan orchestra gave daily concerts. Visayans, as the only Christians, uniformly struck white Americans as "one of the highest types of native civilization," as the *New York Times* put it. Edmund Mitchell, in the *Los Angeles Times*, wrote: "They are the lightest type of the semi-civilized natives." "They are a tall and handsome race, dress well, have a stringed orchestra that produces pleasing music, and observe church ceremonies of a primitive kind."[9] The "primitive" ceremonies included the Catholic mass.

"In contrast with the gentle Visayans," commented Alfred C. Newell in *The World's Work* magazine, "are the fierce Moros. . . ." All of the Moros were Muslims. "There are three tribes of Moros. Two of them, the Samal and the Lanao, are deadly enemies, and an armed guard is maintained between the villages." The Samal Moros lived along the coast of Mindanao. Edmund Mitchell reported for the *Los Angeles Times* that they were "the fierce pirates of the eastern seas, a fanatical, bloodthirsty, and treacherous race, who were never subdued by the Spaniards, and still give trouble to the Americans." He added: "To show the tenacity of their hatred, it may be mentioned that when news came to St. Louis of a recent Moro ambuscade in which over a score of American soldiers lost their lives, straightway a feast was declared in one of the Moro villages, and despite all protests, rejoicings were openly carried on for several days."[10]

Naked Samal boys entertained fairgoers by expertly paddling their boats on the lake.

The Lanao Moros lived in tree houses, to protect themselves from enemies. "The Bogobos wear more clothes than the Samal and Lanao Moros," Newell observed. "They are expert bead-workers, wear multi-colored beads, and are the most pompous of the native tribes." How he determined this last characteristic is unclear.[11]

The last Filipino village on the reservation was that of the Negritos. "Here are fourteen of the island aborigines, small, black people, amiable and cordial to visitors," wrote Newell. A special attraction for visitors was a display of archery put on by five small boys who would shoot at nickels at a distance of 20 to 25 feet. They got to keep those they hit. Newell described them as "pure pagans."[12]

The Board of Lady Managers of the Louisiana Purchase Exhibit reported that "No other one exhibit was so widely commented upon in the press and by the public as the Insular Exhibit. Everybody who went to the Exposition visited the Filipino village."[13]

Visitors did not only see seminaked villagers engaging in "dog dances" and "Moro Moro" dances complete with spears. They also witnessed Filipino Scouts and other soldiers who had cooperated with the American effort to crush the insurrection on the islands. Newell described the scene:

> If you leave the Igorot Village just before half-past five o'clock in the afternoon, you will hear a bugle; and, if you climb the short hill to the parade-ground, you will see emerging from the huge barracks called the cuartel 200 khaki-clad Filipinos. With heads erect and swinging stride they hold a dress-parade. The American flag waves over them, and a Filipino band of eighty-five musicians plays patriotic music. These men are a battalion of native constabulary, the native police, organized to keep the peace on the islands. They are selected from the various provinces and tribes. . . .
>
> The constabulary on the islands number 6,000. They have distinguished themselves in campaigns against native outlaws, and have suppressed brigandage.
>
> Hardly have the constabulary marched from the parade-grounds, when another bugle sounds, and, on a stretch of level turf behind which rise the tents of a military camp, march the Filipino scouts, clad in the regulation United States blue, with service forage caps and with a Filipino band playing. These are the picked representatives of a brigade of 5,000 native soldiers, whose mettle was tested during the insurrection, when they remained loyal to their oath of allegiance to the United States and fought their own countrymen. This efficient organization has grown from a band of scouts that led the way for General Lawton through Luzon jungles. They, too, form in line to salute the Stars and Stripes. It is an impressive sight—this long line of Filipinos in blue, stretching down the green parade-ground at sunset. It shows the real work accomplished in the Philippines—the bringing of law and order and discipline out of insurrection and ignorance—the lesson of good government.[14]

It was, in fact, the lesson of "The White Man's Burden," as the British poet Rudyard Kipling memorably phrased it. Americans had a moral obligation to bring their superior civilization to "Your new-caught, sullen peoples, Half-devil and half-child." White Americans visiting the Philippine Reservation could find its meaning in Kipling's lines. They were fighting:

> The savage wars of peace—
> Fill full the mouth of Famine
> And bid the sickness cease;
> And when your goal is nearest
> The end for others sought,
> Watch sloth and heathen Folly
> Bring all your hopes to nought.

But, since they were Americans, they lacked Kipling's pessimism about the outcome. They would take their "little brown brother" and Americanize him. They would teach him to speak English, to wear Western clothing, to adopt modern agricultural techniques, to become a Christian (Catholicism would do, but Protestantism would be far superior), and swear allegiance to the Stars and Stripes. The Philippine Reservation was white supremacy at its most self-confident.

THE LYNCHING OF ED JOHNSON, IN CHATTANOOGA, TENNESSEE, 1906

Ed Johnson was one of thousands of African Americans lynched in the opening decades of the twentieth century. In some respects his story is all too typical; in others, it is unique.

Typical is the crime he allegedly committed, the rape of a young white woman. Ida Wells Burnett, the crusading black journalist who led the campaign against lynch law for more than 40 years, found that, of the 160 African Americans lynched in 1892, 46 were accused of rape (28.75 percent) and 11 more of attempted rape (6.875 percent). The only charge more commonly alleged was murder.

The young woman was Nevada Taylor, the daughter of the superintendent of Forest Hills cemetery. She and her father and brother lived in a cottage on the grounds. After work she caught the 6:00 P.M. trolley and got off around 6:30 P.M. She heard footsteps, but, before she could even turn around, her assailant drew a strap around her neck. She screamed, but not loudly enough to summon help, and attempted to break free. Her attacker tightened the strap until she could barely breathe. Taylor apparently passed out due to lack of oxygen. When she revived, her clothing was "all disturbed," and there was "a feeling of torture in the region of her throat," the *Chattanooga Times* reported.[15]

She managed to get home and tell her father and brother what had happened. Next, "as if by magic the citizens congregated, each one armed with some sort of firearm and the search began with the ill-suppressed purpose of dealing death to the brute if he should be caught." Sheriff Joseph Shipp was alerted, and he and "a posse of deputies" and several bloodhounds headed for the scene of the crime. The hounds tracked the scent of the rapist back to the trolley stop, where they lost the trail. Taylor's description of the perpetrator was vague. He had dark skin, was about five foot six inches tall, and wore dark clothes and a black hat. The strap was found at the scene.

Two days later, Ed Johnson was arrested and charged. Will Hixson, a young white man, informed the sheriff that he had seen a black man twisting a strap at about 5:50 P.M. on the night of the crime. He later identified the man as Johnson. Sheriff Shipp, correctly fearing that a mob might seek to lynch Johnson, took the prisoner to Nashville. Nevada Taylor and her brother went to the Nashville jail. Shipp brought in two blacks and questioned them so that Taylor could hear their voices as well as see them. She said she "believed" that Johnson was the guilty party. The word "believed" mattered. Later, at Johnson's trial, she refused to say she was certain.

While Johnson was in Nashville, a mob did attack the Chattanooga jail. They were determined to lynch all three blacks who happened to be inside. A judge finally persuaded them to name a committee to inspect the inmates so that they could see for themselves that Johnson was not there. This defused the situation. But the actions of the mob and the sheriff's deputies on that night proved two things. One was that lynch law almost prevailed even before Johnson had been indicted, much less tried. The other was that the deputies were capable of holding off a mob. The *Chattanooga Times* told the story: Three deputy sheriffs stared down a mob of hundreds of enraged whites who chanted "Hang 'em!" and "Burn 'em!" and "various other shouts" that "mingled in a bedlam of sounds." At least 20 in the mob had guns.[16]

Less than three months later a much smaller mob of about 25 would encounter no comparable resistance. There would be no deputies on duty, only the jailer. The mob battered down two iron doors, a task that took them two hours. They then marched Johnson outside. During all that time, as the *Times* noted, "no policeman came around the premises."[17]

But, after the first mob had been turned aside, it looked for a while as though the legal process would prevail. Johnson was quickly indicted and almost as quickly put on trial. He had an alibi; 13 people swore that they had seen him in the Last Chance Saloon on the day and evening of the crime. He was there not to drink but to run errands for tips from the white customers. No one could be sure that he had not slipped away for perhaps half an hour or more. None had seen him leave. None had seen him return. What convicted him was Hixson's testimony that he had seen him with a strap and Taylor's testimony that she "believed" he was the rapist. At the jury's request, she was recalled to the stand on the third and last day of the trial. Juror J. L. Wrenn asked her, "Miss Taylor, can you state positively that this Negro is the one who assaulted you?" Taylor responded, "I will not swear he is the man, but I believe he is the Negro who assaulted me." Wrenn asked again: "In God's name, Miss Taylor, tell us positively—is that the guilty Negro? Can you say it? Can you swear it?" In tears, Taylor replied, "Listen to me. I would not take the life of an innocent man. But, before God, I believe this is the guilty Negro."

The jury initially divided eight to four over the verdict but soon reached unanimity. Johnson's white lawyers indicated that he would not appeal. The state, it appeared, would hang Ed Johnson.[18]

It did not. Two black lawyers took over the case. They appealed, first to the trial judge, for a new trial. He refused. They appealed to the state supreme court.

It turned down their request. The execution remained set for March 13. Next, Johnson's lawyers turned to the federal court, and lost. But the federal judge did grant a 10-day stay of execution so that they could take the case to the U.S. Supreme Court. On March 18, Associate U.S. Justice John Marshall Harlan granted the requested writ of habeas corpus. As the *Chattanooga Times* reported, "the granting of an appeal nullifies all previous orders of the state court and necessitates a resentencing of the prisoner in any event, if indeed it does not occasion a new process from indictment to trial and verdict."[19] There was no longer any execution date. Depending upon what the full Supreme Court decided, there might never be one.

Some two dozen white men decided to mete out their own version of justice. A few, according to the *Chattanooga Times*, wore bandanas to cover the lower halves of their faces. The majority, however, made no effort to disguise themselves. Sheriff Shipp, who would later be tried before the Supreme Court in the only criminal proceeding ever held in that court, was not at the jail. He had not assigned any deputies. Only the jailer was there. The mob demanded that he open the two metal doors that stood between them and Johnson. He refused. "Then began the work of battering the two heavy doors down" with hammer and axe. "Men streaming with perspiration yielded their implements to others as their strength gave out and the work went on steadily." After two hours, during which not a single deputy appeared but a sizable crowd collected outside, they pried open the doors.

As the vigilantes led Johnson down the corridor, the crowd cheered. Some shouted, "Kill him now!" but "men from the section where the crime was committed . . . had no intention of permitting a shooting in the jail." They wanted to hang Johnson from the Walnut Street bridge. Two men climbed up on "the ironwork and pulled the rope, one end of which was around Johnson's neck, over the beam." Some wanted Johnson to confess; "he would only say 'I'm ready to die, but I never done it.'" "Eager hands began to pull," but the rope slipped. They had to begin again. But, as some pulled, "the now frenzied lynchers could restrain themselves no longer, and a fusillade of shots was turned loose." One bullet cut the rope and "the body came tumbling to the bridge floor." Lynchers gathered around the body and emptied their revolvers. Somehow Johnson did not die. "Then a big, broad-shouldered man, who had done much of the work, slowly refilled the chambers of his revolver. When his weapon was loaded to his satisfaction, he walked up to the Negro, stood directly over the body and fired five shots into it." The coroner said Johnson was shot more than 50 times. One of the mob pinned a note to Johnson's body: "To Justice Harlan. Come and get your nigger now." Johnson's body remained unattended on the bridge for upwards of an hour while "a large crowd of the curious" came by to see it.[20]

Sheriff Shipp claimed he had tried to "appease the spirit of the mob." He also claimed, although he spoke to several individuals who were not wearing masks or other disguises, that he could not identify any of the participants. And he said that it was the Supreme Court that was responsible for the lynching.[21] Apparently he believed that attempting to provide a black person some measure of protection under the law was sufficient provocation and justification for a lynching. The Supreme Court did not agree.

After unanimously ruling that it had jurisdiction, the Court sent a deputy clerk to Chattanooga to collect evidence. Perhaps the most damning witness for the prosecution was John Stonecipher, a building contractor who had talked with members of the mob in a saloon several hours before they invaded the jail. He testified that one of them, Frank Ward, said to him, "We want you to help us lynch that damn nigger tonight." Stonecipher replied, "I believe Sheriff Shipp would shoot the red-hot stuff out of you." "No," said Ward, "it is all agreed. There won't be a sheriff or deputy there." Stonecipher also testified concerning conversations he had after the lynching with the defendants Ward, Henry Padgett, Alf Handman, and William Mayes. Ward complained to him, "You are the first damn man from Georgia ever I saw that didn't have nerve enough to kill a nigger."[22] After testifying, Stonecipher received a letter from "The Lynchers" threatening to blow up his house.

In March 1909, the Supreme Court met to consider the case. U.S. Attorney General Charles Bonaparte made the case for the prosecution. He argued that the rule of law was at stake when local officials could decide to set aside a ruling of the highest court. The defense conceded that Sheriff Shipp had exercised poor judgment. He should have stationed deputies at the jail. He should have prepared for the possibility of a mob. But these mistakes did not add up to criminal contempt. This argument convinced three of the justices. The other five ruled that "Shipp not only made the work of the mob easy, but in effect aided and abetted it."[23] They convicted him, the jailer, and four members of the mob. They sentenced Shipp and two members of the mob, including Luther Williams, who fired the final five shots into Johnson, to 90 days in jail. The others got 60 days. Sheriff Shipp returned to Chattanooga after serving his sentence. A crowd of more than 10,000 greeted him with a rousing rendition of "Dixie."

Justice Oliver Wendell Holmes said, upon hearing of the lynching, "In all likelihood, this was a case of an innocent man improperly branded a guilty brute and condemned to die from the start."[24] Historians who have studied the case agree. In this regard, Ed Johnson was one of thousands so branded. His was the only case to make it to the Supreme Court, however. And Sheriff Shipp was perhaps the only white law enforcement official to be held accountable in any way for a lynching. White people assumed, correctly, that they had what amounted to a license to kill black people. They also assumed that the local police and sheriffs would cooperate, as Shipp did in removing his deputies from the jail—normally at least eight were on duty at night. Johnson's lynching changed none of that.

PUBLICATION OF *THE VANISHING RACE*, 1913

In 1913, Joseph K. Dixon, a former preacher and salesman for the Eastman Kodak camera company, published *The Vanishing Race*, about North American

Indians.[25] The book was part of a much larger campaign, underwritten by the Wanamaker department stores, to capture the "truth" about these first peoples. Dixon was no ethnologist and no linguist. He had no training in anthropology. What he did have, in addition to enormous persistence and considerable talent as a photographer, was a genius for salesmanship. First, he sold John Wanamaker and his son Rodman on the notion that they should sponsor a vast educational effort, led by him, that would record and preserve Indian practices, dances, legends, beliefs, and artifacts. Then he sold the materials he created to Wanamaker customers, schoolchildren in New York and Philadelphia, and the media as genuine reproductions of native life. He also sold officials of the Bureau of Indian Affairs on the merits of his project. Their cooperation was necessary if Dixon was to use hundreds of native peoples in his various productions. These were numerous. Recording and preserving the ways of the Indians for Dixon meant photography but also cinema, lectures (by Dixon), pamphlets, and a *Wanamaker Primer on the North American Indian* for schoolchildren to accompany a film version of "Hiawatha" directed and scripted by Dixon, in addition to *The Vanishing Race*.

The Wanamakers, whose stores largely redefined retail marketing, were not the only prominent American capitalists to finance a project to create a record of the Indian way of life. The banker J. P. Morgan subsidized Edward Sheriff Curtis's monumental effort to photograph all of the native peoples west of the Mississippi. Curtis and Morgan, like Dixon and the Wanamakers, assumed that the Indian was in fact vanishing. The closing of the frontier and the massacre of the Ghost Dancers at Wounded Knee in 1890 meant that the tribes could no longer live according to ancestral practices. The Dawes Severalty Act of 1886 sought to break up remaining tribal lands by apportioning 160 acres to each household. All land left over, and it added up to millions of acres, would be sold on the open market. The idea was to transform Indians from tribal peoples into family farmers no longer living in Indian communities but mixed in with whites. The U.S. Bureau of Indian Affairs also actively sought to "Americanize" its charges. It ran schools in which Indian children had to renounce traditional ways, adopt English (including an English name), dress in conventional American fashion, and learn some useful trade. The head of Carlisle College in Pennsylvania, the first institution of higher education for native peoples, famously remarked, "We must kill the Indian to save the man."[26]

Far from contradicting this policy of extirpating native cultures, the Wanamaker/Dixon and Morgan/Curtis projects complemented it. All assumed the Indian was vanishing. All agreed that this was inevitable—all except for the Indians themselves. But their voices went unheeded. Everyone else knew that their disappearance was for the best. And, because their vanishing was so imminent, it was essential—so Dixon and Curtis believed—that a record of their lives be created. As Dixon wrote in his *Primer*:

> Because the Indian is fast moving toward his last frontier; . . . because the Indian was the first American; . . . because the platforms of the Wanamaker Auditoriums in New York and Philadelphia have for their purpose the educa-

tional uplift and stimulus of the community; and because the rising generation needs to know more about the early history of our great country—an expedition was planned . . . to study the North American Indian on his own ground, in his own home, and in a manner that would compel a true photographic, geographic, historic and ethnic record.[27]

Would it actually be *their* lives that Dixon and Curtis would record? An important clue, so far as the Wanamaker projects are concerned, is the early decision to make a film version of Henry Wadsworth Longfellow's epic poem "The Song of Hiawatha." Now mostly unread, "Hiawatha" was enormously popular when first published in 1855 and was routinely assigned in grammar schools through the early decades of the twentieth century. Longfellow largely based his poem on the work of Henry Rowe Schoolcraft, who had married an Ojibway and who published several volumes of tales told to him by her mother and other relatives.[28] Longfellow turned these into a myth of the creation of native cultures, finding his own model in the Icelandic sagas. Longfellow's Hiawatha is an Indian Prometheus. He discovers how to cultivate corn. He invents pictorial writing. He defeats various monsters, magicians, and tricksters. And then he gracefully accepts the inevitable primacy of the "White Foot" and gets into his bark canoe and paddles off into eternity. He is, in sum, a white man's Indian.

Choosing to stage *Hiawatha—The Passion Play of the American Indian* with native peoples playing the roles meant that Dixon, and the Wanamakers, wanted to preserve certain white myths about Indians. Any resemblance between these myths and actual Native American beliefs, practices, or legends would be largely coincidental. Instead, Indians would become actors following the dictates of a white director (Dixon) and reciting lines written by a white poet who knew Old Norse but not any Native American languages.

It was a form of minstrelsy. In minstrel shows, white performers "corked up" and pretended to be slaves. Toward the end of the nineteenth century, blacks began to play some of these roles. But they had to use the same makeup, sing the same sorts of songs, and tell the same sorts of racist jokes. They could not be black; they had to perform blackness according to white stereotypes. So, too, the Indians who played in *Hiawatha*. Children who attended showings sometimes asked Dixon if the performers were "real Indians." They were Native Americans, but their characters were no more real Indians than those played by African American minstrel performers were real blacks.

Normally, performance requires audience members to suspend their knowledge that they are watching people *pretend*. They know that the actor is not Hamlet, for example. But they react as though he were. Casting real Indians made this suspension of disbelief easier. So did shooting the film on location. So, too, did the *Wanamaker Primer on the North American Indian*. It turned the movie into a lesson. For example, the second edition of the *Primer* included "Ten Commandments from the Red Man to the White Man." These enjoined hard work ("Thou shall do thy share of the world's work as it comes to thee"), kindness to others, and learning, among other conventional values.[29] Note the use of "thou," "thy," and "thee." The only Americans who used such language were Quakers. Dixon, more likely, borrowed from the King James edition of the Bible. In the process, he assimilated Hiawatha into the Judeo-Christian tradition. Like Moses, he was a lawgiver. Like Jesus', his story became a "passion play."

Schoolchildren learned other things besides ersatz commandments. Irma Price from New York City, sent Joseph Dixon a poem, "The Passing of the Red Man," as a way of expressing her delight at "The Song of Hiawatha." She wrote, "My little brother and I bought Indian suits at Wanamakers. We are dancing the war dance at home. We have arrows, too, and we are shooting and playing Indians in the little park before our house."[30] Irma indicated in the title of her poem that she also grasped the largest lesson. Native peoples' traditional ways of life were disappearing.

Ironically, the traditions Dixon and the Wanamakers sought to capture in images, film, text, and performance were in no danger of disappearing, not so long as schoolchildren could dress up and shoot arrows and do the war dance. Such white man's Indian traditions had other sources of support. In 1913, for example, the U.S. Mint issued the Indian head nickel; the Indian embodied the "liberty" all Americans cherished, even as hundreds of thousands were penned up on reservations. On the reverse side of the nickel was the buffalo, so closely associated with the Plains Indians and, like them, supposed to be vanishing.[31]

Edward Sheriff Curtis, like Joseph K. Dixon, made the preservation of the folkways of native peoples a life's work. He, however, did not seek a mass audience. His 20 portfolios of photographs, printed on the finest paper, were for the elite, those like J. P. Morgan, Andrew Carnegie, and Theodore Roosevelt, who could afford the hundreds of dollars each volume cost. One of his most celebrated photographs is "The Lost Trail," from his first portfolio, *Apache, Jicarilla, Navaho*. In this, as for many of his images, Curtis had Apaches, no longer hunters or warriors, re-enact an event from their past lives.[32] Because he did not provide a script for the Indians, Curtis could claim that he was faithfully recording the truth.

Images like "The Lost Trail" captured how the Apaches *had* lived—but not how they had lived before encountering the "White Foot." The Spanish introduced horses to the Americas. Native Americans, as the historian James Merrell puts it, also lived in a "New World" once Europeans arrived.[33] Curtis would not encounter Indians largely unchanged by contact until the very end of his quest when, in Alaska, he found natives still living as their ancestors had for centuries. This was not so for the Apache, the Navaho, or the other tribes he photographed. Their lives had been changing as rapidly and as drastically as those of the whites who had pushed them on to the reservations.

Curtis, too, created a mythical Indian, one whose virtues could counterbalance some of the excesses of modern America. Like Dixon's, his Indians lived in harmony with nature. It was the wholesale transformation of the landscape by the white man that made their "vanishing" inevitable. Railroads meant the end of the great herds of buffalo. Farms meant barbed wire fences and irrigation projects.

The discovery of gold, silver, copper, and coal meant the sinking of mining shafts, the construction of smelters, and the rise of boomtowns. All threatened to make Nature vanish, as well. Not coincidentally, the rise of the conservation movement occurred at the same time that white Americans also sought to preserve records of tribal customs and beliefs.

White Americans preserved a variety of mythical Indians. William Cody, aka Buffalo Bill, produced an annual "Buffalo Bill's Wild West and Congress of Rough Riders of the World Show" from the 1880s until World War I.[34] Theodore Roosevelt borrowed the name Rough Riders for the regiment he organized and led during the Spanish-American War. Buffalo Bill also claimed authenticity for his spectacles. One season Sitting Bull was a featured performer in a re-enactment of the Battle of Little Big Horn. But Buffalo Bill specialized in white fantasies about the Wild West in which Indians attacked wagon trains and were driven off, at the last moment, by the cavalry. The real cavalry had many African American troops, the so-called Buffalo Soldiers. But all the troopers in the Wild West Show were white. Authenticity never trumped racial stereotypes.

Buffalo Bill and other heroes of the Wild West like Kit Carson inspired unknown numbers of hack writers to crank out unknowable numbers of stories in pulp magazines like *The New Buffalo Bill Weekly* (1913–1919).[35] Most featured Indians. Some were loyal, brave, and helpful to whites. The majority were "savages" and "renegades," irretrievably wild and dangerous, especially to white women, who then had to be rescued by the white heroes.

Movies took over these themes and stereotypes. The Western became a staple genre. And the studios followed the lead of Dixon, Curtis, and Cody in hiring "real" Indians, not for leading roles—those were reserved for whites made up to look Indian—but for the battle scenes in which they would cry out their war whoops while riding their ponies bareback. In 1913, the first feature-length film, *The Squaw Man*, was made by Cecil B. DeMille. It was about an Indian woman who commits suicide to protect her white husband and their child. The film was so successful that DeMille remade it twice, in 1918 and then in 1931 as a talkie.[36]

It all amounted to still one more chapter in a long history of expropriation. The white man took the Indian's land. He destroyed his tribes. And he turned him into an array of diversions and entertainments.

VOICES OF THE DECADE

RUDYARD KIPLING

Kipling's poem had an enormous impact on the American debate over empire. It appeared in February 1899, just as the newly founded Philippine Republic declared war upon the United States. The United States had refused to withdraw its troops following the surrender of Spain and also had refused to recognize the new Republic. In 1899, Rudyard Kipling was nearing the peak of his literary career. In 1907, he would win the Nobel Prize. Only 34 years old in 1899, he had already published best-selling children's books, collections of stories, and volumes of poetry. Many of his tales were set in India, where he had been born and raised. India was, Prime Minister Benjamin Disraeli told Queen Victoria, the "jewel in the crown," the most important possession of the British Empire. Kipling considered himself a product of that empire, and he became a staunch advocate of Western imperialism. It brought "civilization" to "new-caught sullen peoples." It was, in fact, a moral obligation. Favored nations and races had the responsibility to "take up the White Man's burden." Kipling wrote the poem to urge the United States to take over the Philippines. It was time for the United States to take its proper place as an imperial power.

> Take up the White Man's burden—
> Send forth the best ye breed—
> Go, bind your sons to exile
> To serve your captives' need;
> To wait, in heavy harness,
> On fluttered folk and wild—
> Your new-caught sullen peoples,
> Half devil and half child.
>
> Take up the White Man's burden—
> In patience to abide,
> To veil the threat of terror
> And check the show of pride;
> By open speech and simple,
> An hundred times made plain,
> To seek another's profit
> And work another's gain.
>
> Take up the White Man's burden—
> The savage wars of peace—
> Fill full the mouth of Famine,
> And bid the sickness cease;
> And when your goal is nearest
> (The end for others sought)
> Watch sloth and heathen folly
> Bring all your hope to nought.
>
> Take up the White Man's burden—
> No iron rule of kings,
> But toil of serf and sweeper—
> The tale of common things.

The ports ye shall not enter,
The roads ye shall not tread,
Go, make them with your living
And mark them with your dead.

Take up the White Man's burden,
And reap his old reward—
The blame of those ye better
The hate of those ye guard—
The cry of hosts ye humour
(Ah, slowly!) toward the light:—
"Why brought ye us from bondage,
Our loved Egyptian night?"

Take up the White Man's burden—
Ye dare not stoop to less—
Nor call too loud on Freedom
To cloak your weariness.
By all ye will or whisper,
By all ye leave or do,
The silent sullen peoples
Shall weigh your God and you.

Take up the White Man's burden!
Have done with childish days—
The lightly-proffered laurel,
The easy ungrudged praise:
Comes now, to search your manhood
Through all the thankless years,
Cold, edged with dear-bought wisdom,
The judgment of your peers.

From Rudyard Kipling, "The White Man's Burden," *McClure's Magazine,* February 1899, p. 290.

SEN. BENJAMIN ("PITCHFORK BEN") TILLMAN

One of those most impressed by Kipling's poem was Senator Benjamin ("Pitchfork Ben") Tillman of South Carolina, an opponent of the U.S. decision to annex the Philippines. On February 7, 1899, Tillman made a speech in the Senate in which he tried to use Kipling's poem against itself, to turn it into a call to reject imperialism. Tillman's opposition was based upon his commitment to white supremacy. He was a well-known racist demagogue.

As though coming at the most opportune time possible, you might say just before the treaty [with Spain that ceded sovereignty over the Philippines in return for $20 million] reached the Senate, or about the time it was sent to us, there appeared in one of our magazines a poem by Rudyard Kipling, the greatest poet of England at this time. This poem, unique, and in some places too deep for me, is a prophecy. I do not imagine that in the history of human events any poet has ever felt inspired so clearly to portray our danger and our duty. It is called "The White Man's Burden." With the permission of Senators I will read a stanza, and I beg Senators to listen to it, for it is well worth their attention. This man has lived in the Indies. In fact, he is a citizen of the world, and has been all over it, and knows whereof he speaks.

> "Take up the White Man's burden—
> Send forth the best ye breed—
> Go, bind your sons to exile,
> To serve your captive's need;
> To wait, in heavy harness,
> On fluttered folk and wild—
> Your new-caught sullen peoples,
> Half devil and half child."

I will pause here. I intend to read more, but I wish to call attention to a fact which may have escaped the attention of Senators thus far, that with five exceptions every man in this chamber who has had to do with the colored race in this country voted against the ratification of the treaty. It was . . . because we understand and realize what it is to have two races side by side that can not mix or mingle without deterioration and injury to both and the ultimate destruction of the civilization of the higher. We of the South have borne this white man's burden of a colored race in our midst since their emancipation and before.

It was a burden upon our manhood and our ideas of liberty before they were emancipated. It is still a burden, although they have been granted the franchise. It clings to us like the shirt of Nessus [a centaur killed by Hercules; a shirt soaked in his blood later poisoned Hercules], and we are not responsible, because we inherited it, and your fathers as well as ours are responsible for the presence amongst us of that people. Why do we as a people want to incorporate into our citizenship ten millions more of different or of differing races, three or four of them?

But we have not incorporated them yet, and let us see what this English poet has to say about it, and what he thinks.

> "Take up the White Man's burden—
> No iron rule of kings,
> But toil of serf and sweeper—
> The tale of common things.
> The ports ye shall not enter,
> The roads ye shall not tread,
> Go, make them with your living
> And mark them with your dead."

Ah, if we have no other consideration, if no feeling of humanity, no love of our fellows, no regard for others' rights, if nothing but our self-interest shall actuate us in this crisis, let me say to you that if we go madly on in the direction of crushing these people into subjection and submission we will do so at the cost of many, many thousands of the flower of American youth. There are 10,000,000 of these people, some of them fairly well civilized, and running to the extreme of naked savages, who are reported in our press dispatches as having stood out in the open and fired their bows and arrows, not flinching from the storm of shot and shell thrown into their midst by the American soldiers there. . . .

The city of Manila is surrounded by swamps and marshes, I am told. A few miles back lie the woods and jungles and mountains. These people are used to the climate. They know how to get about, and if they mean to have their liberties, as they appear to do, at what sacrifice will the American domination be placed over them? There is another verse of Kipling. I have fallen in love with this man. He tells us what we will reap:

"Take up the White Man's burden,
And reap his old reward—
The blame of those ye better
The hate of those ye guard—
The cry of those ye humor
(Ah, slowly!) toward the light:—
'Why brought ye us from bondage,
Our loved Egyptian night?'"

Those peoples are not suited to our institutions. They are not ready for liberty as we understand it. They do not want it. Why are we bent on forcing upon them a civilization not suited to them and which only means in their view degradation and a loss of self-respect, which is worse than the loss of life itself?

From a speech delivered in the U.S. Senate, February 7, 1899.

THEODORE ROOSEVELT

One of the most influential advocates of imperialism was Theodore Roosevelt. He had organized a regiment, the Rough Riders (a name he took from the Buffalo Bill Wild West shows), which he led in a celebrated charge up San Juan Hill in Cuba during the war with Spain. In 1900, he was governor of New York and the Republican nominee for vice president. In 1901, President McKinley was assassinated, and "that damned cowboy," as one disgruntled Republican leader called T.R., became president. Noteworthy is the way in which Roosevelt found parallels between the wars against Native Americans and the conquest of the Philippines:

Every expansion of civilization makes for peace. In other words, every expansion of a great civilized power means a victory for law, order, and righteousness. This has been the case in every instance of expansion during the present century, whether the expanding power were France or England, Russia or America. In every instance the expansion has been of benefit, not so much to the power nominally benefited, as to the whole world. In every instance the result proved that the expanding power was doing a duty to civilization far greater and more important than could have been done by any stationary power. Take the case of France and Algiers. During the early decades of the present century piracy of the most dreadful description was rife on the Mediterranean, and thousands of civilized men were yearly dragged into slavery by the Moorish pirates. A degrading peace was purchased by the civilized powers by the payment of tribute. Our own country was one among the tributary nations which thus paid blood-money to the Moslem bandits of the sea. We fought occasional battles with them; and so, on a larger scale, did the English. But peace did not follow, because the country was not occupied.

Our last payment was made in 1830, and the reason it was the last was because in that year the French conquest of Algiers began. Foolish sentimentalists, like those who wrote little poems in favor of the Mahdists against the English, and who now write little essays in favor of Aguinaldo [the leader of the Filipino independence movement] against the Americans, celebrated the Algerian freebooters as heroes who were striving for liberty against the invading French. But the French continued to do their work; France expanded over Algiers, and the result was that piracy on the Mediterranean came to an end, and Algiers has thriven as never before in its history. On an even larger scale the same thing is true of England and the Sudan. The expansion of England throughout the Nile valley has been an incalculable gain for civilization. Any one who reads the writings of the Austrian priests and laymen who were prisoners in the Sudan under the Mahdi [a Muslim religious and political leader] will realize that when England crushed him and conquered the Sudan she conferred a priceless boon upon humanity and made the civilized world her debtor. Again, the same thing is true of the Russian advance in Asia. As in the Sudan the English conquest is followed by peace, and the endless massacres of the Mahdi are stopped forever, so the Russian conquest of the khanates of central Asia meant the cessation of the barbarous warfare under which Asian civilization had steadily withered away since the days of Jenghiz Khan, and the substitution in its place of the reign of peace and order. All civilization has been the gainer by the Russian advance, as it was the gainer by the advance of France in North Africa; as it has been the gainer by the advance of England in both Asia and Africa, both Canada and Australia. Above all, there has been the greatest possible gain in peace. The rule of law and of order has succeeded to the rule of barbarous and bloody violence. Until the great civilized nations stepped in there was no chance for anything but such bloody violence.

So it has been in the history of our own country. Of course our whole national history has been one of expansion. Under Washington and Adams we expanded westward to the Mississippi; under Jefferson we expanded across the continent to the mouth of the Columbia; under Monroe we expanded into Florida; and then into Texas and California; and finally, largely through the instrumentality of Seward, into Alaska; while under every administration the process of expansion in the great plains and the Rockies has continued with growing rapidity. While we had a frontier the chief feature of frontier life was the endless war between the settlers and the red men. Sometimes the immediate occasion for the war was to be found in the conduct of the whites and sometimes in that of the reds, but the ultimate cause was simply that we were in contact with a country held by savages or half-savages. Where we abut on Canada there is no danger of war, nor is there any danger where we abut on the well-settled regions of Mexico. But elsewhere war had to continue until we expanded over the country. Then it was succeeded at once by a peace which has remained unbroken to the present day. In North America, as elsewhere throughout the entire world, the expansion of a civilized nation has invariably meant the growth of the area in which peace is normal throughout the world.

The same will be true of the Philippines. If the men who have counseled national degradation, national dishonor, by urging us to leave the Philippines and put the Aguinaldan oligarchy in control of those islands, could have their way, we should merely turn them over to rapine and bloodshed until some stronger, manlier power stepped in to do the task we had shown ourselves fearful of performing. But, as it is, this country will keep the islands and will establish therein a stable and orderly government, so that one more fair spot of the world's surface shall have been snatched from the forces of darkness. Fundamentally the cause of expansion is the cause of peace. . . .

Nations that expand and nations that do not expand may both ultimately go down, but the one leaves heirs and a glorious memory, and the other leaves neither. The Roman expanded, and he has left a memory which has profoundly influenced the history of mankind, and he has further left as the heirs of his body, and, above all, of his tongue and culture, the so-called Latin peoples of Europe and America. Similarly to-day it is the great expanding peoples which bequeath to future ages the great memories and material results of their achievements, and the nations which shall have sprung from their loins, England standing as the archetype and best exemplar of all such mighty nations. But the peoples that do not expand leave, and can leave, nothing behind them.

It is only the warlike power of a civilized people that can give peace to the world. The Arab wrecked the civilization of the Mediterranean coasts, the Turk wrecked the civilization of southeastern Europe, and the Tatar desolated from China to Russia and to Persia, setting back the progress of the world for centuries, solely because the civilized nations opposed to them had lost the great fighting qualities, and, in becoming overpeaceful, had lost the power of keeping peace with a strong hand. Their passing away marked the beginning of a period of chaotic barbarian warfare. Those whose memories are not so short as to have forgotten the defeat of the Greeks by the Turks, of the Italians by the Abyssinians, and the feeble campaigns waged by Spain against feeble Morocco, must realize that at the present moment the Mediterranean coasts would be overrun either by the Turks or by the Sudan Mahdists if these warlike barbarians had only to fear those southern European powers which have lost the fighting edge. Such a barbarian conquest would mean endless war; and the fact that nowadays the reverse takes place, and that the barbarians recede or are conquered, with the attendant fact that peace follows their retrogression or conquest, is due solely to the power of the mighty civilized races which have not lost the fighting instinct, and which by their expansion are gradually bringing peace into the red wastes where the barbarian peoples of the world hold sway.

From "Expansion and Peace," *The Strenuous Life: Essays and Addresses* (New York: The Century Co., 1900), 1.

IDA B. WELLS-BARNETT

Ida Wells-Barnett devoted her adult life to the campaign against lynching. Her early newspaper articles led to her being forced to leave the South, under threat of death. She moved to Chicago and carried on the fight. The essay, "Lynching and the Excuse for It," excerpted here, came in response to one by the famed settlement house pioneer Jane Addams. Addams had condemned lynching but had conceded, if only for the sake of argument, the white southern claim that they occurred in response to heinous crimes. Barnett was determined to set the record straight.

> It was eminently befitting that the *Independent's* first number in the new century should contain a strong protest against lynching. The deepest dyed infamy of the 19th century was that which, in its supreme contempt for law, defied all constitutional guarantees of citizenship, and during the last fifteen years of the century put to death 2,000 men, women, and children by shooting, hanging, and burning alive. Well would it have been if every preacher in every pulpit in the land had made so earnest a plea as that which came from Miss Addams' forceful pen.
>
> Appreciating the helpful influences of such a dispassionate and logical argument as that made by the writer referred to, I earnestly desire to say nothing to lessen the force of the appeal. At the same time, an unfortunate presumption used as a basis for her argument works so serious, though doubtless unintentional, an injury to the memory of thousands of victims of mob law that it is only fair to call attention to this phase of the writer's plea. It is unspeakably infamous to put thousands of people to death without a trial by jury; it adds to that infamy to charge that these victims were moral monsters, when, in fact, four-fifths of them were not so accused even by the fiends who murdered them.
>
> Almost at the beginning of her discussion, the distinguished writer says: "Let us assume that the Southern citizens who take part in and abet the lynching of Negroes honestly believe that that is the only successful method of dealing with a certain class of crimes."
>
> It is this assumption, this absolutely unwarrantable assumption, that vitiates every suggestion which it inspires Miss Addams to make. It is the same baseless assumption which influences ninety-nine out of every one hundred persons who discuss this question. Among many thousand editorial clippings I have received in the past five years, 99 percent discuss the question upon the presumption that lynchings are the desperate effort of the Southern people to

Ida B. Wells. Courtesy of Library of Congress.

protect their women from black monsters, and, while the large majority condemn lynching, the condemnation is tempered with a plea for the lyncher—that human nature gives way under such awful provocation and that the mob, insane for the moment, must be pitied as well as condemned. It is strange that an intelligent, law-abiding, and fairminded people should so persistently shut their eyes to the facts in the discussion of what the civilized world now concedes to be America's national crime.

This almost universal tendency to accept as true the slander which the lynchers offer to civilization as an excuse for their crime might be explained if the true facts were difficult to obtain; but not the slightest difficulty intervenes. The Associated Press dispatches, the press clipping bureau, frequent book publications, and the annual summary of a number of influential journals give the lynching record every year. This record, easily within the reach of everyone who wants it, makes inexcusable the statement and cruelly unwarranted the assumption that Negroes are lynched only because of their assaults upon womanhood.

For an example in point: For fifteen years past, on the first day of each year, the *Chicago Tribune* has given to the public a carefully compiled record of all the lynchings of the previous year. Space will not permit a résumé of these fifteen years, but as fairly representing the entire time, I desire to briefly tabulate here the record of the five years last past. The statistics of the ten years preceding do not vary; they simply emphasize the record here presented.

The record gives the name and nationality of the man or woman lynched, the alleged crime, the time and place of the lynching. With this is given a résumé of the offenses charged, with the number of persons lynched for the offenses named. That enables the reader to see at a glance the causes assigned for the lynchings, and leaves nothing to be assumed. The lynchers, at the time and place of the lynching, are the best authority for the causes which actuate them. Every presumption is in favor of this record, especially as it remains absolutely unimpeached. This record gives the following statement of the colored persons lynched and the causes of the lynchings for the years named.

With this record in view, there should be no difficulty in ascertaining the alleged offenses given as justification for lynchings during the last five years. If the Southern citizens lynch Negroes because "that is the only successful method of dealing with a certain class of crimes," then that class of crimes should be shown unmistakably by this record. Now consider the record.

It would be supposed that the record would show that all, or nearly all, lynchings were caused by outrageous assaults upon women; certainly that this particular offense would outnumber all other causes for putting human beings to death without a trial by jury and the other safeguards of our Constitution and laws.

But the record makes no such disclosure. Instead, it shows that five women have been lynched, put to death with unspeakable savagery, during the past five years. They certainly were not under the ban of the outlawing crime. It shows that men, not a few but hundreds, have been lynched for misdemeanors, while others have suffered death for no offense known to the law, the causes assigned being "mistaken identity," "insult," "bad reputation," "unpopularity," "violating contract," "running quarantine," "giving evidence," "frightening child by shooting at rabbits," etc. Then, strangest of all, the record shows that the sum total of lynchings for these offenses—not crimes—and for the alleged offenses which are only misdemeanors greatly exceeds the lynchings for the very crime universally declared to be the cause of lynching.

A careful classification of the offenses which have caused lynchings during the past five years shows that contempt for law and race prejudice constitute the real cause of all lynching. During the past five years, 147 white persons were lynched. It may be argued that fear of the "law's delays" was the cause of their being lynched. But this is not true. Not a single white victim of the mob was wealthy or had friends or influence to cause a miscarriage of justice. There was no such possibility; it was contempt for law which incited the mob to put so many white men to death without a complaint under oath, much less a trial.

In the case of the Negroes lynched, the mobs' incentive was race prejudice. Few white men were lynched for any such trivial offenses as are detailed in the causes for lynching colored men. Negroes are lynched for "violating contracts," "unpopularity," "testifying in court," and "shooting at rabbits." As only Negroes are lynched for "no offense," "unknown offenses," offenses not criminal, misdemeanors, and crimes not capital, it must be admitted that the real cause of lynching in all such cases is race prejudice, and should be so classified. . . . .

No good result can come from any investigation which refuses to consider the facts. A conclusion that is based upon a presumption instead of the best evidence is unworthy of a moment's consideration. The lynching record, as it is compiled from day to day by unbiased, reliable, and responsible public journals, should be the basis of every investigation which seeks to discover the cause and suggest the remedy for lynching. The excuses of lynchers and the specious pleas of their apologists should be considered in the light of the record, which they invariably misrepresent or ignore.

The Christian and moral forces of the nation should insist that misrepresentation should have no place in the discussion of this all important question, that the figures of the lynching record should be allowed to plead, trumpet-tongued, in defense of the slandered dead, that the silence of concession be broken, and that truth, swift-winged and courageous, summon this nation to do its duty to exalt justice and preserve inviolate the sacredness of human life.

From "Lynching and the Excuse for It," *New York Independent* 53 (May 16, 1901). In *Lynching and Rape: An Exchange of Views*, by Bettina Aptheckers (New York: American Institute for Marxist Studies, 1977), 29.

THE JAPANESE AND KOREAN EXCLUSION LEAGUE

The League was a San Francisco-based organization led by Patrick H. McCarthy, general president of the Building Trades Council of San Francisco and a future mayor, and Andrew Furuseth, leader of the longshoremen's union. It began in 1905 with the goal of extending the policy of Chinese exclusion to include Japanese and Koreans.

> The Japanese and Korean Exclusion League held its annual meeting Sunday, and transacted its regular business as contemplated before the disaster [the San Francisco earthquake]. . . . .
>
> Attention was called to the fact that if it had not been for the efforts of the Japanese and Korean Exclusion League, assisted by united labor, the Foster bill would have passed Congress, and thus the Chinese Exclusion act would have been virtually repealed. It would have thrown down the bars and admitted every Chinaman to our shores who desires to come here. . . .
>
> The Foster bill and similar measures are killed as far as this session is concerned, but patriotic Americans may do well to keep their eye on the next Congress, because if we are not mistaken strenuous efforts will be made to admit the coolie hordes of China.
>
> The League has also been working diligently and with great success for the extension of the Chinese Exclusion act to Japanese and Koreans.
>
> At the opening of the present Congress, it was very offensive to say anything detrimental about the Japanese immigration in the presence of a Congressman or a Senator, and the President of the United States was even reported to have

said that if they sent the representatives of the Japanese and Korean Exclusion League to the White House he would deport the members of the committee.

The change which has taken place is notable, not only in the halls of legislation in Washington, but in the industrial and commercial centers of the east.

The literature and statistics sent out by the Japanese and Korean Exclusion League has done wonderful work in educating the public.

Thousands of fair minded and well meaning people who were biased and ignorant on the question of Japanese immigration have during the last year, entirely changed their views on the subject. They have learned the truth that the Japanese coolie is even a greater menace to the existence of the white race, to the progress and prosperity of our country than is the Chinese coolie.

But if there has been danger from Asiatic immigration to our state before, that danger has not lessened now.

On the contrary it has increased.

The great calamity which befell San Francisco will furnish the Orient with lurid tales of opportunity for employment and profit. California, the land of fabulous wealth, revenue and mountains of gold, and San Francisco with its wonderful wages will be exploited before the ignorant coolies until they will come in ship loads like an endless swarm of rats.

Do not for a moment think that the Japanese will keep away on account of the earthquakes. They are raised on earthquakes in Japan, and the earthquake will only make the Nepponese coolies feel more at home in California.

Great as the recent catastrophe has been, let us take care lest we encounter a greater one.

We can withstand the earthquake.
We can survive the fire.

As long as California is white man's country, it will remain one of the grandest and best states in the union, but the moment the Golden State is subjected to an unlimited Asiatic coolie invasion there will be no more California.
From *Organized Labor*, Official Organ of the State and Local Building Trades Councils of California, San Francisco, April 21 and 28 and May 5, 1906 (Combined edition). http://www.sfmuseum.org/1906.2/invasion.html.

GEORGE WASHINGTON PLUNKITT

George Washington Plunkitt was one of the sachems, that is, leaders, of the New York Democratic organization, Tammany Hall. A reporter interviewed Plunkitt and published *Plunkitt of Tammany Hall*. It is a funny and clear-eyed discussion of machine politics. Lincoln Steffens was an investigative reporter who wrote a series of articles about corruption in city politics and then published them as *The Shame of the Cities*. Despite Plunkitt's scorn for Steffins, the reporter claimed to admire "honest crooks" like Plunkitt, that is, machine politicians who made no bones about their intention to use politics to benefit themselves, the organization, and their constituents—and in that order.

I've been readin' a book by Lincoln Steffens on *The Shame of the Cities*. Steffens means well but, like all reformers, he don't know how to make distinctions. He can't see no difference between honest graft and dishonest graft and, consequent, he gets things all mixed up. There's the biggest kind of a difference between political looters and politicians who make a fortune out of politics by keepin' their eyes wide open. The looter goes in for himself alone without considerin' his organization or his city. The politician looks after his own interests, the organization's interests, and the city's interests all at the same time. See the distinction? For instance, I ain't no looter. The looter hogs it. I never hogged. I made my pile in politics, but, at the same time, I served the organization and got more big improvements for New York City than any other livin' man. And I never monkeyed with the penal code.

The difference between a looter and a practical politician is the difference between the Philadelphia Republican gang and Tammany Hall. Steffens seems to think they're both about the same; but he's all wrong. The Philadelphia crowd runs up against the penal code. Tammany don't. The Philadelphians ain't satisfied with robbin' the bank of all its gold and paper money. They stay to pick up the nickels and pennies and the cop comes and nabs them. Tammany ain't no such fool. Why, I remember, about fifteen or twenty years ago, a Republican superintendent of the Philadelphia almshouse stole the zinc roof off the buildin' and sold it for junk. . . . There's a limit to everything, and the Philadelphia Republicans go beyond the limit. It seems like they can't be cool and moderate like real politicians. . . .

Steffens made one good point in his book. He said he found that Philadelphia, ruled almost entirely by Americans, was more corrupt than New York, where the Irish do almost all the governin'. I could have told him that before he did any investigatin' if he had come to me. The Irish was born to rule, and they're the honestest people in the world. Show me the Irishman who would steal a roof off an almhouse! He don't exist. Of course, if an Irishman had the political pull and the roof was much worn, he might get the city authorities to put on a new one and get the contract for it himself, and buy the old roof at a bargain—but that's honest graft. It's goin' about the thing like a gentleman, and there's more money in it than in tearin' down an old roof and cartin' it to the junkman's—more money and no penal code.

One reason why the Irishman is more honest in politics than many Sons of the Revolution is that he is grateful to the country and the city that gave him protection and prosperity when he was driven by oppression from the Emerald Isle. Say, that sentence is fine, ain't it? I'm goin' to get some literary feller to work it over into poetry for next St. Patrick's Day dinner.

Yes, the Irishman is grateful. His one thought is to serve the city which gave him a home. He has this thought even before he lands in New York, for his friends here often have a good place in one of the city departments picked out for him while he is still in the old country. Is it any wonder that he has a tender spot in his heart for old New York when he is on its salary list the mornin' after he lands?

From "On the Shame of the Cities," *Plunkitt of Tammany Hall: A Series of Very Plain Talks on Very Practical Politics, Delivered by Ex-senator George Washington Plunkitt, the Tammany*

Philosopher, from His Rostrum—the New York County Court House Bootblack Stand (New York: McClure, Philipps & Co., 1905). Available at History Matters, http://historymatters.gmu.edu/d/5731/. Viewed July 21, 2008.

HENRY CABOT LODGE

Senator Henry Cabot Lodge (Rep., Mass.) was one of the founders of the Immigration Restriction League, which lobbied to make immigrants pass a literacy test before being permitted to enter the United States. In this 1909 speech, "The Restriction of Immigration," Lodge explains the logic of the bill and, more important, he emphasizes the logic of restriction. It is a logic of race or, we would say, of racism. Lodge candidly admits that there is no such thing as a pure Englishman, much less an American. But he insists that races do exist. Races formed, he claims, because, as he and many others believed, acquired characteristics can be inherited. For example, frontier conditions fostered independence and ingenuity, or so said Lodge's friend Theodore Roosevelt. The children of the pioneers inherited these qualities. This belief, now thoroughly disproved, was called "neo-Lamarckianism." It provided the "scientific" basis for racialized thinking.

> Mr. President: This bill is intended to amend the existing law so as to restrict still further immigration to the United States. Paupers, diseased persons, convicts, and, contract laborers are now excluded. By this bill it is proposed to make a new class of excluded immigrants, and add to those which have just been named the totally ignorant. The bill is of the simplest kind. The first section excludes from the country all immigrants who cannot read and write either their own or some other language. The second section merely provides a simple test for determining whether the immigrant can read or write, and is added to the bill so as to define the duties of the immigrant inspectors, and to assure to all immigrants alike perfect justice and a fair test of their knowledge.
>
> Two questions arise in connection with this bill. The first is as to the merits of this particular form of restriction; the second as to the general policy of restricting immigration at all. I desire to discuss briefly these two questions in the order in which I have stated them. The smaller question as to the merits of this particular bill comes first.... There can be no doubt that there is a very earnest desire on the part of the American people to restrict further, and much more extensively than has yet been done, foreign immigration to the United States. The question before the committee was how this could best be done; that is, by what method the largest number of undesirable immigrants and the smallest possible number of desirable could be shut out....
>
> The third method [proposed] was to exclude all immigrants who could neither read nor write, and this is the plan which was adopted by the committee and which is embodied in this bill. In their report the committee have shown by statistics, which have been collected and tabulated with great care, the emigrants who would be affected by this illiteracy test.... It is found, in the first place, that the illiteracy test will bear most heavily upon the Italians, Russians,

Poles, Hungarians, Greeks, and Asiatics, and very lightly, or not at all, upon English-speaking emigrants, or Germans, Scandinavians, and French. In other words, the races most affected by the illiteracy test are those whose emigration to this country has begun within the last twenty years and swelled rapidly to enormous proportions, races with which the English- speaking people have never hitherto assimilated, and who are most alien to the great body of the people of the United States. On the other hand, immigrants from the United Kingdom and of those races which are most closely related to the English-speaking people, and who with the English-speaking people themselves founded the American colonies and built up the United States, are affected but little by the proposed test. These races would not be prevented by this law from coming to this country in practically undiminished numbers. These kindred races also are those who alone go to the Western and Southern States, where immigrants are desired, and take up our unoccupied lands. The races which would suffer most seriously by exclusion under the proposed bill furnish the immigrants who do not go to the West or South, where immigration is needed, but who remain on the Atlantic seaboard, where immigration is not needed and where their presence is most injurious and undesirable.

The statistics prepared by the committee show further that the immigrants excluded by the illiteracy test are those who remain for the most part in congested masses in our great cities. They furnish, as other tables show, a large proportion of the population of the slums. The committee's report proves that illiteracy runs parallel with the slum population, with criminals, paupers, and juvenile delinquents of foreign birth or parentage, whose percentage is out of all proportion to their share of the total population, when compared with the percentage of the same classes among the native born. It also appears from investigations which have been made that the immigrants who would be shut out by the illiteracy test are those who bring least money to the country and come most quickly upon private or public charity for support. The replies of the governors of twenty-six states to the Immigration Restriction League show that in only two cases are immigrants of the classes affected by the illiteracy test desired, and those are of a single race. All the other immigrants mentioned by the governors as desirable belong to the races which are but slightly affected by the provisions of this bill. It is also proved that the classes now excluded by law—the criminals, the diseased, the paupers, and the contract laborers—are furnished chiefly by the same races as those most affected by the test of illiteracy. The same is true as to those immigrants who come to this country for a brief season and return to their native land, taking with them the money they have earned in the United States. There is no more hurtful and undesirable class of immigrants from every point of view than these "birds of passage," and the tables show that the races furnishing the largest number of "birds of passage" have also the greatest proportion of illiterates. . . . .

I have said enough to show what the effects of this bill would be, and that if enacted into law it would be fair in its operation and highly beneficial in its results. It now remains for me to discuss the second and larger question, as to the advisability of restricting immigration at all. This is a subject of the greatest magnitude and the most far-reaching importance. It has two sides, the economic and the social. As to the former, but few words are necessary. There is no one thing which does so much to bring about a reduction of wages and to injure the American wage earner as the unlimited introduction of cheap foreign labor through unrestricted immigration. Statistics show that the change in the race character of our immigration has been accompanied by a corresponding decline in its quality. The number of skilled mechanics and of the persons trained to some occupation or pursuit has fallen off, while the number of those without occupation or training, that is, who are totally unskilled, has risen in our recent immigration to enormous proportions. This low, unskilled labor is the most deadly enemy of the American wage earner, and does more than anything else toward lowering his wages and forcing down his standard of living.... It is perfectly clear, after the experience of several years, that the only relief which can come to the American wage earner from the competition of low-class immigrant labor must be by general laws restricting the total amount of immigration, and framed in such a way as to affect most strongly those elements of the immigration which furnish the low, unskilled, and ignorant foreign labor....

I now come to the aspect of this question which is graver and more serious than any other. The injury of unrestricted immigration to American wages and American standards of living is sufficiently plain and is bad enough, but the danger which this immigration threatens to the quality of our citizenship is far worse. That which it concerns us to know, and that which is more vital to us as a people than all possible questions of tariff or currency, is whether the quality of our citizenship is endangered by the present course and character of immigration to the United States.

To determine this question we must look into the history of our race. Two hundred years ago Daniel Defoe, in some very famous verses called the "True-born Englishman," defended William III, the greatest ruler, with the exception of Cromwell, whom England has had since the days of the Plantagenets, against the accusation so constantly made at the time that he was a foreigner. The line taken by Defoe is the highly characteristic one of a fierce attack upon his opponents. He declared, in lines which were as forcible as they were rough, that the English-speaking people drew their descent from many sources; that there was no such thing as a pure-blooded Englishman; and that King William was as much an Englishman as any of them. The last proposition, in regard to the King, whose mother was a Stuart, was undoubtedly true. It was also superficially true that Englishmen drew their blood from many strains; but the rest of the argument was ludicrously false if the matter is considered in the light of modern history and modern science.

For practical purposes in considering the question of race and in dealing with the civilized peoples of west Europe and of America, there is no such thing as a race of original purity according to the divisions of ethnical science. In considering the practical problems of the present time we can deal only with artificial races,—that is, races like the English-speaking people, the French, or the Germans,—who have been developed as races by the operation during a long period of time of climatic influences, wars, migrations, conquests, and industrial development. To the philologist and the ethnologist it is of great importance to determine the ethnical divisions of mankind in the earliest historic times. To the scientific modern historian, to the student of social phenomena, and to the statesman alike, the early ethnic divisions are of little consequence; but the sharply marked race divisions which have been gradually developed by the conditions and events of the last thousand years are absolutely vital. It is by these conditions and events that the races or nations which to-day govern the world have been produced, and it is their characteristics which it is important to understand. . . .

Such, then, briefly were the people composing the colonies when we faced England in the war for independence. It will be observed that, with the exception of the Huguenot French, who formed but a small percentage of the total population, the people of the thirteen colonies were all of the same original race stocks. The Dutch, the Swedes, and, the Germans simply blended again with the English-speaking people, who like them were descended from the Germanic tribes whom Cæsar fought and Tacitus described.

During the present century, down to 1875, there have been three large migrations to this country in addition to the always steady stream from Great Britain; one came from Ireland, about the middle of the century, and somewhat later, one from Germany and one from Scandinavia, in which is included Sweden, Denmark, and Norway. The Irish, although of a different race stock originally, have been closely associated with the English-speaking people, for nearly a thousand years. They speak the same language, and during that long period the two races have lived side by side, and to some extent intermarried. The Germans and Scandinavians are again people of the same race stock as the English who founded and built up the colonies. During this century, down to 1875, then, there had been scarcely any immigration to this country except from kindred or allied races, and, no other which was sufficiently numerous to have produced any effect on the national characteristics, or to be taken into account here. Since 1875, however, there has been a great change. While the people who for two hundred and fifty years have been migrating to America have continued to furnish large numbers of immigrants to the United States, other races of totally different race origin, with whom the English-speaking people have never hitherto been assimilated or brought in contact, have suddenly begun to immigrate to the United States in large numbers. Russians, Hungarians, Poles, Bohemians, Italians, Greeks, and even Asiatics, whose immigration to America was almost unknown twenty years ago, have during the last twenty years poured in in steadily increasing numbers until now they nearly equal the immigration of those races kindred in blood or speech, or both, by whom the United States has hitherto been built up and the American people formed. This momentous fact is the one which confronts us to-day, and if continued, it carries with it future consequences far deeper than any other event of our times. It involves, in a word, nothing less than the possibility of a great and perilous change in the very fabric of our race. The English-speaking race, as I have shown, has been made slowly during the centuries.

Nothing has happened thus far to change it radically here. In the United States, after allowing for the variations produced by new climatic influences and changed conditions of life and of political institutions, it is still in the great essentials fundamentally the same race. The additions in this country until the present time have been from kindred people, or from those with whom we have been long allied and who speak the same language. . . .

. . . .

It being admitted, therefore, that a historic race of fixed type has been developed, it remains to consider what this means, what a race is, and what a change would portend. That which identifies a race and sets it apart from others is not to be found merely or ultimately in its physical appearance, its institutions, its laws, its literature, or even its language. These are in the last analysis only the expression or the evidence of race. The achievements of the intellect pass easily land to land and from people to people. The telephone, invented but yesterday, is used to-day in China, in Australia, or in South Africa as freely as in the United States. The book which the press to-day gives to the world in English is scattered tomorrow throughout the earth in every tongue, and the thoughts of the writer become the property of mankind. You can take a Hindoo, and give him the highest education the world can afford. He has a keen intelligence. He will absorb the learning of Oxford, he will acquire the manners and habits of England, he will sit in the British Parliament, but you cannot make him an Englishman.

Yet, he, like his conqueror, is of the great Indo-European family. But it has taken six thousand years and more to create the differences which exist between them. You cannot efface those differences thus made by education in a single life, because they do not rest upon the intellect. What, then, is the matter of race, which separates the Englishman from the Hindoo and the American from the Indian? It is something deeper and more fundamental than anything which concerns the intellect. We all know it instinctively, although it is so impalpable that we can scarcely define it, and yet is so deeply marked that even the physiological difference between the Negro, the Mongol, and the Caucasian are not more persistent or more obvious. When we speak of race, then, we do not mean its expressions in art or in language, or its achievements in knowledge. We mean the moral and intellectual characters, which in their association make the soul of a race, and which represent the product of all its past, the inheritance of all its ancestors, and the motives of all its conduct. The men of each race possess an indestructible stock of ideas, traditions, sentiments, modes of thought, an unconscious inheritance from their ancestors, upon which argument has no effect.

What makes a race are their mental and, above all, their moral characteristics, the slow growth and accumulation of centuries of toil and conflict. These are the qualities which determine their social efficiency as a people, which, make one race rise and another fall, which we draw out of a dim past through many generations of ancestors, about which we cannot argue, but in which we blindly believe, and which guide us in our short-lived generation as they have guided the race itself across the centuries. . . .

Those qualities are moral far more than intellectual, and it is on the moral qualities of the English-speaking race that our history, our victories, and all our future rest. There is only one way in which you can lower those qualities or weaken those characteristics, and that is by breeding them out. If a lower race mixes with a higher in sufficient numbers, history teaches us that the lower race will prevail. The lower race will absorb the higher, not the higher the lower, when the two strains approach equality in numbers. In other words, there is a limit to the capacity of any race for assimilating and elevating an inferior race; and when you begin to pour in unlimited numbers people of alien or lower races of less social efficiency and less moral force, you are running the most frightful risk that a people can run. The lowering of a great race means not only its own decline, but that of civilization. . . .

Mr. President, more precious even than forms of government are the mental and moral qualities which make what we call our race. While those stand unimpaired all is safe. When those decline all is imperiled. They are exposed to but a single danger, and that is by changing the quality of our race and citizenship through the wholesale infusion of races whose traditions and inheritances, whose thoughts and whose beliefs are wholly alien to ours, and with whom we have never assimilated or even been associated in the past. The danger has begun. It is small as yet, comparatively speaking, but it is large enough to warn us to act while there is yet time and while it can be done easily and efficiently. There lies the peril at the portals of our land; there is pressing the tide of unrestricted immigration. The time has certainly come, if not to stop, at least to check, to, sift, and to restrict those immigrants. In careless strength, with generous hand, we have kept our gates wide open to all the world. If we do not close them, we should at least place sentinels beside them to challenge those who would pass through. The gates which admit men to the United States and to citizenship in the great republic should no longer be left unguarded.

> O Liberty, white Goddess! is it well
> To leave the gates unguarded? On thy breast
> Fold Sorrow's children, soothe the hurts of fate,
> Lift the down-trodden, but with hand of steel
> Stay those who to thy sacred portals come
> To waste the gifts of freedom. Have a care
> Lest from thy brow the clustered stars be torn
> And trampled in the dust. For so of old,
> The thronging Goth and Vandal trampled Rome,
> And where the temples of the Cæsars stood
> The lean wolf unmolested made her lair.

From "The Restriction of Immigration," in *Speeches and Addresses, 1884–1909* (Boston: Houghton Mifflin, 1909), 245–266.

RACE RELATIONS BY GROUP

AFRICAN AMERICANS

The 1900s were a dismal decade for American blacks. Segregation became more pervasive. Lynching continued. The great majority of African Americans still performed farm labor in the South, either as sharecroppers for white landowners or as hired labor. There was a significant minority who owned their own farms and laid the basis for an emerging middle class, but even many of them struggled to make ends meet. Making matters worse was the intellectual respectability of racial theories that justified discrimination. On the plus side, ragtime and dances invented in black communities were very popular. And the modern civil rights movement began with the Niagara Movement and then the founding of the NAACP.

In 1900, Congressman George H. White, an African American Republican from North Carolina, introduced the first bill to make lynching a federal crime. In 1900, more than 100 blacks were executed by white mobs. The same would prove true of 1901. The great majority of these atrocities occurred in the South, where white apologists claimed that such measures were necessary to protect the honor of white women and to deal with what they alleged was the black slide into barbarism. In point of fact, as the African American journalist Ida B. Wells tirelessly pointed out, lynching victims often were black shopkeepers, whose success threatened the prosperity of white competitors, or people falsely accused of a variety of crimes. Lynch mobs almost invariably had the tacit support of local law enforcement officials. And mob members had no need to fear arrest or prosecution. They sometimes posed for pictures, their faces uncovered, in front of the dangling corpse of their victim. These pictures often were sold as postcards.

All of this made congressional action essential. But it was not forthcoming. There would be a long series of antilynching measures introduced. None ever became law. One reason was the ongoing decline in black political power. In 1901, Congressman White gave up his seat. There would not be another black member of the House of Representatives for 28 years. White was the last in the line of African Americans who had entered politics in the South during Reconstruction. There had been black governors, black U.S. senators, and black members of state legislatures, as well as members of Congress. "Redemption," as white supremacists called their regaining of political control in the South, meant the gradual erosion of these black political gains. By 1901, whites held every significant political office. It would take the "Great Migration," the movement of millions of blacks to the urban North and Midwest, which started around 1915, before African Americans could rebuild a political base.

In the meantime, they were dependent upon sympathetic whites, who were in short supply. One measure of this is the outcry that greeted President Theodore Roosevelt's decision to invite Booker T. Washington to dinner. Washington was the most prominent African American of the day. He counseled acceptance of segregation, at least for the time being, and urged blacks to pull themselves up by their own efforts. Despite his accommodationist views, however, howls of protest greeted Roosevelt's invitation. The president defended his decision, saying that the White House was open to all. But he never extended another invitation to an African American.

An even greater howl of disapproval and dismay greeted Jack Johnson's winning the heavyweight boxing title the day after Christmas in 1908. The previous champion, Jim Jeffries, had refused to fight Johnson because he was black. After Jeffries retired, Johnson defeated Tommy Burns for the title. In 1910, Jeffries came back, the first of a long line of "great white hopes" whom Johnson defeated over his seven years as champion. His defeat of Jeffries sparked racial violence in several cities, and his home state of Texas passed a law prohibiting the showing of films of his fights. Adding fuel to the racist fire were Johnson's three marriages, all to white women.

Racism, meanwhile, claimed a high level of intellectual respectability. The new racist theories claimed to rest upon Darwinian evolutionary ideas. Races (and nationality groups) were thought to constitute competing "stocks." The success of whites in imposing their rule over peoples of color in Africa, Asia,

Booker T. Washington. Courtesy of Library of Congress.

including the Philippines, and elsewhere supposedly demonstrated their natural superiority. Scientists measured the skulls of the various races and claimed that their findings showed that the intellectual abilities of whites, especially those whose ancestors came from northern and western Europe, far exceeded those of all others. These ideas fit nicely with those of eugenics. These held that, just as breeders could improve horses and livestock, the state could improve the quality of its citizens by sterilizing the "unfit."

Students in American high schools and colleges dutifully learned that whites were genetically superior. Otherwise, they would fail their biology, anthropology, and psychology courses. With science seemingly confirming prejudice, whites complacently congratulated themselves on their own excellence and just as complacently accepted the notion that blacks should be kept segregated, be denied the vote, and be unable to serve on juries.

As race relations continued to worsen, some younger African Americans openly rejected Booker T. Washington's famous Atlanta Compromise, the name derived from a speech he gave in 1895 in which he argued that in all matters social blacks and whites could be as separate as the fingers and in all matters economic as united as the hand. In 1903, W.E.B. Du Bois published *The Souls of Black Folk*. In it, he rejected Washington's call for blacks to accept segregation and disenfranchisement. Du Bois gave voice to a new generation of black intellectuals. In 1905, they gathered at Niagara, in upstate New York, to launch the Niagara Movement, an event that marks the beginning of the civil rights movement. Later, in 1909, Du Bois, William Monroe Trotter, Kelly Miller, and other members of the movement, along with white supporters such as Mary Ovington White, created the National Association for the Advancement of Colored People (NAACP).

As with the federal antilynching bill, the need was great. In Brownsville, Texas, on August 13, 1906, shooting broke out between white townspeople and black soldiers stationed at Fort Brown. One white was killed and others seriously wounded. Whites claimed that black troops in town had started firing at whites. The vast majority of the black soldiers were on the base during the whole time and were awakened in the middle of the night with orders to defend the fort against a possible attack by townspeople who were enraged because a white woman had been sexually assaulted several days earlier. There was no evidence that any of the soldiers had done anything more than follow orders, given by white officers, that night. A local grand jury refused to issue an indictment. Army investigations turned up no evidence of wrongdoing. Nonetheless, Theodore Roosevelt ordered all 167 black soldiers dishonorably discharged.

A month later, on September 22, a major race riot broke out in Atlanta, Georgia. Dozens of blacks and two whites died as white mobs rampaged through black neighborhoods for three days. The trigger was a series of sensational newspaper accounts of sexual assaults upon white women by black men. The papers carried stories of four such attacks on September 22 alone. None of the stories had any validity, it later turned out. But they were enough to set off the riot. One of those with a firsthand view of the violence was the 13-year-old Walter White, who would devote his life to fighting racism as the longtime head of the NAACP. He and his family barely escaped with their lives.

Two years later, in 1908, the first race riot in the North in half a century raged in Springfield, Illinois, from August 14 through the 19th. Once again, the trigger was the accusation, again baseless, that a black man had raped a white woman. Even though its members knew that the alleged rapist was being held elsewhere, the white mob set off to destroy the black neighborhood. Despite the decision of the governor to send thousands of militia immediately, a second mob formed and killed and then lynched an elderly black man.

The 1900s ended as inauspiciously as they began. In 1910, the Baltimore City Council adopted an ordinance that drew boundaries defining black and white neighborhoods. It was the first measure to make residential segregation mandatory. Dallas, Texas; Greensboro, North Carolina; Louisville, Kentucky; Norfolk, Roanoke, and Richmond, Virginia; Oklahoma City, Oklahoma; and St. Louis, Missouri, all quickly followed.

Not everything was bleak, however. In 1901, the vaudeville stars Bert Williams and George Walker recorded several of their comic songs for the Victor Talking Machine Company. It was a sign of the influence black Americans were beginning to have in shaping American popular culture. Even white racists paid top dollar to see Williams and Walker perform. Even they bought piano rolls made by Scott Joplin, whose "Maple Leaf Rag" began the ragtime music craze that lasted for two decades. Even they joined in the new dance craze, learning the steps to the "cakewalk" and the "black bottom," dances that originated in African American dance halls and clubs.

Black religion also became a major influence in American Protestantism. In 1906, in an African American church on Azusa Street in Los Angeles, a black minister, William J. Seymour, launched the Azusa Street Revival. It was the beginning of Pentecostalism. Whites heard about the all-day and all-night services, about people falling down and then jumping up and speaking in tongues, and they started to come to the Azusa Street Church, too. Seymour's services were among the few integrated activities anywhere in the country and quite possibly the only ones in which an African American played the leading part. Pentecostals have formed dozens of denominations in the century since, but their services owe certain characteristics to African American religious practices. One is the active role assigned to the congregation. It is common for members to cry out "Amen!" and "Yes, Lord, yes!" This draws upon the call-and-response mode of black preaching and singing, although many white Pentecostals may be unaware of the influence.

AMERICAN INDIANS

Policies put in place at the end of the nineteenth century continued to shape the lives of Native Americans. The government hoped to break up the tribes and to get the next generation to adopt white ways. The Carlisle Indian Industrial School in Pennsylvania, the school attended by Jim Thorpe, arguably the greatest athlete of the twentieth century, exemplified this approach. Students did not return to their families during vacations but lived with white families. They were expected to become Christians, make English their everyday language, and thus assimilate into American culture. Those who chose to remain with their own people found little opportunity on the reservations. There were few jobs. Murder, suicide, and alcoholism rates soared. The land usually had few resources. When there were resources to be exploited, the tribal lands were opened to settlers, as in Oklahoma starting in 1889.

In 1901 Congress acted to make the Indians in Oklahoma American citizens. The Indians were not consulted, perhaps because the primary objective was not to assimilate them but to speed up the territory's application for statehood. This required a minimum number of residents. Indians, as noncitizens, did not count toward the necessary total. Citizenship also simplified and speeded up the transfer of property to non-Indians. Oklahoma was rich in oil and natural gas deposits. Many of the most valuable minerals were on tribal land. Citizenship dissolved the tribes, divided tribal holdings among individual Indians, and eliminated the role of the Bureau of Indian Affairs, whose purpose supposedly was to protect Native Americans. In practice, the bureau rarely offered real protection from greedy whites.

Statehood came for Oklahoma in 1907 when Congress merged the Oklahoma and Indian territories. All of this land had originally been the Indian Territory before Congress carved the Oklahoma Territory out of it. Statehood put the territories together again. It also opened more land to white acquisition.

Indian school, Cantonment, Oklahoma. Courtesy of Library of Congress.

In 1903, in *Lone Wolf v. Hickcock,* the Supreme Court made the transfer of tribal lands to non-Indians easier still. The Kiowas and the Comanches had sued the Secretary of the Interior, who supervised the Bureau of Indian Affairs, to prevent the sale or disposal of any tribal lands without the consent of the members of the tribe involved. This was one of the provisions of the 1867 Treaty of Medicine Lodge. The Court ruled that the treaty did not apply because the U.S. government held the land in trust for the tribes. As a result, Congress could override the treaty. The decision was not simply a defeat for these two tribes. It transferred power over tribal holdings from all tribes to Congress. It also gave Congress the power to nullify any treaty provision it chose.

In 1906, Congress passed the Burke Act, which further speeded up the transfer of tribal lands to non-Indians. Under the terms of the Dawes Severalty Act of 1886, reservation lands were to be divided up among individual members of the tribes as soon as they "adopted the habits of civilized life," a phrase that meant that they had adopted English and white values and dress and occupations. Until that time, the federal government was to hold the lands in trust. The Burke Act expanded the powers of the Secretary of the Interior to remove individual tracts from the trust. As with the decision to make all Native Americans in Oklahoma citizens whether they wished it or not, the law made it easier for white land speculators to acquire tribal lands.

Also in 1906 Congress enacted the Antiquities Bill. This addressed an issue that remains controversial today. Some of the land owned by the federal government had been used in previous centuries as Indian burial grounds. Universities and organizations like the National Geographic Society had begun to sponsor expeditions to excavate these sites. Native Americans protested that these lands were sacred, that the bones being dug up belonged to their ancestors, and that, therefore, they should be left in peace and not put on display in museums. The Antiquities Act determined that the human remains and Indian artifacts found on federal land belonged to the United States and not to tribes or individual Indians.

In 1908, a Supreme Court decision finally favored Native Americans. This was *Winters v. United States.* Indians from the Fort Belknap reservation, in Montana, sued a white land developer who wanted to dam the Milk River. This would have diverted water from the reservation. The Court held that Congress, in establishing reservations, implicitly guaranteed that their inhabitants would have enough water to survive. It was a small victory, and the first in a long time.

In 1910, Walter Camp named Jim Thorpe, a Sac and Fox from Oklahoma, to his All-Star football team. Thorpe received the same honor in 1911 and 1912. In 1912, he led his Carlisle Indian team to the national championship. One of their victories was a 27–6 win over Army. In that game Thorpe had a 92-yard touchdown run called back because of a penalty. On the next play, he ran 97 yards for the score. Being named to the All-American team marked the initial recognition of Thorpe, whom many consider the finest American athlete of the first half of the twentieth century. Thorpe excelled in every sport he took up. In the 1912 Olympics, in Stockholm, he won both the decathlon and the pentathlon. The pentathlon consisted of the long jump, the javelin throw, the 200-meter dash, the discus throw, and the 1,500-meter run. The decathlon had 10 events: the 100-yard dash, the 220, the 440, the 880, the mile, the 120-yard high hurdles, the 220-yard low hurdles, the broad jump, the high jump, the pole vault, the shot put, the javelin, and the discus throw. Thorpe placed first in 8 of the 15 events and set a record in the decathlon that was not broken for 20 years. The Swedish king, in presenting Thorpe with his medals, called him the greatest athlete in the world. Controversy arose when it was discovered that Thorpe had played semiprofessional baseball during the summers of his college career, and he was forced to return the medals. He went on to play professional football for many years.

ASIAN AMERICANS AND PACIFIC ISLANDERS

Asian immigrants formed a tiny portion of the American population in 1900. The Chinese had been excluded from coming to the United States since 1882. And there were virtually no Pacific Islanders in America outside of Hawaii. Nonetheless, many of the racial and ethnic controversies of the decade swirled around these groups. One major reason was the debate over whether the United States ought to become an imperial power by taking over the Philippines. The presidential election of 1900 turned into a referendum on this issue, with the imperialists in the persons of the incumbent, William McKinley, and his vice presidential nominee, Theodore Roosevelt, winning a decisive victory. Another reason was the growing stream of Japanese immigrants to the West Coast, many having come to Hawaii first. Their arrival triggered a repetition of the anti-Chinese campaign of 20 years earlier. White Americans, especially those in California, Oregon, and Washington, proved equally hostile to immigrants from Korea and India, even though the number of immigrants was very small.

The United States decided to shoulder "the white man's burden," as the British poet Rudyard Kipling called the civilizing mission of supposedly superior whites, in the wake of the Spanish-American War. He wrote his poem, published first in the American magazine *McClure's*, in 1899, to add his voice to those of Theodore Roosevelt and other American imperialists who saw the American acquisition of the Philippine Islands as providing a stepping stone to China.

The opportunity to seize the Philippines grew out of the war with Spain of 1898. The battle cry of the conflict for Americans was "Remember the *Maine*," in honor of an American naval vessel that blew up in Havana harbor, a disaster incorrectly blamed upon Spain. But the fighting began halfway across the planet with the destruction of the Spanish fleet in Manila harbor by the American Pacific fleet. Assistant Secretary of the Navy Theodore Roosevelt had given Commodore George Dewey the order to attack the fleet in the event of war. Spain was engaged in putting down an insurrection on the islands. The United States decided to ally with the "Insurrectos," and their combined forces quickly forced the Spanish to surrender. The Filipinos thought that the United States would assume the same policy toward them that it had toward Cuba, namely a guarantee of their independence and a pledge to take no land for itself. Instead, the United States purchased Spain's claim to the Philippines for $20 million. The "Insurrectos," led by Ernesto Aguinaldo, proclaimed their independence, and the War in the Philippines began in early 1899. It would officially last until July 4, 1902, when Theodore Roosevelt proclaimed victory. The fighting, however, continued for another decade. In all, some 12,000 Americans and at least a quarter of a million Filipinos died in what was a war of extreme brutality on both sides. The "Insurrectos" sometimes buried their prisoners up to their necks, forced molasses down their throats, and left them to be eaten alive from the inside out by fire ants. The Americans retaliated by putting whole villages to the torch, killing everyone regardless of gender or age.

Hostility to Asian immigrants mounted in the 1900s, especially against the Japanese and, to a lesser extent, Koreans. The first major anti-Japanese rally was organized by several labor unions in California in 1900, coincident with the movement of Japanese farm workers from Hawaii. As with the "Chinese Must Go!" campaign of the 1870s and 1880s, spokespeople described the Japanese as a threat to the American standard of living. The Japanese and the Koreans, they charged, would take jobs from Americans by accepting lower wages. Further, like the Chinese, they would bring Oriental vices with them. Since white Californians knew almost nothing about the Japanese or their culture, their attacks drew heavily upon well-established stereotypes of the Chinese.

Newspapers also campaigned against the Japanese. On February 23, 1905, the front page of the *San Francisco Chronicle* read: "The Japanese Invasion: The Problem of the Hour." Pacific Coast papers competed to see which could run the most alarming stories. A few months after the *Chronicle* launched its anti-Japanese campaign, the Asiatic Exclusion League was formed, in San Francisco, on May 14, 1905. Union members and European immigrants formed the bulk of the membership. This began the formal organization of the anti-Japanese movement.

Meanwhile, hostility to the Chinese remained intense. In 1900, a bubonic plague scare in San Francisco led public authorities to quarantine Chinatown. It was a common belief among doctors that particular racial groups were more likely to carry particular diseases than were others, a theory in keeping with the overall racial ideas of the time. Nor was anti-Chinese sentiment limited to the West Coast. In 1902, federal immigration officials and Boston police swept through the Hub's Chinatown and arrested almost 250 illegal immigrants.

Also in 1902, Congress renewed and made permanent the Chinese Exclusion Act. The original measure had been due to expire that year. Exclusion was not enough for members of the Asian Exclusion League, formed in 1905. The same interest groups—labor unions, European immigrant associations, real estate brokers, and newspaper publishers—who had led anti-Chinese activities for decades formed the League's leadership. In that same year, Congress created the Border Patrol to prevent illegal Asian immigration via Mexico and Canada. In 1905 as well, California's Civil Code outlawed marriage between whites and "Mongolians," such as Chinese, Japanese, and Koreans. Most states prohibited marriage between blacks and whites. California was the first to broaden the definition of miscegenation to include Asians.

The decision to treat Asians as legally equivalent to African Americans underlay the decision by the San Francisco Board of Education in 1906 to prohibit Chinese, Japanese, and other Asian American children from attending white schools. That year, 1906, was the year of the great San Francisco earthquake and fire, a calamity that destroyed all municipal records, including those concerning immigration. As a result, Chinese immigrants were able to claim they were U.S. citizens. As nonwhites, they were not eligible for citizenship, so they had to claim to have been born in the United States. With no birth or immigration records, city officials could not contest their assertions. Citizens enjoyed the right to bring wives and children to America. This led to an influx of so-called picture-book brides, women who married immigrants by proxy while still in China and then came to America. This redressed what had been a very lopsided gender ratio and guaranteed new generations of Chinese-Americans.

Members of the Asian Exclusion League wanted Congress to ban Japanese immigration as it had that from China. But, while China's imperial regime was teetering on the brink of collapse, Japan was emerging as a major Pacific power. Theodore Roosevelt helped negotiate the end of the Russo-Japanese War, during which, for the first time in centuries, an Asian nation defeated a European country. President Roosevelt had no desire to insult the government of Japan, So, in 1907–1908, he worked out the so-called Gentlemen's Agreement. Under its terms, the United States agreed not to prohibit Japanese immigration, and Japan agreed not to issue passports to Japanese laborers. Japanese women could come, if they were married to men already in the United States. This, as with the Chinese, led to widespread use of the "picture brides" system of proxy marriage. And, as with the Chinese, it guaranteed a new generation of Japanese-Americans who, because born in the United States, would be American citizens.

The United States also agreed to seek to end discrimination against Japanese-Americans. Japan was particularly concerned with California laws such as that which required the children of Japanese immigrants to attend segregated schools. California retained these laws and passed still others. On the other hand, President Theodore Roosevelt issued Executive Order 589 in 1907. This prohibited Japanese with passports for Hawaii, Mexico, or Canada to re-emigrate to the United States.

Immigrants from India, despite their very small numbers, also encountered violent hostility. In 1908, a white mob expelled Indians from Bellingham, Washington. The same thing happened the next year in Live Oak, California.

A measure of the widespread nature of anti-Asian prejudice is the popularity of the Sax Rohmer novels featuring the arch-villain Fu Man Chu. Rohmer based the character on Professor Moriarty of the Sherlock Holmes stories. His hero, in fact, was Holmes's nephew. Like his uncle, he thwarted the schemes of the criminal mastermind with the assistance of a close friend, a medical doctor. Why would such derivative fare attract so many readers and, later, so many moviegoers? Simply put, Fu Man Chu embodied the "Yellow Peril."

EUROPEAN IMMIGRANTS

Immigration, overwhelmingly from Europe, reached new heights. A total of 8,795,386 people immigrated from Europe during the first 10 years of the twentieth century. In 1905, for the first time, more than a million immigrants came to the United States, and in 1907, approximately 1.25 million immigrants entered the country via Ellis Island, in New York harbor. Tens of thousands more came through Boston, Baltimore, and other ports. They came for the same reasons earlier immigrants had. They hoped to find economic opportunity, to rejoin family members who had already made the journey, and to live in a country with political and religious freedom. Some came to avoid persecution. In 1903, for example, the Kishinev Massacre occurred within the Pale of Settlement, the area of Russia where Jews could live. It was one of a series of pogroms in which Russian soldiers murdered and raped Jews and burned their villages. The tsars routinely used anti-Semitism to deflect discontent. The result was a Jewish exodus from Russia. Many, aided by American Jews, settled on the Lower East Side of Manhattan. There they also encountered anti-Semitism. In 1902, for example, an Irish-American mob attacked a Jewish funeral procession in Manhattan. But Jews in America encountered nothing equivalent to the pogroms.

Not all immigrants stayed. Many came as seasonal labor, so-called Birds of Passage, and returned to their home countries. Some of these made the round trip several times. Others remained in America for a number of years, saving up enough money to pay off a mortgage or purchase land, before going back. French Canadians often promised themselves that they would return to Quebec. And, as steamboats fares declined and the trip itself took less and less time, Greeks, Poles, Italians, and other European migrants went back and forth between the United States and their countries of origin. Russian Jews, on the other hand, had no wish to return. The Irish also saw themselves as permanent residents. They waxed nostalgic about the "ould sod," but the bitter poverty they had escaped made them save up to bring brothers, sisters, and other relatives to the United States, rather than to finance their own return.

The upshot of all of this movement was that first- and second-generation immigrants came to form the majority of the population in many American cities. This caused old-stock Americans to fear that the newcomers would take over the country. Many blamed ethnic voters for the machine politics and corruption in New York, Boston, Chicago, and other cities. Many feared the growth of Roman Catholicism. Others espoused an increasingly strident anti-Semitism. This merely began their list of concerns. The menace of the alien radical also preyed upon their minds.

Russian Jew on a bench, New York City, c. 1910. Courtesy of Library of Congress.

Ever since the Haymarket Bombing of 1886, in which several Chicago police officers died, nativists had charged that some immigrants brought with them un-American political beliefs such as anarchism and socialism. On September 6, 1901, a man popularly misidentified as a Polish immigrant shot President McKinley as he visited the Buffalo World's Fair. McKinley's death eight days later heightened anti-immigrant sentiments, and Congress adopted the Anarchist Exclusion Act. Unlike the Chinese Exclusion Act, this measure had little practical effect. U.S. consuls in European ports had no effective way of determining the political sympathies of those applying for visas. Immigration inspectors at Ellis Island, required to process thousands of newcomers each day, speaking scores of languages, could only ask them to swear they were not anarchists. Since the immigrants knew that confessing their radical leanings would earn them a quick passage back to their home country, few did so.

Yet another fear was that immigrants from southern and eastern Europe were genetically inferior to earlier newcomers from northern and western Europe. The American Breeders Association in 1903 created a Committee on Eugenics to lobby for laws requiring the involuntary sterilization of those deemed mentally defective, unwed mothers, and the offspring of those alleged to be hereditary criminals. It was an appropriate beginning. Member of the Breeders Association carefully traced the bloodlines of champion horses, cattle, dogs, and other animals. Surely the same methods would work with humans, as well. David Starr Jordan, president of Stanford University, was a leading supporter, as was Prescott Hall, founder of the Immigration Restriction League. They achieved their initial legislative success in 1907 when Indiana adopted the first involuntary sterilization law. By 1930, most other states had followed its lead.

All of these fears led to calls for immigration restriction. The literacy test was the preferred method. Many immigrants could neither read nor write. As a result, the Immigration Restriction League and other organizations argued that a simple test would eliminate the great majority of migrants from eastern and southern Europe while allowing those from western and northern Europe to continue to enter the country. President Roosevelt opposed the measure, in part because the Republican Party had strong support among urban workers who were often themselves immigrants or the children of immigrants. The best the restrictionists could do was to create the Dillingham Commission in 1907 to study the impact of immigration on the American economy, polity, and society.

Congress did take one step toward the literacy test in 1906. The Naturalization Act of that year required that all applicants for citizenship had to be able to speak and read English. The law also placed the supervision of the naturalization process in the hands of the newly established Immigration and Naturalization Service. Previously, state and municipal courts had controlled access to citizenship. Good-government reformers had long complained that machine politicians appointed compliant judges who admitted to citizenship any and all applicants who were likely to vote as the machine wanted.

Congress took another step to control immigration in 1907, passing the Expatriation Act. This took away the citizenship of American-born women who married a foreign national. Since women could not vote in national elections or serve on juries in most jurisdictions, the act was largely symbolic. It stigmatized marriages between the native-born and aliens and emphasized the wife's subservience to the husband. *His* citizenship defined them both. In the 1920s, when Congress established immigration quotas based upon national origins, the Expatriation Act suddenly had a practical impact. American-born women who traveled abroad to visit their husband's families or for any other reason could return to the United States only if they could obtain a visa. Since some of the quotas were exceedingly small, many women who had lived their whole lives in the United States found themselves marooned in Europe. Congress had to repeal the law.

Israel Zangwill's play *The Melting Pot* opened in New York City in 1908. It provided a metaphor for defenders of open immigration that continues to shape popular debate today. Zangwill, a Jewish immigrant to England, proclaimed that the mixture of diverse peoples and cultures would produce a stronger America, just as certain alloys prove stronger than the metals that produce them. It was an idea with a long intellectual pedigree. Hector St. John de Crevecoeur had asked, "Who is this American, this new man?" in the eighteenth century. He answered that the American combined the best of all the European nations. It was an answer that

Two women strikers on picket line during the "Uprising of the Twenty Thousand," New York City, February 1910. Courtesy of Library of Congress.

directly contradicted the claims of the eugenicists. They believed in racial purity, not in amalgamation. Their term for the melting pot was "mongrelization." And their views were the ones taught in high school and college biology courses.

Yet, one group of so-called new immigrants from southern and eastern Europe did win a remarkable degree of popular support. In 1909–1910, Jewish and Italian shirtwaist workers went on strike in New York City in what became known as the "Uprising of the Twenty Thousand." At first the strike attracted little attention. Then middle- and upper-class women turned up on the picket lines and in the courts, since, as was usual, the police did their best to disrupt the strikers by arbitrarily arresting them. These "allies" were members of the Women's Trade Union League, affluent reformers who believed that the most effective way to fight prostitution was to increase the wages working women could earn. Their support attracted new allies, including suffragists. The banker J. P. Morgan's daughter Ann supported the strike. So did the socialist newspaper *The New York Call* and the leading Yiddish-language paper, also socialist, *The Forward*. It was a remarkable, perhaps unique, instance of sorority that cut across ethnic, religious, class, and political lines. The strike was a qualified success. Most manufacturers, but not the largest, recognized the union. The union, the International Ladies

Garment Workers, became a force in the garment industry and in New York City politics.

This was the exception, not the rule. Most newcomers worked long hours for low wages in terrible conditions. Most unions were limited to skilled trades dominated by Yankees and members of the old immigration from Great Britain, English-speaking Canada, Germany, and Scandinavia. It was a hard life. But immigrants shared in the American Dream, and some of them and more of their children began to achieve positions of wealth and power. In 1903, for example, Theodore Roosevelt appointed Oscar Strauss Secretary of Labor and Commerce; he was the first Jew to hold a cabinet position. Another key example, because of their visibility, were urban politicians such as the Irish-Americans who ran Tammany Hall, the Democratic political machine in New York City. Still others, such as the Jewish attorney Louis Brandeis, who argued important cases before the Supreme Court, began to achieve success in professions previously dominated by white Anglo-Saxon Protestants.

Overall, it was a mixed picture of increasing nativism, anti-Catholicism, anti-Semitism, and calls for immigration restriction on the one hand and increasing influence and opportunity for European immigrants on the other. Both trends would continue for the next two decades.

LATINOS

Large-scale emigration from Mexico, Puerto Rico, and the rest of Latin America had not yet begun. The great majority of Latinos in the United States, as a result, were the descendants of those Mexicans who lived in the provinces seized by the United States during the Mexican War. Tens of thousands of residents of Arizona, New Mexico, California, Nevada, and Utah remained in those territories after the war. Their children and grandchildren became American citizens by birth. A few prominent families managed to hold on to their lands, but many were dispossessed by Anglo-Americans. Still more had no land to begin with. They continued to work as farm laborers, cowboys, cooks, and domestics and in other menial jobs. Most learned at least some English but continued to speak primarily Spanish. Their children were usually bilingual.

Despite their citizenship, Mexican-Americans faced a great deal of prejudice, as the Arizona Orphan Abduction case shows. This involved a group of 40 orphan children who were sent from a Catholic orphanage in New York City to live with Mexican Catholic families in Arizona in 1904. Such "orphan trains" were common in the late nineteenth and early twentieth centuries. Orphanages in the East would send orphans off in search of adoptive families. The train would pull into a town, and prospective adoptive parents would look the children over and choose their favorite. Usually the choice depended upon the family's need for labor. The train would then continue on to the next town until all or most of the children had been adopted. This case was different. The train's final destination was Clifton-Morenci, Arizona, where Mexican-American Catholics had pledged to take all 40 of the remaining orphans. White Arizonians, especially white Protestant women, objected to Mexican-Americans adopting white children. So they literally kidnapped the orphans. The case went to the Supreme Court, which ruled in favor of the kidnappers, as had the lower courts. Race trumped all other considerations, including the fact that the nuns who escorted the children represented their legal guardian, the New York Foundling Hospital.

Mexican-Americans faced discrimination in the job market and in housing and education. But there was little or no concern about immigration from Mexico. In 1905, when Congress established the Border Patrol, it sought to prevent Chinese, Japanese, and Korean workers from entering the United States from Hawaii via Mexico or Canada. Mexicans were welcome to cross the border at will. Those who did so usually came for seasonal farm jobs or to work as maids in border cities like El Paso and San Diego.

In 1910, the Mexican Revolution broke out. As the fighting raged, thousands of refugees came to the United States. This began a major migration. Over the next 20 years, more than a million Mexicans would cross the border. And resistance to Mexican immigration would build. But, that was in the future.

In 1910, there was a measure of actual progress. Mexican-American delegates to the New Mexico constitutional convention managed to insert a provision that stipulated that both Spanish and English be used for all state business. This had been agreed to by the United States and Mexico in 1848 in the Treaty of Guadalupe Hidalgo, which ended the Mexican War. But the United States had made no effort to live up to its commitment. California, Arizona, and the other areas captured during the war did not recognize Spanish as one of the two official languages. Only New Mexico did.

LAW AND GOVERNMENT

Both court decisions and legislative actions reflected the racism that so strongly characterized the United States during the first decades of the twentieth century. The most crucial Supreme Court decision had come earlier, in 1896, in *Plessy v. Ferguson*. The Court held that a black man had no legal right to ride in a "whites only" railway car. The railroad could provide "separate but equal" facilities, instead. The decision made segregation of all kinds the law of the land and effectively repealed the "equal protection" clause of the Fourteenth Amendment. Justice John Marshall Harlan's dissenting opinion proved prophetic. He argued that the "separate but equal" formula clearly violated the meaning and intent of the Fourteenth and Fifteenth Amendments, both adopted to secure the civil rights of freed slaves. Worse, the formula created a double standard in the law. Blacks could be discriminated against merely because it pleased whites to do so.

The decision, he predicted, would ultimately prove as notorious as the *Dred Scott* Decision.

Plessy did join *Dred Scott* at the top of the list of the worst Supreme Court decisions. It had exactly the dire consequences Justice Harlan predicted. And it would take almost 60 years for the Court to reverse itself, in *Brown v. Board of Education* (1954), when it finally accepted Harlan's view that separate meant unequal treatment. No key cases involving the rights of African American arose in the 1900s. In part this was a result of the policy of accommodation to segregation preached by the black educator Booker T. Washington. And in part it was a result of the sweeping nature of *Plessy*, which made challenges to segregation difficult if not impossible.

The City Council of Baltimore in 1910 approved the first ordinance that specified the boundaries of black and white neighborhoods, creating legally mandated housing segregation. This was a direct consequence of *Plessy*. It was followed by similar measures in Dallas, Texas; Greensboro, North Carolina; Louisville, Kentucky; Norfolk, Virginia; Oklahoma City, Oklahoma; Richmond, Virginia, and Roanoke, Virginia; and St. Louis, Missouri.

In 1900, Congressman George H. White (Rep., N.C.) introduced a bill making lynching a federal crime. More than 100 African Americans had been lynched the previous year, continuing a dreadful trend that had already lasted for decades and would continue throughout the 1900s. Local and state law enforcement authorities routinely did nothing to prevent lynching. On the contrary, they often actively cooperated with the lynch mobs. White's bill did not become law. Neither did the scores of similar measures proposed over the next 40 years. They were defeated by Southerners, who argued that their states already had laws against murder. When confronted by the fact that the laws were never enforced against lynchers, they replied that only such vigilante justice could protect southern white women from would-be black rapists. As the journalist Ida B. Wells pointed out, this was a lie.

In most of its other important decisions, the Supreme Court also upheld the standard of white supremacy. In *Lone Wolf v. Hickock* (1903), it ruled against the Kiowas and Comanches who had sued the Secretary of the Interior to stop the transfer of tribal lands. According to the Treaty of Medicine Lodge of 1868, tribes had to consent to any such transfer. But the Court held that the land did not belong to the tribes. Congress instead held it in trust for them. As the trustee, Congress had the power to make any alterations in the status of the land it thought beneficial. The ruling effectively eviscerated not only the Treaty of Medicine Lodge but all similar agreements between tribes and the United States. In *Winters v. United States*, the Supreme Court actually ruled in favor of Indians from the Fort Belknap reservation in Montana. They had sued to prevent a white property owner from damming the Milk River above the reservation. At issue was whether, in establishing the reservation, the United States had implicitly guaranteed the Indians enough water to survive on the land. The Court determined that it had.

Congress, meanwhile, continued to pass measures that further restricted tribal rights and holdings. Several had to do with Oklahoma statehood. Originally, the entire area was Indian Territory, land set aside for the tribes forced to evacuate their homes east of the Mississippi in the 1830s. In 1861, the Indian Territory seceded from the United States and joined the Confederate States of America. Defeat entailed a significant loss of land. In 1889, the United States divided almost 3 million so-called unassigned acres into 160-acre lots. Whites from adjoining states lined up at the territory's borders for what was literally a race to get the best parcels. This was the first of several land runs as the government opened lands purchased from tribes to settlement. The last great land opening was on August 6, 1901, when the surplus acreage of the Kiowa and Comanche country, amounting to 3.5 million acres, was opened to settlers. This time there was no run. Instead, would-be settlers had to file claims in advance.

The rapid influx of white settlers, along with the discovery of petroleum, put Oklahoma on the fast track for statehood. To expedite this, in 1901 Congress granted citizenship to all Indians living outside the remaining reservations. This allowed the territory to reach the minimum population required for statehood more quickly. And, in 1907, Oklahoma was admitted as a state. All of the remaining reservation land, Congress decided, would become part of the new state. Individual Indians and families would each receive a portion of the former reservations. Since they could now sell these properties, the measure opened the lands to whites.

In 1906, Congress passed two laws that contributed further to the ending of reservations and of tribal rights. One was the Antiquities Act. Tribes claimed that graves and other relics of their history should be protected. Universities and museums argued that the bones and artifacts should be available for scientific study. This is an argument that continues today, with the difference that tribes are far more likely to prevail. In the Antiquities Act, Congress decided that neither tribes nor individual Indians had any claim on anything found on federal land. Also in 1906, Congress adopted the Burke Act; it amended the Dawes Severalty Act of 1886, which had set a schedule for dividing tribal lands among individual Indian families. In the meantime, it had provided that these lands be held in trust. This provided the legal basis for *Lone Wolf v. Hitchcock* (1903). The Burke Act gave the Secretary of the Interior the power to accelerate the schedule if he decided that individuals and groups of Indians had "adopted the habits of civilized life."

Congress devoted much attention throughout the decade to Asian immigrants, beginning with the Organic Act of 1900, which ended contract labor in Hawaii. Japanese, Chinese, and Filipino farm laborers had contracted to work for specific planters while still in their homelands. The intent of the law was to discourage their migration to the islands by making them find work only after they had paid for and completed their journeys. An additional purpose was to protect the workers from exploitation. Contracts often paid lower wages than migrants could negotiate in the open market. The measure achieved this second goal but did nothing to stem the flow of Asians and Pacific Islanders to Hawaii and then on to the United States. As a result, Congress created the Border Patrol, in 1905, to prevent Chinese immigrants from entering the United States via Mexico or Canada. Congress had already renewed the Chinese Exclusion Act in 1902. The original 1882 law was about to expire; the new law had no expiration date.

Japanese and Korean workers in Hawaii were still able to enter the United States, and it was not long before white Americans on the West Coast demanded their exclusion, as well. President Theodore Roosevelt strenuously opposed congressional action. He had negotiated the peace treaty that ended the Russo-Japanese War of 1904–1905 and correctly regarded Japan as a major Pacific power. He had no desire to insult the Japanese government by prohibiting immigration from there. Making the situation more complex was a series of actions by San Francisco and California authorities. In 1905, the state outlawed intermarriage between whites and "Mongolians," that is, Chinese, Japanese, and Koreans. The following year, the city's board of education required the children of these same groups to attend segregated schools. The measures effectively classified Asians with African Americans.

In 1907–1908, the president negotiated a diplomatic agreement with Japan. In return for not being excluded by the United States, the Japanese government agreed not to permit its nationals to emigrate to America. Exceptions were to be made for government officials, Japanese citizens traveling on business, and students. A bigger exception permitted Japanese nationals already living in the United States to bring over their wives and children. The great majority of these nationals were unmarried males. But Japan recognized proxy marriages, that is, marriages where one of the parties was not physically present but instead was represented by another. This allowed thousands of Japanese men living in the United States to select brides from so-called picture books, marry them by proxy, and bring them to America. President Roosevelt next issued Executive Order 589, which prohibited Japanese with passports for Hawaii, Mexico, or Canada to re-emigrate to the United States. He also promised Japan that he would work for the repeal of discriminatory state and local measures. These nonetheless remained in effect.

Congress also acted to limit the immigration of people holding radical political views and of peoples from eastern and southern Europe. The first effort, which took the form of the Anarchist Exclusion Act of 1901, was triggered by the assassination of President William McKinley, while attending the Buffalo World's Fair, by Leon Czolgosz, a Polish-American anarchist. As would be the case later with the assassination of John F. Kennedy, many people refused to believe that assassin had acted alone. Instead, conspiracy theories proliferated. But this exclusion act had only symbolic value. The United States had no way of investigating the political beliefs of the hundreds of thousands who crowded Ellis Island and other ports of entry every year beyond asking the newcomers to swear that they were not anarchists.

Calls for the restriction of immigration continued to mount. The Immigration Restriction League campaigned for a literacy test. Immigrants would have to be capable of reading 40 words in some language. League partisans, such as Senator Henry Cabot Lodge (Rep., Massachusetts), believed that, since many newcomers from southern and eastern Europe were illiterate, the test would effectively reduce their numbers while not impacting desirable immigration from northern and western Europe. Faced with a veto from President Theodore Roosevelt, advocates of restriction agreed to drop their demands, at least for the present, in return for the creation of a commission to study the overall impact of immigration, a study they were certain would validate their arguments. The Dillingham Commission was created in 1907 and issued its 42-volume report in 1911. Few read beyond the first two volumes, which purported to summarize the findings. In fact, they misrepresented the findings, which tended to show that immigrants did not increase crime or unemployment or lower wages or otherwise become burdens upon society. The summaries presented the opposite as true.

Congress created the Immigration and Naturalization Bureau in 1906 to enforce the growing number of restrictions and exclusions and to oversee the citizenship process. This latter task was aimed at weakening urban political machines, such as Tammany Hall in New York City. The machines allegedly appointed judges who then naturalized immigrants loyal to political "bosses." The new bureau would also enforce a new law that required all applicants for citizenship to be literate in English.

The most important state law was Indiana's involuntary sterilization measure, the initial legislative victory for the new eugenics movement. Eugenics held that society needed to protect itself from hereditary defects such as feeblemindedness by preventing those with such deficiencies from reproducing. The list of supposedly inherited defects was dishearteningly long and included what would now be regarded as behaviors, such as criminal acts, rather than physical traits. The reason that criminality was thought to be hereditary was that most scientists believed that acquired characteristics could be inherited. So, for example, many believed that centuries of living without a country of their own meant that Jews lacked the genetic makeup for patriotism. By the same logic, the child of a criminal who followed in his father's footsteps supposedly did so not because of his home environment but because he had inherited his father's antisocial tendencies. Ultimately, more than 30 states followed Indiana's example. Tens of thousands were sterilized against their will in the ensuing decades.

MEDIA AND MASS COMMUNICATIONS

Print media dominated mass communications in the 1900s. Newsstands in middle-size and large cities offered a choice of several English-language dailies, along with papers in German, Polish, Yiddish, Italian, and other languages. In

1905, Robert Abbott founded the *Chicago Defender*. It quickly became the most influential African American paper. Customers could also choose among hundreds of magazines. Some, like *Harper's Weekly*, offered heavily illustrated compilations of news, fiction, book reviews, and cartoons. Others specialized in sensationalized stories of sin, crime, and sports. *The Police Gazette* was the original, and it had many imitators. There were no movie magazines, yet. There were fashion magazines. Another *Harper's, Harper's Bazaar*, led the way. On the covers of most of these publications was a beautiful girl. There was even a popular song about "The Girl on the Magazine Cover." She was drawn by one of a coterie of illustrators who effectively set the standard of American feminine beauty. The most celebrated was Charles Dana Gibson. His "Gibson Girl," tall, with fair skin and regular features, was clearly a descendant of the white Anglo-Saxon pioneers. No member of a minority ethnic group needed apply to model for Gibson and his colleagues. No African Americans, Asians, or Hispanics needed to, either. Where readers would have seen blacks, Indians, and Asians, as well as knife-wielding Italian criminals and bomb-throwing anarchists from eastern Europe, was on the covers of dime novels and so-called penny dreadful magazines. These contained stories of maidens rescued at the last minute from the clutches of evildoers by Buffalo Bill or any one of hundreds of entirely fictitious heroes. Often the villains were Chinese, such as Sax Rohmer's Fu Man Chu. Or they might be renegade Indians or members of the "Black Hand," as Italian extortionists were called.

Newspapers competed by reducing stories to headlines. These could be disconcerting. "The Japanese Invasion: The Problem of the Hour" read the front page of the *San Francisco Chronicle* for February 23, 1905. Sensationalized crime stories and dramatic trials made possible the job of newsboys hawking their paper with cries of "Extra! Extra! Read all about it!" on street corners. Papers also competed on the "funny pages." Comics were a new art form with deep roots in the immigrant experience. "The Yellow Kid," which featured an Irish-American street urchin and his ethnic pals, was so popular that the Hearst and Pulitzer newspaper chains got into a bidding war for the rights to publish it, a competition that gave us the phrase "yellow journalism." Many of the first comic strip authors were themselves children of immigrants who drew upon their own life experiences.

Papers routinely assigned their best writers to the sports pages. Baseball was the national pastime. And many of the leading players were also second-generation immigrants like Honus Wagner of the Pittsburgh Pirates. The poem "Casey at the Bat" celebrated and spoofed this ethnic pride as all in Mudville hope against hope that "mighty Casey" will get to bat. Boxing was another popular sport with strong racial and ethnic links. For several years, Jack Johnson could not get a shot at the heavyweight title because the Irish-American champ, Jim Jeffries, refused to fight a black man. Jeffries then came out of retirement in an attempt to reclaim the title, becoming the first in a long series of "great white hopes" who fought Johnson and lost.

Beyond professional sports were the many contests sponsored by churches, ethnic and racial organizations, and schools. Ethnic and African American newspapers covered these faithfully. Coverage in the English-language dailies was more hit-or-miss, but still very important. One's prospects in America, blacks, Asians, and white ethnics knew, depended in large measure on the standing of one's group. As a result, it mattered if the Polish team beat the Lithuanians or vice versa. It mattered all the more because the opportunities for Poles or Lithuanians or members of other ethnic and racial groups to gain public notice were few and far between. Honus Wagner, Jack Johnson, and Jim Thorpe held iconic status in their ethnic and racial groups.

CULTURAL SCENE

Movies were in their infancy as the new century began. The first movies lasted but a minute or two but already showed the medium's power to shape the culture in profound and unpredictable ways. Among the first films shown commercially were recreations of Philippine War battles, shot by the Edison Company using the New Jersey State Militia. They showed heroic white Americans stoutheartedly advancing upon and then vanquishing the enemy. In the real battles, many of the American soldiers were African Americans, veterans of the Indian Wars and of the war in Cuba. But, in the movies, U.S. troops were white. Hollywood would continue this distortion of history for another half-century as uncounted westerns had white cavalry troops arriving in the nick of time to rescue the wagon train or stagecoach from marauding Indians.

It is unknown how many people saw these early war movies. They were often shown in storefronts. Admission cost a nickel. And filmgoers tended to be blue-collar workers and their families. As films became longer, audiences grew larger. Scores of film companies, most initially located on Long Island, sprang up. They drew upon vaudeville performers, chorus girls, and unemployed actors for their casts. The plots grew more complicated, and excitement became the norm for movie scripts. *The Great Train Robbery* set the pattern. Initially, making movies required little capital. The entrepreneur rented a camera, hired someone to operate it, leased some open space, shot the movie in a matter of days, and distributed it to other small entrepreneurs who showed it in so-called nickelodeons. Film companies came into existence and then disappeared with barely a trace with great frequency in these early years. But some companies thrived. They signed actors to long-term contracts, built studios, purchased the best equipment, and turned out longer, better, and more gripping pictures. So, too, some of the nickelodeon operators put their profits into building larger theatres. Many of these early entrepreneurs were first- and second-generation immigrants. Jews were especially prominent in the emerging motion picture industry. This did not mean so much in the 1900s. By 1920, however, the motion picture business was one of the largest industries in the country. The fact that so many immigrants and their children were running the studios, producing and distributing the pictures and, in many cases, starring in them as well, would give them control of an extraordinarily potent force in shaping American culture.

Another new medium was the phonograph recording, also pioneered by Thomas Edison. The initial sound quality was poor. Yet, consumers gobbled up recordings of Sousa marches, Caruso singing arias, and, after 1901, George Walker and Bert Williams performing original comic songs. Walker and Williams were the first African Americans to sign a contract with the Victor Recording Company. Other black performers would soon follow their lead. So would countless vaudeville acts, many of them, as with the movie industry, first- and second-generation immigrants. Even more popular than the phonograph, in large measure because the sound quality was so good, were piano rolls. They were used with player pianos. One inserted the roll, and the piano played itself. Since this was the age of ragtime, many of the most popular rolls were made by black composers and musicians like Scott Joplin, whose "Maple Leaf Rag" touched off the ragtime craze. The new music inspired new dances. These also originated in the African American community, as names like the "black bottom" made plain.

A more profound cultural development began in April 1906 in an African American church in Los Angeles. This was the Azusa Street Revival, an event that sparked the Pentecostal movement first in the United States and then in the world. Pentecostal churches are now the fastest-growing of all Christian denominations. The pastor of the Azusa Street Church, the Rev. William J. Seymour, did not give sermons. Instead, he walked among the congregation, reading an occasional verse from a miniature Bible. Meanwhile, members of the church would shout out, fall in a faint, shake violently (early Pentecostals were sometimes called Holy Rollers), and then jump up and begin to speak in tongues. This was, they believed, the same blessing as that bestowed upon the apostles 50 days after Jesus' resurrection. According to the "Acts of the Apostles" in the New Testament, tongues of fire appeared over the heads of the apostles. When they began to preach, each person heard them in his or her own language. The Azusa Street converts spoke in what sounded like an unknown language.[37] Later they testified to feeling the power of the Holy Spirit passing through their bodies. Not infrequently, they claimed that they had been cured of sicknesses and disabilities.

As word of the revival spread, largely through the Los Angeles newspapers, whites began to attend the Rev. Seymour's services. Many, no doubt, were simply curious and wanted to see for themselves. Enough stayed on to worship, however, for the Azusa Street Revival to become a truly interracial experience and to last for four years. Many, hearing of the revival, had similar experiences. One was an Irish immigrant named Robert Semple, who embarked upon a revival tour of southern Ontario. There he met, converted, and married a teenaged agnostic. She would later become the most famous Pentecostal preacher of the 1920s and 1930s, Aimee Semple McPherson.

Most African Americans did not become Pentecostals. They primarily worshipped as Baptists or Methodists. Their churches formed the core of their communities, and their ministers frequently served as spokesmen for blacks in pressing for higher budgets for schools and other city services and in defending their communities from racist accusations. The churches offered spiritual solace from the dehumanizing impact of discrimination. They also provided a network of clubs, sports teams, choirs, and other organizations that enabled ordinary blacks to achieve prominence within their communities. The choir member who sang the solo on Sunday was an important person, even if she worked as a maid for some white family the other days of the week.

Even the churches, however, could not completely offset the omnipresent reminders of white supremacy. Unsurprisingly, many African Americans internalized some of this ideology. There was racial prejudice within the black community. Those with lighter skin, and thus with more white ancestors, looked down upon those with darker complexions. In 1907, Madame C. J. Walker of Denver took commercial advantage of the desire among blacks to look white by marketing her hair-straightening method. She followed it with products that she claimed would lighten skin tones. Within a few years, she became the first African American millionaire.

Religion was as important among immigrant groups as it was for African Americans, and for the same reasons. Each group wanted its own church or synagogue and often competed to make its own the largest and most lavish. In Worcester, Massachusetts, for example, two Catholic churches, one Irish, one French-Canadian, stood directly across the street from each other. Each had its own parochial school, its own athletic teams, its own dramatic society, and its own array of social programs for young and old. Each group kept a wary eye on the other, determined not to be outdone. The same sort of rivalry existed in virtually all of the industrial cities and towns of the North, Midwest, and West.

As racial and ethnic subcultures developed and thrived, the larger culture slowly and unevenly became more pluralistic. One example was the success of Irish-American singer, dancer, composer, and playwright George M. Cohan. Cohan's songs often celebrated his Irish background, as with "Mary," with its refrain "It's a grand old name." Irish families routinely named the first daughter Mary. Yet Cohan also emphasized his American patriotism in shows like *Yankee Doodle Dandy*. Another example, already noted, was the popularity of Scott Joplin's rags. Joplin thought of ragtime as a form of classical music and of himself as an African American Chopin. White amateur piano players who bought the sheet music and tried to learn to play "The Entertainers" or any other of his hits soon learned what he meant. The songs were melodic, fun to dance to, and devilishly hard to play.

Also vital in providing ethnic and racial visibility was vaudeville. We might not ordinarily think of it as a form of mass communication, but that is what it became in terms of dispersing black and ethnic cultural styles. Vaudeville theaters in various cities were linked in "circuits." Entertainers signed up to play the circuit, that is, to go from city to city, usually doing three shows a day. There were nine acts on the bill. The biggest name came on eighth, "next to closing." Variety was the order of the day. There were acrobats, trained animal acts, singers, dancers, comedians, jugglers, whatever the booking agent putting the bill together thought would appeal. The swimmer Annette Kellerman, for example, swam in a large glass tank to great acclaim. Part of the secret of her success was her one-piece bathing costume, something considered so daring that she was arrested in Boston for indecent exposure.

However rigidly segregated the rest of America was becoming, vaudeville was open to all. Walker and Williams, a black comedy duo, were headliners, although they stayed out of the South. After the team split up, Bert Williams starred in the Ziegfeld Follies for years. The Follies was the pinnacle, the highest a vaudeville performer could climb. White ethnics also excelled. Harrigan and Hart, an Irish-American comedy team, became huge stars. Gallagher and Sheen, an Irish- and-Jewish duo, poked fun at ethnic stereotypes and religious misunderstandings. Fanny Brice, born to a German-Jewish family, acquired a Yiddish accent to do comic songs like "Second Hand Rose" and "I'm an Indian Too." She, too, headlined at the Follies. The racial and ethnic makeup of vaudeville had the effect, largely unnoticed at the time, of turning black, Irish, Swedish, and Jewish performers into models. Audience members told jokes they learned from the Marx Brothers, tried to sing like Al Jolson, or attempted Bert Williams's shuffle dance.

At the same time, WASPs continued to control what has been called "the command posts of culture," such as the big book publishing houses. They monopolized the faculties of the leading colleges and universities. They edited the most prestigious magazines and journals. They were the ministers in the largest and most prosperous churches. Newspapers published by fellow WASPs published their sermons. They also wrote most of the best-sellers. But a new genre, the novel recounting the immigrant experience, was emerging. One of the earliest and best was Abraham Cahan's *The Rise of David Levinsky*. Cahan was the editor and publisher of the largest Yiddish-language newspaper in the country, *The Forward*, and did much to foster Yiddish literature. But he wrote *The Rise of David Levinsky* in English. It tells of a young Jew from eastern Europe starting out on New York's Lower East Side. David finds a job in a sweatshop and starts the long process of "yellowing," that is, going from greenhorn to acculturated Jewish American. He soon learns that there are two main paths. One leads through trade unionism toward a socialist future. The other demands that he somehow raise some capital and go into business. It is the entrepreneurial path that David chooses, to his worldly profit and spiritual loss.

Old-stock American novelists were also discovering the immigrant experience. Upton Sinclair's *The Jungle*, set in the Chicago stockyards, begins with a Lithuanian wedding and then follows the young couple for the next several years as they seek to build a future. What drew most attention, however, was not Sinclair's careful and sympathetic description of Chicago's ethnic communities but his exposé of conditions in the stockyards. He wanted to touch the heart of middle America, he recalled, and instead punched it in the stomach.

WASP predominance continued, but, in movies, music, comics, and sports, blacks and ethnics were coming to the fore. The importance of this cannot be exaggerated. As Irving Berlin, the dean of American popular songwriters over the first half of the twentieth century, observed: "Let others write the laws; I want to write the music." Berlin published his first big hit, "Alexander's Ragtime Band," in 1910. It was the first of hundreds he would compose over the next 50 years.

INFLUENTIAL THEORIES AND VIEWS OF RACE RELATIONS

Several racial theories developed in the late nineteenth century continued to shape beliefs about African Americans, Asians, and immigrants from southern and eastern Europe. One, first developed by Francis Amasa Walker, president of M.I.T. and a director of the U.S. Census Bureau, held that white Americans of northern and western European backgrounds confronted the likelihood of "race suicide." Walker pointed to the declining birth rates among old-stock Americans. These were falling to below replacement levels. As a result, the United States depended upon immigration for population growth. The newcomers, moreover, had comparatively high birth rates. This meant the inevitable decline of old-stock Americans and their replacement over time by the descendants of the immigrants. Walker explained the declining birth rates among WASPs in terms of the low standard of living of immigrants. Native-born Americans insisted upon an "American" standard of living. But immigrants competed for their jobs and were willing to accept lower wages. Or so Walker claimed. This led to smaller families as old-stock families adjusted to the competition.

Walker's theory drew upon several sources. One was Darwinism. The crucial measure of "fitness" was the birth rate. Decline indicated approaching extinction. And, since this decline resulted from choices made by old-stock families, it amounted to "race suicide." Another source was the stereotype that immigrants would work for less than the native-born. The phrase "coolie wages" expressed this belief with regard to Asians. A similar charge was made against each new immigrant group in turn. There was a measure of truth in these claims. New immigrants, so-called greenhorns, were often exploited—usually by members of their own nationality groups, who took advantage of their unfamiliarity with America. As newcomers became more knowledgeable, they insisted upon the same wages as the native-born received.

Walker had many influential followers. One was Charles W. Eliot, the long-time president of Harvard. Eliot undertook a study of the fertility of Harvard graduates and discovered that affluent WASPs had even fewer children than their working-class counterparts. The cause, he determined, was that the typical Harvard graduate did not marry until his late twenties or early thirties, that is, not until he had carved out a career for himself. Eliot's first proposed solution was to speed up the amount of time it took to graduate. Harvard students, however, preferred four years of college to three. Eliot next turned to expanding the pool of Harvard applicants. Instead of continuing to focus on students at a handful of elite preparatory schools, he called for standardized admission tests. The goal was to interest gifted students in St. Louis or San Francisco in applying to Harvard. This approach succeeded brilliantly. Indeed, it transformed the college application process. It did nothing, however, to increase the birth rates of Harvard families.

Another of Walker's acolytes was Theodore Roosevelt, himself a Harvard graduate. T.R. used his "bully pulpit," as he called the presidency, to call upon old-stock Americans to have more children. And he set a personal example, fathering six. None of this exhortation had any effect. As a result, many of Roosevelt's contemporaries turned to restrictions on immigration as a defense against too-fertile immigrants. Roosevelt himself did not. It was his opposition to the literacy test requirement, which his friend Senator Henry Cabot Lodge (Rep., Mass.) thought would block southern and eastern Europeans, that led to the creation of the Dillingham Commission, in 1907, to study the overall impact of immigration on American society. The Vermont Republican senator William P. Dillingham knew in advance what his investigation would disclose. He, too, feared "race suicide."

An even more pernicious racial theory held that African Americans, freed from white control, were in the process of reverting to barbarism. This notion did not have a single father in the way that the "race suicide" theory did. One early advocate of black retrogression was Nathaniel Southgate Shaler, dean of the Lawrence School of Science at Harvard. Shaler, a student of evolution, held that human behavior had evolved, just as had physical traits. Different races, occupying different parts of the planet, had developed different patterns of behavior. Whites, he argued, had become organizers and builders. Blacks were imitative and savage. Held in bondage, their imitativeness had made them copy white behaviors. Once freed, however, they would inevitably revert to savagery. Shaler's ideas depended upon a version of evolutionary theory, neo-Lamarckianism, that owed nothing to Darwin. Writing before Darwin, Lamarck had theorized that acquired characteristics, such as behaviors, could be inherited. For example, he thought that giraffes had acquired their long necks by stretching them in search of food high in trees. They then passed on this acquired characteristic to their offspring, who repeated the process until there was no more need for additional stretching. If behavior is inherited rather than learned, then blacks in America would act the way their ancestors had in Africa. As Shaler put it in an article in *The Atlantic Monthly*, "there will naturally be a strong tendency, for many generations to come, for them to revert to their ancestral conditions." This was especially true in the case of rape. He wrote in 1904 "that the Negro is sexually a very brutal creature who cannot be trusted in contact with white women."

Shaler thus provided scientific legitimacy to the claims of white lynch mob organizers that they needed to protect what they liked to call southern white womanhood. Another advocate of this theory of racial retrogression was Rebecca Latimer Fletcher. In a speech in Georgia in 1897 she claimed:

> When there is not enough religion in the pulpit to organize a crusade against sin; nor justice in the court house to promptly punish crime; nor manhood enough in the nation to put a sheltering arm about innocence and virtue—if it needs lynching to protect woman's dearest possession from the ravening human beasts—then I say lynch, a thousand times a week if necessary.[38]

Latimer's was not a voice crying in the wilderness. She was a best-selling author, and, in 1922, she became the first woman to serve in the U.S. Senate when the governor of Georgia appointed her to fill out the remainder of the term of the late Tom Watson, himself one of the most notorious racist demagogues in American history. And the lynchings continued, not 1,000 a week, but close to 100 a year throughout the 1900s.

Neo-Lamarckianism influenced the practice of medicine, as well. In 1900, for example, a bubonic plague scare swept through San Francisco. Public health authorities quarantined the city's Chinatown because they believed that particular races were especially likely to be carriers of specific diseases. It was simply another acquired characteristic become hereditary.

Feeding off the "race suicide" theory, notions of racial retrogression, and neo-Lamarckian ideas generally, the American Breeders Association created a Committee on Eugenics in 1903. Within a few years, the committee would spawn the American Eugenics Society. This group would then lead the campaign to improve the American "breed" by lobbying states to adopt involuntary sterilization measures. Indiana's sterilization law, passed in 1907, was the first. Eugenicists were interested in more than preventing the mentally defective from reproducing. Like Theodore Roosevelt, who endorsed several of their campaigns, they wanted to encourage the "best" people to have more children. And they wanted governments to do more for these children. School programs for the "gifted and talented" are local reminders of their considerable success.

Was there an opposition to racist theorizing? Yes, but it was just beginning. In 1911, Franz Boas, a professor at Columbia University, would publish *The Mind of Primitive Man*. In it, he would make the case that culture, not heredity, explained behavior and that the different races were all equal. In 1908, Israel Zangwell's play *The Melting Pot* opened in New York. In this work, Zangwell gave expression to the notion that each group in America contributed something valuable and that the resulting American culture was more than the sum of its parts. The message anticipated Boas's. The popularity of the play suggested that at least some Americans were ready to heed it.

RESOURCE GUIDE

SUGGESTED READING

"Our Little Brown Brothers" at the Louisiana Purchase Exposition

Board of Lady Managers. *Report to the Louisiana Purchase Exposition Commission.* Cambridge, MA: Riverside Press, Houghton, 1905.

Breitbart, Eric. *A World on Display: Photographs from the St. Louis World's Fair, 1904.* Albuquerque: University of New Mexico Press, 1997.

Correspondence Relating to the War with Spain: Including the Insurrection in the Philippine Islands and the China Relief Expedition, April 15, 1898, to July 30, 1902. Washington, DC: Center of Military History, U.S. Army, 1993, 2002.

Feuer, A. B. *America at War: The Philippines, 1898–1913.* Westport, CT: Praeger, 2002.

Hoganson, Kristin L. *Fighting for American Manhood: How Gender Politics Provoked the Spanish-American and Philippine-American Wars.* New Haven, CT: Yale University Press, 1998.

Parezo, Nancy J., and Don D. Fowler. *Anthropology Goes to the Fair: The 1904 Louisiana Purchase Exposition.* Lincoln: University of Nebraska Press, 2007.

Welch, Richard E. *Response to Imperialism: The United States and the Philippine-American War, 1899–1902.* Chapel Hill: University of North Carolina Press, 1979.

The Lynching of Ed Johnson in Chattanooga, Tennessee, 1906

The Autobiography of Ida B. Wells, ed. Alfreda M. Duster. Chicago: University of Chicago Press, 1970. Wells led the antilynching campaign and helped found the NAACP.

Curriden, Mark, and Leroy Phillips Jr. *Contempt of Court: The Turn-of-the-Century Lynching That Launched a Hundred Years of Federalism.* New York: Faber & Faber, 1999.

Webb, Michael. "'God Bless You All—I Am Innocent': Sheriff Joseph F. Shipp, Chattanooga, and the Lynching of Ed Johnson." In *Trial and Triumph: Essays in Tennessee's African American History,* ed. Carroll Van West. Knoxville: University of Tennessee Press, 2002, 281–309.

Publication of *The Vanishing Race,* 1913

Adams, David Wallace. *Education for Extinction: American Indians and the Boarding School Experience 1875–1928.* Lawrence: University Press of Kansas, 1995.

Buffalo Bill and the Wild West. Catalog for an exhibit, November 21, 1981–April 4, 1982, at the Brooklyn Museum and the Museum of Art at the Carnegie Institute. Pittsburgh: The Brooklyn Museum, the Museum of Art at the Carnegie Institute, and the Buffalo Bill Historical Center.

Leach, William R. *Land of Desire: Merchants, Power, and the Rise of a New American Culture.* New York: Vintage Books, 1994. Explores the careers of the Wanamakers.

Lyman, Christopher M. *The Vanishing Race and Other Illusions: Photographs of Indians by Edward S. Curtis.* New York: Pantheon Books in association with the Smithsonian Institution, 1982.

Marsden, Michael T., and Jack Nachbar. "The Indian in the Movies." In *History of Indian-White Relations*, ed. Wilcomb E. Washburn, Vol. 4, *Handbook of North American Indians*, ed. William C. Sturtevant. Washington, DC: Smithsonian Institution, 1988.

Trachtenberg, Alan. *Shades of Hiawatha: Staging Indians, Making Americans, 1880–1930*. New York: Hill & Wang, 2004.

Rudyard Kipling

Gilmour, David. *The Long Recessional: The Imperial Life of Rudyard Kipling*. New York: Farrar Straus & Giroux, 2002.

Sen. Benjamin ("Pitchfork Ben") Tillman

Kantrowitz, Stephen David. *Ben Tillman and the Reconstruction of White Supremacy*. Chapel Hill: University of North Carolina Press, 2000.

Theodore Roosevelt

Morris, Edmund. *Theodore Rex*. New York: Random House, 2001.

Ida B. Wells-Barnett

McMurry, Linda O. *To Keep the Waters Troubled: The Life of Ida B. Wells*. New York: Oxford University Press, 1998.

Schechter, Patricia Ann. *Ida B. Wells-Barnett and American Reform, 1880–1930*. Chapel Hill: University of North Carolina Press, 2001.

The Japanese and Korean Exclusion League

Daniels, Roger. *Guarding the Golden Door: American Immigration Policy and Immigrants since 1882*. New York: Hill & Wang, 2004.

Ichioka, Yuji. *The Issei: The World of the First Generation Japanese Immigrants, 1885–1924*. New York: Free Press, 1988.

Henry Cabot Lodge

Daniels, Roger. *Guarding the Golden Door: American Immigration Policy and Immigrants since 1882*. New York: Hill & Wang, 2004.

African Americans

Kellogg, Charles Flint. *NAACP: A History of the National Association for the Advancement of Colored People, 1909–1920*. Baltimore: Johns Hopkins University Press, 1967.

Lane, Ann J. *The Brownsville Affair: National Crisis and Black Reaction*. Port Washington, NY: Kennikat Press, 1971.

McPherson, James M. *The Abolitionist Legacy: From Reconstruction to the NAACP*. Princeton: Princeton University Press, 1975.

European Americans

Bodnar, John E. *The Transplanted: A History of Immigrants in Urban America*. Bloomington: University of Indiana Press, 1985.

Handlin, Oscar. *The Uprooted: The Epic Story of the Great Migrations That Made the American People*. Boston: Little, Brown, 1951.

Latinos

Gonzales, Manuel G. *Mexicanos: A History of Mexicans in the United States*. Bloomington: University of Indiana Press, 1999.
Gordon, Linda. *The Great Arizona Orphan Abduction*. Cambridge, MA: Harvard University Press, 1999.
Gutiérrez, David. *Walls and Mirrors: Mexican Americans, Mexican Immigrants, and the Politics of Ethnicity*. Berkeley: University of California Press, 1995.
Kiser, George C., and Martha W. Kiser, eds. *Mexican Workers in the United States: Historical and Political Perspectives*. Albuquerque: University of New Mexico Press, 1979.
Sanchez, George J. *Becoming Mexican American: Ethnicity, Culture and Identity in Chicano Los Angeles, 1900–1945*. New York: Oxford University Press, 1993.

Asian Americans

Chan, Sucheng, ed. *Entry Denied: Exclusion and the Chinese Community in America, 1882–1943*. Philadelphia: Temple University Press, 1991.
Daniels, Roger. *Asian American: Chinese and Japanese Americans in the United States since 1850*. Seattle: University of Washington Press, 1988.
Daniels, Roger. *The Politics of Prejudice: The Anti-Japanese Movement in California and the Struggle for Japanese Exclusion*. Berkeley: University of California Press, 1962.

FILMS/VIDEOS

Nonfiction

Crucible of Empire: The Spanish-American War, production of Great Projects Film Company, in association with the South Carolina Educational Television Network; written and produced by Daniel A. Miller and Daniel B. Polin; directed by Daniel A. Miller (1999).
Library of Congress's American Memory Web site: http://lcweb2.loc.gov/ammem/sawhtml/sawsp5.html. Several are documentaries about the war in the Philippines shot by the Biograph Company; others are re-creations filmed by the Edison Company.
The Rise and Fall of Jim Crow, a co-production of Quest Productions, Videoline Productions, and Thirteen/WNET New York; produced by Bill Jersey, Sam Pollard, and Richard Wormser; directed by Bill Jersey and Richard Wormser; written by Bill Jersey and Richard Wormser (2002).

Fiction

The Godfather, Part II (1974), based upon the novel by Mario Puzo; produced and directed by Francis Ford Coppola; released by Paramount Pictures. Brilliant recreation via flashbacks of Italian immigrant life in turn-of-the-century New York.
Hester Street (1976), based upon a short story by Abraham Cahan; produced by Raphael D. Silver; directed by Joan Micklin Silver; distributed by First Run Features. Engrossing drama of Jewish immigrant life on the Lower East Side of New York.

Life of Buffalo Bill (Pawnee Bill Film Company, 1912) and *The Indian Wars* (Essanay, 1913). William Cody plays himself in both of these.

Meet Me in St. Louis, screenplay by Irving Brecher and Fred F. Finklehoffe; produced by Arthur Freed; directed by Vincente Minnelli for Metro-Goldwyn-Mayer, 1944. Hit musical comedy about a young woman who falls in love with the boy next door during the 1904 World's Fair.

Ragtime (1981), based upon the novel by E. L. Doctorow; produced by Dino De Laurentiis Company; directed by Milos Forman; distributed by Paramount Pictures. Oscar-winning story of ethnic and racial relations in early-twentieth-century New York.

The Squaw Man (1914), based upon the 1906 play produced by David Belasco; produced by the Jesse L. Lasky Feature Play Company; directed by Cecil B. DeMille and remade by him in 1918 and 1931 (as a talkie). The first full-length western, it includes many references to the "vanishing" of the Indian nations.

WEB SITES

"The Booker T. Washington Era," http://lcweb2.loc.gov/ammem/aaohtml/exhibit/aopart6.html, part 6 of the African American Odyssey at the Library of Congress's American Memory Web site (http://lcweb2.loc.gov/ammem/aaohtml/exhibit/aointro.html).

"Carlisle Indian Industrial School," http://home.epix.net/~landis/, created by Barbara Landis with support from the Viola White Water Foundation, offers a historical overview, images, and other materials relating to the school.

Edward S. Curtis's "The North American Indian" site, http://curtis.library.northwestern.edu/, Northwestern University Digital Library Collections, contains the entire 20 volumes of photographs and commentary.

"A History of Japanese Americans in California," http://www.jimcrowhistory.org/home.htm, was created by the National Park Service.

"A History of Jim Crow," http://www.ferris.edu/news/jimcrow/index.htm, presents the "Jim Crow Museum of Racist Memorabilia" at Ferris State University. Companion site to the PBS documentary series *The Rise and Fall of Jim Crow*. Contains a large collection of cartoons, book and magazine covers, artifacts, and other materials. All are highly offensive but historically important.

"Lynching in America: Statistics, Information, Images," http://www.nps.gov/history/history/online_books/5views/5views4.htm, was created by the University of Missouri School of Law, Kansas City.

New York Public Library online exhibition "The War of 1898: A War in Perspective: 1898–1998," http://www.nypl.org/research/chss/epo/spanexhib/, is another excellent starting place.

"The 1904 World's Fair: Looking Back at Looking Forward," http://www.mohistory.org/Fair/WF/HTML/About/, created by the Missouri Historical Society, features collection of objects from the Fair and a virtual recreation of its most popular attractions.

"The Silent Western: Early Movie Myths of the American West," http://xroads.virginia.edu/~HYPER/HNS/Westfilm/west.html, by the University of Virginia, includes a segment on the portrayal of Native Americans and Mexicans in early westerns. Also at the University of Virginia Web site is a section devoted to Buffalo Bill's Wild West Show; at http://xroads.virginia.edu/%7EHYPER/HNS/BuffaloBill/home.html.

"The Trial of Sheriff Joseph Shipp et al. for the Lynching of Ed Johnson, 1907," http://www.law.umkc.edu/faculty/projects/ftrials/shipp/shipp.html, created by Douglas Linder for his Famous American Trials project at the University of Missouri, Kansas City, Law School, features trial documents, newspaper reports, and an introductory essay by Professor Linder.

"The White Man's Burden" and "To the Person Sitting in Darkness," http://www.assumption.edu/users/mcclymer/His130/P-H/burden/default.html, created by John McClymer at Assumption College, explores the debate over imperialism during and after the War with Spain, including the role of Sen. Benjamin "Pitchfork Ben" Tillman.

"The World of 1898: The Spanish-American War." The Library of Congress's American Memory site, http://www.loc.gov/rr/hispanic/1898/, is a good place to begin.

NOTES

1. *Plessy v. Ferguson*, 163 U.S. 537 (1896), available at http://supreme.justia.com/us/163/537/case.html. Viewed July 21, 2008.

2. *Buck v. Bell*, 274 U.S. 200 (1927), available at http://supreme.justia.com/us/274/200/index.html. Viewed July 21, 2008.

3. "Native Filipinos in a Natural Environment/Typical Life of the Islands Revealed in the St. Louis Fair Exhibit," *New York Times*, July 17, 1904.

4. American spelling of Philippine names varied. Igorot, for example, was sometimes rendered Igorrote and sometimes Igorrot. I have not attempted to correct any misspellings. They are evidence of the way in which white Americans viewed Filipinos.

5. *Official Guide to the World's Fair*, St. Louis, 1904.

6. The teacher, Pilar Zamora, became a celebrity. See, for example, "Filipino Belle at the St. Louis Fair," *Washington Post*, April 3, 1904.

7. Alfred C. Newell, "The Philippine Peoples," *The World's Work* 8 (August 1904).

8. Ibid.

9. Edmund Mitchell, "Splendid Exhibit from Philippines," *Los Angeles Times*, June 26, 1904.

10. Ibid.

11. Newell, "The Philippine Peoples."

12. Ibid.

13. Report to the Louisiana Purchase Exposition Commission (Board of Lady Managers of the Louisiana Purchase Exposition, 1905).

14. Newell, "The Philippine Peoples."

15. *Chattanooga Times*, January 24, 1906.

16. *Chattanooga Times*, January 26, 1906.

17. *Chattanooga Times*, March 20, 1906.

18. *Chattanooga Times*, February 7–10, 1906.

19. *Chattanooga Times*, March 19, 1906.

20. *Chattanooga Times*, March 20, 1906.

21. Associated Press, May 28, 1906.

22. Examination of John Stonecipher by Assistant Attorney General Sanford, February 14, 1906, available at http://www.law.umkc.edu/faculty/projects/ftrials/shipp/stoneciphertestimony.html. Viewed July 28, 2008.

23. Opinion for the Court by Chief Justice Fuller in *United States v. Shipp*. No. 5, Original. Supreme Court of the United States 214 U.S. 386, available at http://www.law.umkc.edu/faculty/projects/ftrials/shipp/shippcase.html#MR.%20CHIEF%20JUSTICE. Viewed July 28, 2008.

24. Quoted in *The Shipp Trial: An Account* by Douglas Linder, available at http://www.law.umkc.edu/faculty/projects/ftrials/shipp/shipp.html. Accessed July 28, 2008.

25. Joseph Kossuth Dixon, *The Vanishing Race: The Last Great Indian Council* (Garden City, NY: 1914 [c.1913]). Alan Trachtenberg, *Shades of Hiawatha: Staging Indians, Making Americans, 1880–1930* (New York: Hill and Wang, 2004), discusses the Dixon/Wanamaker project, as well as that of Edward S. Curtis, in great detail and with great insight.

26. Richard Henry Pratt, *Battlefield and Classroom: Four Decades with the American Indian, 1867–1904* (Norman, OK: University of Oklahoma Press, 2004). Pratt founded Carlisle.

27. Quoted in Trachtenberg, *Shades of Hiawatha*, pp. 242–243.

28. Henry Row Schoolcraft, *Algic Researches* (New York, 1839) and *The Myth of Hiawatha and Other Oral Legends* (Philadelphia, 1856), in addition to Henry Wadsworth Longfellow, *The Song of Hiawatha* (Boston, 1855).

29. Quoted in Trachtenberg, *Shades of Hiawatha*, p. 240.

30. Quoted in Trachtenberg, *Shades of Hiawatha*, p. 248.

31. The U.S. Mint had earlier (1859–1909) issued an Indian head penny. This featured an Indian princess with a laurel wreath on the reverse.

32. The entire work is available online at Northwestern University's "Edward S. Curtis's The North American Indian" site at http://curtis.library.northwestern.edu/.

33. James Merrell, "The Indians' New World: The Catawba Experience," *William and Mary Quarterly* 41 (1984): 537–565.

34. *Buffalo Bill and the Wild West* (Pittsburgh, 1981), a catalog produced by the Brooklyn Museum, the Museum of Art at the Carnegie Institute, and the Buffalo Bill Historical Center for an exhibit, November 21, 1981–April 4, 1982, in Brooklyn and Pittsburgh.

35. The dime novels and penny dreadfuls online collection at Stanford University, available at http://www-sul.stanford.edu/depts/dp/pennies/home.html, contains 31 issues of magazines using Buffalo Bill in the title. It has more than 200 magazine covers with images of Native Americans in the collection.

36. Michael T. Marsden and Jack Nachbar, "The Indian in the Movies," in *History of Indian-White Relations*, ed. Wilcomb E. Washburn. Vol. 4. of *Handbook of North American Indians*, ed. William C. Sturtevant (Washington, DC: Smithsonian Institution, 1988), p. 610.

37. Experts in linguistics refer to this phenomenon as glossalia. Speakers articulate sounds common to their native languages, in this case American English. They do not use actual words. Constance Holden, "Tongues on the Mind," *ScienceNOW Daily News* November 2, 2006.

38. *Atlanta Journal*, August 12, 1897.

1910s

TIMELINE

1910–1920	Two million Italians immigrate to the United States; if World War I had not drastically reduced immigration, the total might easily have been twice that.
1911–1920	A total of 5,735,811 immigrants come to the United States.
1911	A total of 60 black Americans are lynched.
	The Dillingham Commission issues its 42-volume Report. The first two, which supposedly summarize its findings, systematically distort the evidence to "prove" that immigrants from southern and eastern Europe lower wages, increase crime rates, and are more likely to wind up in poorhouses and insane asylums.
March 25	The Triangle Factory Fire in New York City kills 145, most of them young working women. Most are Jewish or Italian immigrants. The fire leads to the creation of the Factory Safety Commission by New York State. Chief investigator Frances Perkins, who would serve as Secretary of Labor during Franklin Roosevelt's presidency, later maintains that the New Deal really began with the creation of the Commission.
May 15	The City Council of Baltimore approves the first city ordinance stipulating the boundaries of black and white neighborhoods. It is followed by similar ones in Dallas, Texas; Greensboro, North Carolina; Louisville, Kentucky; Norfolk, Virginia; Oklahoma

	City, Oklahoma; Richmond, Virginia; Roanoke, Virginia; and St. Louis, Missouri. This formally begins the legal process of residential segregation.
December 15	The United States abrogates the treaty of 1832 with Russia because Russia refuses to honor the passports of Jewish Americans.
1912	A total of 61 black Americans are lynched.
January–March	A successful strike in the textile mills of Lawrence, Massachusetts, unites French-Canadian, Italian, Polish, and Irish workers, along with workers from numerous other ethnic groups, under the leadership of the Industrial Workers of the World (IWW). Employers historically hired workers of diverse backgrounds as a way of preventing union organization.
	Alliance College is founded by the Polish National Alliance to enable Polish Americans to learn about Poland's culture, history, and language. It would close in 1987.
1913	A total of 51 black Americans are lynched.
January 1	African Americans celebrate the fiftieth anniversary of the Emancipation Proclamation.
February–July	Another strike of immigrant textile workers, this time in Paterson, New Jersey, is organized by the IWW. As a way of gaining publicity and raising money, the strikers stage a "pageant" to which a variety of radically inclined intellectuals and artists contribute.
April 11	The Wilson administration begins government-wide segregation of workplaces, restrooms, and lunchrooms. Wilson, born in Virginia and a supporter of white supremacy, would continue to segregate the federal government.
May	California passes the Alien Land Law, barring "all aliens ineligible for citizenship" from owning land. This later grows to include a prohibition on leasing land; 12 other states adopt similar laws.
July 28–August 26	The trial of Leo Frank in Atlanta for the murder of the teenage Mary Phagan and his subsequent lynching lead to the founding of the Anti-Defamation League of B'nai B'rith to protect Jews from discrimination and ill treatment.
October 20	In *United States v. Sandoval*, the Supreme Court upholds the application of a federal liquor-control law to the New Mexico Pueblos, despite the fact that Pueblo lands have never been treated as a reservation. The Court rules that an unbroken line

of federal legislative, executive, and judicial actions has "attributed to the United States as a superior and civilized nation the power and duty of exercising a fostering care and protection over all dependent Indian communities within its borders."

1914–1918	World War I interrupts mass immigration to the United States.
1914	A total of 51 black Americans are lynched.
	More than 23,000 Poles in the United States volunteer to join the French Campaign as the Polish Legion. Poland ceased to exist as an independent country when Prussia (later Germany), Austria, and Russia partitioned it. Poles in America, as well as those in Europe, see in the war a chance to reconstitute Poland.
April 21	President Woodrow Wilson sends troops to Vera Cruz, Mexico, to depose President Victoriano Huerta, who then resigns. We must teach the Mexicans to elect "good men," Wilson declares.
November 27	The American Jewish Joint Distribution Committee is founded by American Jews to assist Jews displaced by World War I.
1915	A total of 56 black Americans are lynched.
	The "Great Migration" of African Americans from the rural South to the urban North gathers steam. By 1920, hundreds of thousands have relocated to Detroit, Chicago, New York, and other northern cities.
February 8	*Birth of a Nation*, D. W. Griffith's glorification of the Ku Klux Klan and white supremacy, opens to great critical and popular acclaim despite the efforts of the NAACP to prevent it from being shown.
1916	A total of 50 black Americans are lynched.
	Madison Grant writes *The Passing of the Great Race*, which argues that inferior "stocks" from southern and eastern Europe will soon outnumber people of northern and western European heritage. The result will the "mongrelization" of the American people.
March 15	General John J. ("Black Jack") Pershing, soon to command the American Expeditionary Force in France, leads 10,000 American soldiers into Mexican territory in retaliation for

a raid on Columbus, New Mexico, by General Francisco "Pancho" Villa. Pershing got his nickname because he led African American soldiers as a junior officer. After 11 months, Pershing returns to the United States without ever catching up with Villa.

June 5   Louis Dembitz Brandeis becomes the first Jew appointed to the U.S. Supreme Court. Brandeis had successfully argued several important cases before the court.

1917   A total of 36 black Americans are lynched.

February 5   Congress passes a literacy test for immigrants over President Woodrow Wilson's veto. The law stipulates that immigrants have to be able to read 40 words in some language. It also prohibits immigration from Asia, except for Japan (covered by the "Gentlemen's Agreement") and the Philippines (which is an American dependency) by enacting an "Asiatic Barred Zone." In addition, the legislation requires the deportation of aliens who preach revolution or sabotage any time after their entry into the United States. Attorney General A. Mitchell Palmer would attempt to use this last provision to deport thousands during the Red Scare of 1919–1920.

March 2   The Jones-Shafroth Act makes Puerto Ricans American citizens and also makes them eligible for the draft.

April 2   The United States enters World War I.

A total of 17,000 Indians serve in the armed forces. Some, however, resist the draft because they are not citizens and cannot vote. In 1919, Indian veterans of the war are granted citizenship.

Millions of unnaturalized immigrants from the Austro-Hungarian, German, and Ottoman empires become "enemy aliens" when the United States enters the war. As such, they cannot work in militarily sensitive occupations, visit the District of Columbia, or fly in a plane, among other restrictions. They also are ineligible for the draft.

A total of 370,000 African Americans serve in the military; more than half are in the French war zone. Black veterans bring a new militancy home from France and are at the forefront of the emergence of the "New Negro" in the 1920s.

June 15   Congress passes the Espionage Act. It imposes fines and prison sentences for antiwar activities. One of the first targets is the IWW. In September, the government raids IWW offices around the country and arrests 165 union officials.

July 1–3	One of the bloodiest race riots in the nation's history takes place in East St. Louis, Illinois. A congressional committee reports that between 40 and 200 people were killed, hundreds more injured, and 6,000 driven from their homes. The vast majority of the killed and injured were black, as were virtually all of those who were made homeless.
July 12	In Bisbee, Arizona, more than 1,000 striking copper workers, many of them immigrants from Europe or native-born Mexican-Americans, are rounded up by vigilantes organized by the copper companies and deported, that is, put in railroad boxcars and shipped off to New Mexico. The owners claim that the strikers, led by the Industrial Workers of the World (IWW), which opposes American entry into World War I, intend to subvert the war effort. The federal government investigates and determines that there is no basis for the deportations and that the strikers' civil rights have been violated. The Justice Department also decides that no federal laws have been violated. Arizona puts one vigilante on trial. A jury finds him not guilty. Other cases are then dismissed.
July 28	Thousands of African Americans, organized by the NAACP, march down Manhattan's Fifth Avenue, protesting lynchings, race riots, segregation, and discrimination.
August 23	A riot erupts in Houston between black soldiers and white citizens; 2 blacks and 11 whites are killed. The riot grows out of tensions between Houston's white police and black military police. More than 100 African American soldiers take their rifles and march on the city; 18 black soldiers are later hanged for their participation in the riot.
November 2	The Balfour Declaration expresses Britain's support for a Jewish national homeland in Palestine. This, along with the overthrow of the Russian tsar in the February Revolution, clears the way for American Jews to rally around the American entry into World War I. Anti-Jewish pogroms, brutal assaults upon Jewish villages within the Pale of Settlement in Russia, had made the tsar a universally hated figure among Jews everywhere.
1917–1918	The Wilson administration cracks down on dissent and makes immigrants special targets. The Committee on Public Information censors foreign-language newspapers and organizes public

events, such as "I Am an American Day" (July 4, 1918), at which immigrants have to display their loyalty to the United States. State Councils of Defense harass immigrants whose loyalty their members doubt.

1918	A total of 60 black Americans are lynched.
March	The government puts 101 IWW officials on trial for allegedly violating the Espionage Act. IWW president William "Big Bill" Haywood is sent to jail along with other defendants. The fines effectively empty the IWW treasury. To all intents and purposes, the IWW is defunct.
July 25–28	A race riot occurs in Chester, Pennsylvania, and three blacks and two whites are killed.
July 25–29	A race riot occurs in nearby Philadelphia, and three blacks and one white are killed.
1919	A total of 76 black Americans are lynched.
April–October	A total of 26 race riots occur between the months of April and October. The riots occur in a variety of cities, including:
	Charleston, South Carolina (May 10)
	Gregg and Longview counties, Texas (July 13)
	Washington, DC (July 19–23)
	Chicago (July 27–August 3)
	Elaine, Arkansas (October 1–3)
June 28	Poland becomes an independent country under the Treaty of Versailles as a result of the defeat of Germany and Austria and the "separate peace" signed between the new Soviet Union and Germany in 1918.
November 10	In a sign of the times, the House of Representatives refuses to seat socialist Victor Berger, who had been elected to Congress from a largely Polish section of Milwaukee.
1919–1920	The First Red Scare continues the harassment of immigrants, especially those from the former Russian Empire, who are suspected of sympathizing with the Bolshevik revolution of October 1917. Also targeted are those who subscribe to radical newspapers or who joined the Industrial Workers of the World.

1920	A total of 53 black Americans are lynched.
	Five Socialist Party assemblymen (August Claessens, Samuel A. De Witt, Samuel Orr, Charles Solomon, and Louis Waldman) are expelled from the New York State Assembly on the grounds that membership in the Socialist Party constitutes disloyalty to the United States.
August 1	Marcus Garvey's Universal Improvement Association holds its national convention in Harlem, in New York City. Garvey's African nationalist movement is the first black American mass movement; Garvey campaigns for black self-sufficiency and urges his followers to identify with their African roots. The NAACP fiercely opposes Garvey's movement.
November	California enacts a more stringent Alien Land Law.

OVERVIEW

The 1910s saw a dramatic worsening of race and ethnic relations. One clear indicator was the enormous success of *The Birth of a Nation*, D. W. Griffith's epic movie that glorified the Ku Klux Klan and caricatured blacks as drunkards and rapists seeking to prey upon innocent white women. The film's popularity, despite a determined campaign by the recently founded National Association for the Advancement of Colored People (NAACP), led to the founding of the second Ku Klux Klan in Georgia in 1915. The new KKK championed white supremacy, but it placed equal emphasis on the supposed dangers of immigration, especially of Catholics and Jews. It was this nativist appeal that allowed the Klan to recruit successfully in places like Maine, Indiana, and Washington State, where there were few blacks.

Hostilities were not limited to conflicts between whites and blacks or between self-styled real Americans and immigrants. They also raged among racial and ethnic groups and were exacerbated by the war. Even before the United States entered the conflict, in 1917, southern blacks had begun the so-called Great Migration to northern and midwestern cities. Labor shortages, caused by the sharp reduction in the number of immigrants from Europe after 1914 and by the mobilization of millions of white workers in the military in 1917 and 1918, led hundreds of thousands of African Americans to leave the South and farm labor for factory jobs in Detroit, Chicago, Pittsburgh, New York, and other cities. There they found new economic and cultural opportunities. The industrialist Henry Ford hired blacks at the Ford Motor Company as a way of blocking union organization, since unions often refused to permit nonwhites to become members.

Other employers followed his lead. Jobs on the assembly line or in the steel mills or meatpacking plants paid far better than farm labor in the South. And, as pioneers in Detroit and elsewhere described their new life in letters back home, their friends and relatives decided to head north themselves.

Opportunities in the North meant that blacks competed with whites, especially with white ethnics, for housing and employment. The resulting tensions led to riots, that is, white assaults on black neighborhoods, in East St. Louis, Illinois, Chicago, Washington, DC, and Tulsa, Oklahoma, among other cites. And lynching remained common, including in places like Indiana and Minnesota.

The most famous lynching victim in the 1910s was not an African American. The victim was Leo Frank, a New York-born and -educated Jew who ran a pencil factory in Atlanta, Georgia. In 1913, a 13-year-old employee named Mary Phagan was found murdered in the factory basement. Frank was arrested, tried, and convicted. Since there was a plausible black suspect, only anti-Semitism, combined with a fear of northern capitalists preying upon white southern workers, can explain why suspicion instead fell upon Frank. On the last day of his term, June 20, 1915, Georgia governor John Slaton commuted Frank's sentence to life in prison. On August 16, 1915, Frank was abducted from the penitentiary by some 25 men. Early on the morning of August 17, they lynched him just outside Marietta, hometown of Mary Phagan. The lynchers, who called themselves the "Knights of Mary Phagan," were guests of honor a few months later at the founding ceremony of the Knights of the Ku Klux Klan.

The American Jewish community responded by forming the Anti-Defamation League to combat anti-Semitism. Numerous other ethnic groups created similar organizations. Anti-immigration sentiment ran high, nevertheless. In 1916, both Theodore Roosevelt, who sought the Republican nomination for president, and President Woodrow Wilson warned of the menace posed by the "hyphen," that is, the ethnic American. T.R. called upon immigrants and their children to adopt what he called "100 Per Cent. Americanism" by renouncing any loyalty to the old country. They must be pro the United States in every way, Roosevelt thundered, and not pro anywhere else at all. Wilson emphatically agreed. This cast millions as potential traitors. German-Americans, for example, had rallied behind Wilson's call for the United States to be neutral and vigorously complained about what they correctly charged was his support for Great Britain. Irish American organizations also criticized this pro-British tilt, as did Swedish-Americans, who distrusted Russia, England's ally. Meanwhile, those who supported Great Britain or France faced no criticism for supporting their homelands.

When the United States did enter the war, the Wilson administration embarked upon a vigorous campaign to heat patriotism to a "white-hot" level, according to George Creel, who headed the Committee on Public Information (CPI) and who had charge of the job. The CPI censored the foreign-language press, invented safe ethnic associations like the American Friends of German Democracy or the American-Hungarian Loyalty League, and transformed July 4,

1918, into "I Am an American Day," during which ethnic groups marched in native costumes while holding American flags. Meanwhile, the national Council of Defense, which oversaw the mobilization of the economy, organized state committees. These often engaged in activities that Creel later described as illegal. Local and state committees targeted immigrants who did not subscribe to Liberty Loans (war bonds), for example, sometimes vandalizing their homes.

Such activities amounted to government-sanctioned vigilantism. America had a long, if dishonorable, tradition of so-called vigilante justice. Lynching provides the most notorious example. The Bisbee Deportation affords another. Bisbee, Arizona, was home to copper mines. The war had led to a sharp increase in copper prices (from 13 cents per pound before 1914 to 37 cents by 1917) and thus in company profits. That, along with the sharp rise in other prices, led miners to go out on strike. They were organized by the radical Industrial Workers of the World (IWW), which had led strikes in Lawrence, Massachusetts (the "Bread and Roses" strike), and Paterson, New Jersey, among other places. The IWW sought to organize those workers that craft unions, that is, those composed of skilled workers like plumbers or masons, historically had ignored.

The Wobblies, as IWW members were known, also sought to organize workers across ethnic lines. The copper miners in Bisbee were a mix of old-stock Americans, Latinos descended from the Mexican inhabitants of Arizona, and immigrants. On July 12, 1917, armed vigilantes, organized by the mine owners, rounded up more than 1,000 strikers and "deported" them; they forced them on to boxcars and took them by rail to New Mexico. They then patrolled the roads leading back into Bisbee to make certain that no one tried to return. It took several months for the Wilson administration to begin an investigation. The President's Mediation Commission concluded that the IWW had not engaged in any disloyal or illegal activities, as the mine companies had charged, and that the deportations were illegal. It also concluded that no federal law was involved and that the state and local authorities had jurisdiction. In the end, the one person tried for this mass kidnapping was found innocent. Cases against other defendants were then dropped.

In general, the war years saw a blind lashing out at all things foreign. Iowa, for example, prohibited the use of any language other than English in public, including over the telephone or in religious services, a measure directly aimed at Catholics who used Latin and at Jews who used Hebrew in their services. Concert orchestras refused to play the works of Mozart, Beethoven, and Brahms. Restaurants renamed hamburger Salisbury steak, and sauerkraut was dubbed liberty cabbage. More lasting, the frankfurter became the hot dog.

Many immigrants were technically enemy aliens. Austria and Prussia (later Germany) had, along with Russia, divided Poland among themselves in the nineteenth century. As a result, many Poles in America were legally defined as German or Austrian citizens, despite the fact that they had no love for their legal homelands. Hungary was also part of the Austrian empire. On April 16, 1917, when the

United States declared war on the German and Austrian empires, all males older than 14 who were still "natives, citizens, denizens, or subjects" of those countries became alien enemies. In 1918, Congress placed women age 14 and over in the same category. Also on April 16, 1917, President Wilson issued regulations limiting the rights of alien enemies. They could not own firearms, aircraft, or radio equipment. They could not publish an "attack" upon any branch of the U.S. government. They could not live in areas listed as "prohibited" by the president. They could be removed by presidential order to what in World War II would be called relocation camps. Alien enemies could not leave the country without permission, and they had to carry a registration card. On November 16, 1917, additional regulations limited alien enemies' access to docks, railroads, and warehouses. They could not fly in planes, even as passengers, and could not visit the District of Columbia.

Millions of immigrants officially became objects of suspicion. They were, therefore, not subject to the military draft. This gave rise to complaints that immigrants were not doing their fair share in the war effort. Those immigrants who volunteered for military service, and huge numbers did, had to become American citizens before shipping out for France. Otherwise, if they were captured, they would be treated not as prisoners of war but as traitors who were subject to execution. The United States waived naturalization rules for these recruits, and they and their immediate families became Americans in several mass ceremonies.

Despite the evident patriotism of immigrants, old-stock Americans continued to suspect their loyalty, especially that of newcomers from eastern Europe. This was a result of more than existing prejudice and administration policies. The Bolshevik Revolution of 1917, in Russia, had the effect of intensifying nativism. The new Soviet Union entered into negotiations with Germany and, in March 1918, signed a separate peace that permitted the Germans to concentrate their forces on the western front. Anyone from Russia, Finland, or Hungary, where a Communist uprising broke out in 1919, fell under suspicion. So did immigrants associated with anarchist or socialist organizations. In 1917, the Socialist Party in the United States had condemned the American entry into the war, and its leader, Eugene V. Debs, went to prison for speaking out against the military draft.

Once the war ended, a Red Scare gripped the nation. Major strikes, in some instances led by socialists and communists, wracked the economy in 1919. The most important was the steel strike. It was led by William Z. Foster, who became the presidential nominee of the new Communist Party of the United States in 1920. A large percentage of the strikers were immigrants from Poland, Lithuania, and Hungary. Local, state, and national officials warned darkly of Bolshevik plots to overthrow the republic. Attorney General A. Mitchell Palmer played a conspicuous part in this scaremongering. President Wilson, preoccupied with the struggle to get the U.S. Senate to ratify American entry into the League of Nations and then disabled by a stroke, did nothing to rein in Palmer. The Scare cul-

Anarchists marching, New York City, 1914. Courtesy of Library of Congress.

minated in the Palmer Raids on New Year's Day, 1920. Federal agents rounded up thousands, usually without any substantial evidence, and held them for deportation. Fortunately, Louis F. Post, an Assistant Secretary of Labor who oversaw the Immigration and Naturalization Bureau, had the final say. He refused to deport anyone against whom there was no conclusive evidence. This led to calls for his removal from office and a congressional investigation. Post persevered and won. Several hundred anarchists were deported on the *Buford,* nicknamed the "Soviet Ark." Everyone else was released.

It was in the midst of this wave of anti-immigrant sentiment that Congress adopted the restriction law of 1917. It required that all immigrants be literate in some language. The idea was that immigrants from northern and western Europe would continue to come and those from eastern and southern Europe would be barred, since a large majority of these so-called new immigrants were illiterate. In the event, the measure failed completely. If literacy was the price of admission, immigrants would learn to read and write. The numbers of newcomers in 1919 and 1920 quickly reached prewar levels, the great majority from countries like Poland, Greece, and Italy. Congress then passed the Emergency Immigration Law of 1921, which established quotas for each European country based upon the 1910 census. Congress chose 1910, rather than 1920, because it would further reduce the numbers of southern and eastern Europeans who could enter the country.

Underlying both laws was the racial theory of eugenics. Proponents held that the different European, and other, peoples constituted distinctive and competing "stocks." The choice of the term "stock" provides an important clue. Eugenicists held that, just as ranchers bred better livestock, the United States and other "Anglo-Saxon" countries could breed better people. There was, they believed, a hierarchy of peoples. At the pinnacle were northern Europeans—Anglo-Saxons, Vikings, Aryans. Next came so-called Alpine stocks, such as the Swiss, the French, and northern Italians. Then came those evolution had always left behind, as the University of Wisconsin sociology professor Edward A. Ross put it in his best-selling *The Old World in the New* (1914). These lesser breeds threatened to "mongrelize" the American people. They allegedly undercut the American standard of living by working for less than what was needed to support an "American" family. This was the same charge leveled first at Chinese and then at Japanese workers. Even more menacing was the high birthrate among these less desirable immigrant groups. Americans of Anglo-Saxon descent, eugenicists pointed out, produced fewer offspring every generation. This meant, in the title of Madison Grant's bestseller, *The Passing of the Great Race* (1916).

World War I gave the eugenicists new evidence. The military administered the new Intelligence Quotient (IQ) tests to recruits. The results showed that old-stock Americans were by far the most intelligent and that only blacks performed less well on the tests than immigrants from southern and eastern Europe. Later generations of scholars would explain the scores by showing the ways in which the test questions presumed a middle-class background few blacks and new immigrants possessed. But, at the time, the scientific validity of the results went largely unchallenged.

African Americans did not receive the same chance to fight for their country that enemy aliens did. Woodrow Wilson segregated the military and relegated blacks to mostly noncombat roles. The "War to Make the World Safe for Democracy" was a white man's crusade. Even so, blacks volunteered for service in large numbers, and the NAACP campaigned for their equal treatment—to no avail.

On the home front, race relations deteriorated. Competition between blacks and white ethnics in northern cities sparked riots, 18 between 1915 and 1919 alone. The one in East St. Louis, Illinois, in which 9 whites and an estimated 39 blacks died, illustrates how and why the races came into violent conflict. East St. Louis was an industrial city with excellent rail connections and easy access to soft coal. As of 1910, virtually all of its residents were white. Then African Americans started to move in, lured by the availability of jobs. During the 1916 election, the local Democratic Party charged that the Republicans were attempting to "colonize" blacks, who could not vote in the South but could in Illinois. Also in the late fall of 1916, the Aluminum Ore Company started to fire pro-union activists and replace them with black workers. In 1913, there had been only 19 or 12 African Americans at work at Aluminum Ore. In November

1916, there were 280 (out of a total of 1,900 workers). The next month, there were 410. By February 1917, there were 470. Almost all of the new hires were migrants from the South. In May, there was a hearing at City Hall to air union charges that "Negro and cheap foreign labor" were being imported "to tear down the standard of living of our citizens" and that "imported gunmen, detectives, and federal injunctions are being used to crush our people." An overflow crowd lined the streets and, after the hearing, went on a rampage through the black section of town.

This was a preamble to the great riot of July 2, 1917. The previous evening, a group of unknown whites in a Ford Model T had driven through an African American neighborhood firing wildly into houses. A few minutes later, another Model T, this one driven by an East St. Louis police detective, drove down the same streets. All Model Ts were black. This one was unmarked. Residents riddled it with bullets and killed the officer. The next morning, enraged whites set out to get revenge.

Even as racial and ethnic relations went from bad to worse, African American and immigrant roles in the popular culture continued to expand. They wrote much of the music, invented the dances, told the jokes, and made the movies. When the American Expeditionary Force left for France, its anthem was "Over There," written by the Irish-American and Catholic showman George M. Cohan. An Army private, Irving Berlin, a Jew born in Russia, wrote a show to raise money for a recreation center. His *Yip, Yip, Yaphank*—Yaphank was the name of the town on Long Island where Berlin did his basic training—had a successful Broadway run and gave the nation its most popular wartime song aside from "Over There," "Oh! How I Hate to Get up in the Morning."

Further, the Great Migration led to the emergence of Harlem as the unofficial capital of black America. Harlem provided a setting for musicians, poets, novelists, painters, and intellectuals to exchange ideas and respond to each other's works. The roots of the Harlem Renaissance lay in the late 1910s. Chicago, too, became a cultural center, especially for musicians. When the trumpeter Louis Armstrong left New Orleans, he headed for Chicago.

KEY EVENTS

THE TRIANGLE FIRE, MARCH 25, 1911

Late in the afternoon on Saturday, March 25, 1911, a fire broke out at the Triangle Shirtwaist Company, located on Washington Square in New York City. The factory occupied the top three floors of the nine-story Asch Building. The fire started on the seventh floor and, despite the fact that the building was fireproof, quickly engulfed the two floors above. There were large amounts of flammable

Crowds at the scene of the Triangle Shirtwaist Company fire, New York City, March 26, 1911. Courtesy of the Library of Congress.

material on all three floors. The seventh was where the patterns for the waists, as women's blouses were called, were cut. Surplus fabric was tossed into wooden bins underneath the cutting tables. The fire started in one of these bins. This was not an uncommon event. Usually, it would be extinguished immediately. There were several buckets set aside for just this purpose. This time, however, the fire spread too quickly. As the cotton and lace burned, the heat became so intense that it blew out the windows. Since heat rises, the fire next blew in the windows, first on the eighth floor, where the sewing was done, and then on the ninth, where the company's offices were.[1]

Workers on the seventh floor managed to escape, many by the elevators, which never reached the floors above. Others fled onto the stairs. The crush was so great that people could barely move. A policeman ran into the building and restored a semblance of order. In doing this, he saved scores of lives. So did the elevator operators, one a volunteer who took over when one of the two regular operators panicked. They made trip after trip until the heat became too intense.

Workers on the ninth floor escaped to the roof. The Asch Building adjoined another that belonged to New York University's School of Law. NYU students not only helped those on the roof but even went down into the building and rescued several workers who had taken shelter in a washroom.

Those on the eighth floor were trapped. There were two doors, one on either side of the building. One was kept locked. This was to ensure that the women working there did not steal any of the waists. At the end of the day, they had to pass through the second door under the watchful eye of a guard. Keeping one exit locked was a violation of the city fire safety code, one punishable by a $25 fine. When the fire crashed through the windows with a terrifying roar, most started to move in the opposite direction, toward the locked door. Firemen would have to use their axes to break it down. Piled up against it they found dozens of incinerated bodies.

A few workers scrambled to the elevator doors and forced them open. The cars stopped only at the floor below, but several women jumped on top of them and rode to safety. One managed to climb down the steel cable. Her hands were seriously cut and bruised, but she was alive. Most of the remaining workers headed toward the windows and, as the fire licked at their backs, scrambled out onto the ledges. Eighty feet below an enormous crowd was gathering. Most of the shirtwaist shops had been unionized during the "Uprising of the Twenty Thousand" strike the year before. Their workers put in only a half-day on Saturday. That was why the rest of the Asch Building was empty. Word of what was happening spread almost as rapidly as the fire itself. The journalist William G. Shepherd was in the crowd and phoned in an account to the United Press Service that appeared in hundreds of newspapers the next morning.[2]

Firefighters quickly arrived and set up their equipment. The ladder reached the sixth floor. One woman tried to jump from the eighth-story ledge into the outstretched arm of a fireman. But the 20-foot drop meant she was traveling too rapidly to be caught and held. Water pressure was sufficient to reach only the sixth floor. Firemen could not put out the fire. Heat-activated automatic sprinkler systems had been invented. New buildings were required to install them; older buildings, including the Asch, were not. Thousands watched as the tragedy played out.

When the bodies stopped falling, city officials set up an emergency morgue on an unused pier. Thousands struggled to get inside. Anguished police held them back. Some in the crowd, distraught over the loss of a daughter or sister, tried to throw themselves off the pier. Finally, there was enough order for the gruesome task of identifying the dead to begin. The bodies were laid out in rows. Relatives, a handful at a time, peered anxiously into each casket. One young woman identified her fiancé by the pocket watch he carried. When she opened it, she found a picture of herself. Other stories of how bereaved parents determined that a particular body was that of their daughter, equally heartbreaking, filled the next day's newspapers.[3]

All of New York City, all of America, was horrified. The Jewish and Italian immigrant communities clustered on the Lower East Side were enraged, as well. Thousands attended a memorial meeting in Grand Central Palace. The meeting chair called upon all to stand in silence in memory of the dead. First, there was silence, then sobbing, then what the *New York Times* called "the cries of convulsive weeping," then screams and shrieks. One woman fainted, then dozens more. At least 50 had to be carried from the building. When the "wave upon wave of hysteria" ceased, socialist speakers called upon the audience to follow the example of Milwaukee, which had just elected a socialist mayor. Next, an anarchist proposed bombing City Hall.[4]

It was a meeting that frightened many, including local political leaders and progressive reformers. The politicians, proud Democrats and loyal members of Tammany Hall, the most notorious political machine in the country, normally had no use for the reformers. The reformers, for their part, saw the machine as the embodiment of municipal corruption. Yet, they formed an unlikely alliance in the wake of the fire.

The New York state legislature formed a Factory Investigating Commission. To the reformers' dismay, and to the scorn of the socialists on the Lower East Side, its co-chairs were both Tammany stalwarts, Al Smith, the Speaker of the State Assembly, and Robert Wagner, the President of the State Senate. Unexpectedly, they chose Frances Perkins to head the investigation. She was still in her twenties and worked for the National Consumers' League, a progressive organization dedicated to improving working conditions, especially those of working women. More surprising still, Smith and Wagner allowed her to pick the rest of the commission staff.[5] Perkins filled it with people like herself and with people very unlike herself. One was Rose Schneiderman. Perkins was a prototypical "new woman," college-educated, dedicated to improving the world; Schneiderman was a Jewish immigrant who had had to drop out of grammar school to support her mother and her younger brother. She was a capmaker and a union activist.[6] She had helped lead the shirtwaist strike and had given a memorable and fiery speech at the Metropolitan Opera House on April 3, 1911. This was the meeting called to defuse anger on the Lower East Side that led to the creation of the New York Factory Investigating Commission. "I would be a traitor to these poor burned bodies if I came here to talk good fellowship," she began. "We have tried you good people of the public and we have found you wanting." She ended on the same note: "I can't talk fellowship to you who are gathered here. Too much blood has been spilled. I know from my experience it is up to the working people to save themselves. The only way they can save themselves is by a strong working-class movement."[7] It took courage as well as insight to hire Schneiderman to investigate factory safety. Perkins, who would become U.S. Secretary of Labor during the New Deal, had plenty of both. So, it turned out, did Al Smith and Robert Wagner.

Smith would become governor of New York in 1918, lose his bid for reelection narrowly in the Republican landslide of 1920, and then win in 1922, 1924, and 1926. In 1928, he became the first Catholic to run for president. Frances Perkins and Rose Schneiderman worked loyally for Smith throughout his terms as governor and then for his successor, Franklin D. Roosevelt. Robert Wagner, also a Catholic, became a U.S. senator and, in 1935, authored the Wagner Act, which people then and now described as the Magna Carta of American labor. It was this measure that made possible the great union organizing campaigns of the late 1930s.

Frances Perkins always maintained that the New Deal began on March 25, 1911, not March 4, 1933, when FDR took office. It began, that is, with the Triangle Fire. She meant this in several ways. One had to do with the results of the Commission's work. It recommended, and Smith and Wagner pushed through the state legislature, a broad array of reforms designed to protect workers. Many other states subsequently adopted similar measures. Taken together, the laws did more than require fire drills and fire escapes and the like. They helped change the relationship between the citizen and the government.[8] The government existed, in the minds of Schneiderman, Perkins, Smith, Wagner, and (later) Franklin and Eleanor Roosevelt, to benefit ordinary people in their daily lives. This is, Perkins insisted, the real meaning of New Deal liberalism.

The Factory Safety Commission also began the political partnership that grew into the Roosevelt coalition that dominated American politics between 1932 and 1968. It combined urban political machines, immigrant and ethnic voters, especially Roman Catholics and Jews, and intellectuals and reformers with the Democratic Party's traditional base among white Southerners. It was a coalition that explicitly sought to break down prejudices against Catholics, Jews, and white immigrants and their descendants. It did not seek to address racism until after World War II, and then very tentatively. It was strongly pro-labor and pro-union.

THE "BREAD AND ROSES" STRIKE, LAWRENCE, MASSACHUSETTS, 1912

On February 24, 1912, 40 children and their parents gathered at the Boston & Maine railroad station in Lawrence, Massachusetts. The parents were among some 20,000 to 25,000 textile workers striking to protest a wage cut. They intended to send their children to live with supporters in Philadelphia for the duration of the strike. It was a tactic that had been used successfully in France and Italy. The Lawrence strike was six weeks old. Strikers and their families already depended on donations from fellow union members, socialists, and political radicals from around the country for food and other necessities. Sending their children out of town made it easier to make ends meet. It also generated sympathetic publicity. Hundreds of children had already been sent to New York and Vermont, among other destinations.[9]

Col. E. Le Roy Sweetser, commander of the dozen companies of state militia occupying Lawrence and a determined opponent of the strike, decided to end the practice. On February 17, he sent a letter to the ad hoc "strike committee" that was coordinating the strike and that was urging parents to send their children on "vacation." "I will not permit the shipping off of little children away from their parents to other cities unless I am satisfied that this is done with the consent of the parents of said children." The committee had anticipated Sweetser. From the first, it had asked all of the parents to sign a consent form. "It is imperative," the form began, "that the parents of a child, or of children, who wish to go on vacation during the strike of mill workers at Lawrence, Massachusetts, give their consent in writing. . . . No children will be accepted except the parents, father and mother, sign such a card."

When Col. Sweetser's militia and the Lawrence police showed up at the station that Saturday, they did not ask to see the consent forms. They simply commanded the parents to take their children home. When some refused, they charged into the parents and children, beating and arresting them. Thirty were arrested in all, most for "violation of city ordinances," that is, for "congregating." Five women were held on the charge of neglecting their children but were not arrested. The children were also detained. Ultimately, all of the charges were dismissed. Two pregnant women miscarried. Newspapers and magazines all over the country jumped on the story.

A full-page cartoon in *Collier's* magazine typified the coverage. It showed an enormous policeman, wielding a bloody club, wading into the mass of children and their parents. At the upper left, "Sympathy," a figure resembling the Statue of Liberty, said, "Let the children come" to the "homes of the workers of other cities." At the upper right, smokestacks symbolized "Lawrence, Mass., The Hunger City, Dividends for mill-owners, Starvation wages for workers." Senator Miles Poindexter of Washington, an outspoken Republican supporter of progressive reform, rushed to Lawrence and sharply criticized the militia, the police, and the mill owners. The Socialist congressman Victor Berger of Milwaukee headed a congressional investigation. The Senate called upon the U.S. Commissioner of Labor to investigate, as well.

The attack on the children and their parents turned the strikers, the vast majority of whom were immigrants or the children of immigrants, into martyrs. And it helped turn a strike led by the radical Industrial Workers of the World (IWW) into a cause espoused by most Americans. It also enormously increased the pressure on the mills to meet the strikers' demands. On March 12, the largest companies gave in. On the 14th, the strike committee recommended that the workers accept the offer. The strikers had won. For the first time, the textile companies would pay time and a half for overtime. The workers also gained a 5 percent wage increase. And the companies promised not to discriminate against any striker.

The Lawrence strike was a rare victory for labor in this period, and a most unlikely one. Only a handful of workers belonged to a union prior to the walkout, and most of these were skilled workers allied to the American Federation of Labor (AFL) who played no active role in the strike. A few hundred others were dues-paying members of the Industrial Workers of the World (IWW). Most of these were French-speaking weavers from Belgium. They were one of many nationality groups in the mills. There were French-Canadians, Italians, Poles, Lithuanians, Syrians, Jews from Russia and the Austro-Hungarian Empire, and workers of a dozen other ethnicities. Employers favored hiring workers from a multitude of backgrounds. They spoke different languages, worshipped in different churches, shopped in different groceries. Diversity served as an obstacle to organization. Given all of these disadvantages, the national leadership of the IWW urged the Lawrence workers not to strike. There was no leadership in Lawrence, they pointed out. There was no strike fund.

But what there was in Lawrence was a large number of determined workers. The *Lawrence Sun* of Thursday, January 11, printed a two-column story with the headline "Italian Mill Workers Vote to Go Out on Strike Friday/In Noisy Meeting 900 Men Voice Dissatisfaction over Reduced Pay Because of 54-Hour Law."

The 54-hour law went into effect on January 1. It cut the maximum number of hours women and children under 18 could work from 56 to 54. Two years earlier, a similar measure had reduced the maximum from 58 to 56. Then the textile companies had raised hourly and piece rates so that workers earned as much in 56 hours as they had in 58. This time, however, the companies determined that the workers would have to accept a de facto wage cut. The Italians meeting in Ford Hall, according to the *Sun*, wanted "their pay raised to the amount they formerly received." The rival *Lawrence Eagle* reported on Friday, January 12, that Poles and Lithuanians had joined Italian workers at the meeting and that all three groups had voted unanimously to strike. It also noted that there would be a mass meeting on Saturday at City Hall "at which speakers in English, Italian, Polish, and French will be present."[10] Faced with the fact that the strike was on, the IWW leadership changed its mind and sent an experienced organizer, Joe Ettor, to help. The Wobblies, as IWW members were called, aimed at the destruction of the wage system and capitalism.

Marx's influence on the IWW is obvious. But its members were not socialists, although the two groups often cooperated, as in Lawrence.[11] Wobblies were anarcho-syndicalists. That is, they looked to the abolition of the state; that was the anarchist part of their ideology. They wanted to replace it with workers' associations or syndicates. The few hundred Wobblies in Lawrence before the strike[12] may well have been true believers. The overwhelming majority of the strikers, however, were not. They were moved by hunger and desperation, not radical manifestos.

When *Collier's* called Lawrence the "Hunger City," the facts supported the accusation. The *Report on Strike of Textile Workers* of the U.S. Commission of Labor found that "even with fresh milk at 7 cents a quart many families in Lawrence are unable to afford fresh milk and depend entirely upon condensed or evaporated milk," which they diluted with water.[13] Poor diet led to an abnormally high infant mortality rate. In 1909, "for every 1,000 live births in Lawrence there were 172 deaths of infants under 1 year of age." Of 35 cities studied by the U.S. Census Bureau that year, Lawrence ranked 29th in infant mortality; four of the six cities with even worse infant mortality were also textile centers. Manchester, New Hampshire, had the highest rate, a horrifying 263 deaths for every 1,000 live births. The overall death rate was also very high, 17.7 per 1,000 of all ages. In 1910, Census Bureau data again found that only 6 of 35 cities had higher death rates, and once again, 3 of the 6 were textile centers. Nearby Lowell had the highest death rate, 19.7 per 1,000.[14]

Collier's was also right about the mills paying starvation wages. The Commissioner of Labor's *Report* found that most workers (59.8 percent) in the woolen and worsted mills, the largest in the city, earned less than 15 cents per hour and that more than one in four (26.3 percent) made less than 12 cents an hour. Only one in five (22.6 percent) earned more than 20 cents an hour. Virtually no one under 18 earned more than 20 cents per hour; only a small percentage of women workers made that much.[15] These wages meant overcrowded housing, as well as inadequate diets. The Commissioner's *Report* stated that many immigrant households, particularly among Poles, Italians, and Lithuanians, supplemented their earning by taking in lodgers. They would receive $3.00 to $3.50 per month from each. In return, lodgers received a place to sleep and use of the family stove. The kitchen stove was a family's most important single possession. Almost always, it was the only source of heat.

Mill owners disputed the claim that they paid excessively high dividends.[16] William Wood, president of the American Woolen Company, the city's largest employer, in an open letter to the strikers, claimed that "the last two years have been very discouraging years for us and for all manufacturers in our line." After consulting with his board of directors, Wood had "reluctantly and regretfully" concluded that it was impossible to give workers any increase. The strikers rejected Wood's argument completely. "The company has even in the worst of times managed to pay dividends to its stockholders" and over the past several years it had erected new mill buildings out of current revenue. Further, Wood "must bear in mind the fact that these men, women, and children have not gone on strike for light or transient causes, but because they could no longer bear up under the burdens laid upon their shoulders."[17]

What was not in dispute was the fact that the textile industry benefited from a high protective tariff on foreign competitors that effectively kept them out of the American market or the fact that the ostensible reason for this protection was to guarantee textile workers an "American Standard of Living" in the face of cheap foreign labor, or the fact was textile workers were, on average, the most poorly paid workers in any industry.

On Thursday, January 11, 1912, a group of weavers in the Everett cotton mill, most of them Polish women, carrying an American flag, marched from department to department calling out "Strike!" and "All out; come on; all out. Strike!" They grabbed picker sticks as they went and used them to break looms and other machines and slash fabric. On Friday, workers in some departments in the Washington mill stopped work at about 9:00 in the morning. Most were Italian. Word reached the payroll department, and management decided to delay the distribution of pay envelopes. This probably contributed to the ensuing rioting as workers emulated their Everett mill colleagues by stopping machinery and driving other employees from their places. A contingent of police responded but failed to get the workers to leave the mill. More police arrived, and the strikers moved out on to the street. The crowd grew by the minute. After speeches in Italian, they moved toward the Wood mill of the American Woolen Company. They carried an Italian flag and many American flags. The strikers rushed into the Wood mill, shut off the power for the machines, and called on the workers there to join the strike. By now there were thousands moving to the Kuhnhardt and Duck mills, where guards, warned of their advance, succeeded in blocking their entrance by turning hoses on them. Frustrated, the demonstrators picked up chunks of the ice that was rapidly forming on the street and broke all of the mills' windows. The strike had begun.

An IWW organizer, Joe Ettor, arrived by train the next morning. Usually, the Wobblies organized immigrant workers by language groups. But there was no time to set up 15 or 20 separate organizations. Instead, Ettor suggested a "strike committee" composed of two representatives of every major nationality employed in the mills. These representatives had the responsibility of explaining strike tactics and strategy to their fellow ethnics. They also had the task of setting up distribution of food and other necessities. The committee worked with local grocers and bakers, since each nationality had its own dietary preferences. And they coordinated the campaign to send children on vacation. Some members of the committee were IWW members. Others were not. Ettor did not choose them. The striking members of their own ethnic groups elected them. Ettor was elected to chair the committee.

By Sunday, the committee had formulated its demands. Initially, all the strikers had wanted was enough of a pay increase to offset the 54-hour law. Now they demanded a 15 percent hike in wages, double pay for overtime, the abolition of the premium system,[18] and amnesty for strikers. To this list was later added a demand for the release on bail of Joe Ettor and Arturo Giovannitti, publisher of an Italian-language radical newspaper, after their arrest as accessories to murder following the shooting of a striker, Anna Lo Pezzi, on January 29.[19]

Both sides dug in. The strike committee offered to discuss its demands, but the mill owners refused. Whether they had a role in the arrest of Ettor and Giovannitti is unknown, although the strikers assumed that they did. With Ettor in jail, other IWW leaders came to Lawrence, including the union's president, William "Big Bill" Haywood. The strike committee continued to hold the diverse ethnic communities together. The arrest of Ettor was the second attempt to discredit the strike. On January 19, dynamite was discovered in a cemetery, a tailor shop, and a shoe shop. The strikers were accused of planning a series of bombings, and several were arrested. But it turned out that a Lawrence school committee member had planted the dynamite. He pleaded guilty and paid a $500 fine.

Then came the debacle at the train station, congressional investigations that might jeopardize the favorable tariff protections, and a wave of newspaper and magazine reports sympathetic to the strikers. Add to this the money the companies were losing because of the strike and the willingness of the strikers to remain out as long as was necessary, and the companies decided to settle.

THE LYNCHING OF LEO FRANK, 1915

On April 26, 1913, Mary Phagan, a white 13-year-old worker in an Atlanta pencil factory, went to collect her pay. It was the Confederate Memorial Day, a holiday in Georgia, and she intended to spend it watching the big parade. Instead, she was murdered; her body was found in the factory basement by the watchman, Newt Lee, an African American. He called the police.[20]

Initial suspicion fell upon Lee and on Arthur Mullinax, a white streetcar conductor who had sometimes given Phagan rides to and from work in his car. Several others were also arrested. But Atlanta police also suspected Leo Frank, a Jew from New York City, who managed the factory. They had no evidence against him but thought he acted strangely when they first interviewed him. At the inquest, held on April 30, 1913, just four days after the murder, a teenage friend of Mary Phagan named George Epps claimed that she was afraid of Leo Frank because he had flirted with her. Newt Lee, still a prime suspect, said that Frank seemed nervous the day of the murder. On the other hand, two mechanics, who also saw Frank that day, testified that he had behaved normally.

The next day, May 1, the police made another arrest. They found Jim Conley, a black sweeper, washing out a bloodstained shirt in the factory. A week later, on May 8, the coroner's jury ordered both Newt Lee and Leo Frank held for homicide. By this time, more witnesses had come forward. Phagan's foreman claimed that he saw Frank that day and that he was not nervous. He also swore that he knew Frank well and that he would never have done such a thing. The police discounted his testimony, charging that Frank had bribed him. There was no evidence of a bribe, however. Several of Phagan's co-workers also spoke to the police. Frank, they said, had made "improper" advances.

At this point, the police simply did not have a case. But they did have clues. Two of the most important were handwritten notes found next to the body, supposedly scribbled by Phagan with her dying breath, that accused Newt Lee. Tests showed that Jim Conley had written them. He admitted that he had but claimed he did so at the direction of Leo Frank. On May 23, the prosecutor, Hugh Dorsey, indicted Leo Frank for murder. He did not mention the notes to the grand jury. He did not use Jim Conley as a witness. He did not present Frank's statement to the police affirming that he had been in his office at the time of the murder. It was an indictment based simply on suspicions.

The person directly implicated by the evidence was Jim Conley. On May 30, the police took Conley to the pencil factory and had him walk through his version of what happened that day. Frank, he said, had asked him to watch the stairs leading to his office. He had instead fallen asleep. Next, Frank's whistle from his office awakened him. He found Frank shaking so severely he had to hang on to Conley to steady himself. He then dictated the notes. "Why should I hang?" Frank said by way of explanation. Earlier, Conley had sworn that Frank dictated them the day before the murder. Then he and Frank carried the body to the elevator and left it in the basement. This statement was demonstrably false, but the police—and later the defense team—did not realize it. Conley had defecated under the elevator on the morning of the murder. The police noted the "fresh" feces. Had Conley and Frank, or anyone else, used the elevator to go to the basement, the car would have crushed the excrement.

The case against Leo Frank rested on the testimony of Jim Conley. Why would the police believe Conley, a black man, who changed his story time and again as new evidence discredited his earlier claims? Why would an all-white jury believe Conley? His testimony aside, there was no credible evidence against Frank. The judge, even though he sentenced Frank to death, had serious doubts. He later communicated his concerns to the governor, asking him to commute Frank's sentence. Conley's own lawyer had doubts, as well. He later admitted that he thought his client was probably the murderer. Here is a mystery more puzzling than who killed Mary Phagan.

Southern history is filled with cases of innocent blacks convicted of crimes against white women, such as Ed Johnson whose story is detailed in Part 1. They simply found themselves in the wrong place at the wrong time. Conley had the opportunity to murder Phagan. He admitted to being in the pencil factory when she was killed. He admitted that he had helped dispose of the body. He had ready access to the supposed murder weapon. (The cause of death was actually strangulation.) He had a history of violence. He had shot his wife and threatened an employer with a gun. And, according to southern racial convictions, he unquestionably had a motive. All black men were thought to harbor designs of raping white women. Little Mary tried to resist. Conley killed her. If Leo Frank were a southern Protestant, that would have been the prosecution's theory of the case. Or Newt Lee would have been indicted. Both he and Leo Frank were held in jail for weeks. And a lynch mob gathered several nights after Lee was arrested. But Leo Frank was not a southern Protestant. He was a northern Jew, and the police and the prosecutor decided that he was guilty, and they set about finding—in some instances inventing—evidence against him.

Frank had no alibi. He was alone in his office, he testified, between noon and 1 P.M., the time when Phagan was killed. One young white factory worker swore that she went to see him at 12:05 and he was not in his office. This was not much on which to build a case. So, on June 2, the police interrogated Minola McKnight, the Franks' African American cook. Initially, she confirmed Frank's account about when he returned home for lunch and when he returned to the factory. On June 3, after a night in jail and intense questioning by the police, Mrs. McKnight signed a statement in which she alleged that Leo Frank was extremely nervous and drinking heavily the evening of the murder. She claimed that she overheard Frank's wife say that he had threatened to shoot himself. Frank, she also alleged, had confided in her: "It is mighty bad, Minola. I might have to go to jail about this girl, and I don't know anything about it." Finally, she said her wages had been raised as a "tip to keep quiet." Frank's wife, Lucille, bitterly protested the strong-arm tactics: "the action of the solicitor general in arresting and imprisoning our family cook because she would not voluntarily make a false statement against my innocent husband, brings a limit to patience."

Frank's trial began on July 28, 1913, and lasted until August 25, when the jury found him guilty. The following day, the judge sentenced him to death by hanging for the murder of Mary Phagan. The key moments came on August 4, when

Leo Frank hanging from a tree, Marietta, Georgia, August 17, 1915. Courtesy of Library of Congress.

Jim Conley told his tale, and on August 18, when Leo Frank told his. Conley's account had already changed several times; it had also grown more detailed. And the details were so scandalous that the judge ordered the courtroom cleared of women and children. Frank, Conley testified, had often asked him to serve as a lookout on the stairs leading to his office while he "entertained" various women. While not able to provide an eyewitness description of what Frank and these women did on these occasions, Conley implied that they engaged in various deviant sexual acts. He then retold the story of Frank asking him to watch the stairs while he "chatted" with Mary Phagan, of his falling asleep, and of Frank summoning him with a whistle. Frank told him that Phagan had repulsed his advances, that he became angry and struck her, and that she was dead. Then Conley and Frank carried the body to the elevator, took it to the basement, and returned to Frank's office, where Frank promised Conley some money to keep quiet and then dictated the notes to attempt to frame Newt Lee. This was still another shift in Conley's account of the notes. First he had said Frank dictated them the day before the murder, then before they moved the body, and finally after. There was another problem with his story. Someone had indeed struck Phagan, causing her to bleed profusely. But she did not die from the wound. She was strangled. Conley testified that Frank confessed to striking Phagan, not to strangling her with his bare hands.

The defense made much of the changes in his story and of Conley's police record and violent past. They did not, however, get him to give any ground on his main assertions, despite long hours of cross-questioning. This made Frank's testimony all the more crucial. The defense managed to challenge the prosecution's claims that Frank sexually harassed his female employees with testimony from numerous present and former workers at the pencil factory. It discredited the testimony of George Epps about Phagan being afraid of Frank by introducing testimony contradicting his claim that he and Phagan rode together on the streetcar the morning of the murder. But the very large number of character witnesses introduced by the defense effectively acknowledged that what was on trial was Frank's character, not his actions.

How was it possible to turn a moderately successful businessman into a sexual deviant and callous murderer in the popular imagination? Rumors helped. Any number of people *claimed* to know terrible things about Frank. On May 10, for example, the *Atlanta Constitution* printed the claim of Robert House, an ex-policeman, that he had caught Leo Frank and a young girl in the woods at Druid Hills Park engaging in immoral acts. House said that Frank had begged him not to arrest him. House, it turned out, was lying. Presumably, he wanted attention.

More powerful than rumor was anti-Semitism. Whipping up popular hatred of Frank because he was a Jew was former Georgia senator Tom Watson. He published editorials in his *Watson's Magazine* with titles like "The Official Record in the Case of Leo Frank, a Jew Pervert" (September 1915). The phrase "Jew Pervert" played off several phobias at once. One was the Jewish merchant, the Shylock. Another was the Jewish criminal who exploited children, the Fagin. Still a third was the Jewish sexual fiend who lusted after Gentile women in a manner analogous to the black male's alleged obsession with white womanhood.[21]

All of these stereotypes shaped popular perceptions of Frank. As a result, Frank became the embodiment of a generalized misgiving about a rapidly changing white South. Families like the Phagans had moved to the city to escape the dismal poverty of sharecropping. There were opportunities in places like Atlanta. But they entailed young white women going to work in factories like the one Leo Frank ran. There they worked long hours for paltry wages. There they encountered sexual harassment; if not in Frank's factory, then in many others. There they also achieved a modest measure of independence. They had money of their own. They escaped parental supervision, not only during the workday but on other occasions, as well. Mary Phagan went to Atlanta alone. She intended to pick up her pay, watch the Confederate Memorial Day parade, and perhaps meet up with friends. Perhaps a boyfriend. Parents, fathers especially, could not protect their daughters, and they could not control them. Leo Frank, the Northerner, the Jew, embodied these troubling changes. He was not one of them. He did not, so they believed, share their values. He was a menace.

Anti-Semitism, fueled by cultural concerns, briefly trumped racism. Leo Frank faced a death sentence. Jim Conley got one year in jail for helping dispose of the body.

Frank's lawyers immediately launched a series of appeals, first to the trial judge and then to Fulton County Superior Court and to the Georgia State Supreme Court and finally to the U.S. Supreme Court. All were rejected, and Frank's execution was rescheduled for June 22, 1915. On June 20, his last day in office, Georgia governor John Slayton commuted Frank's sentence to life in prison. He was convinced that Frank was innocent. He and his wife, knowing how unpopular the commutation would prove, left the state immediately and did not return for months.

On July 18, a fellow prisoner slashed Frank's throat. Two nearby convicts, both physicians, stopped the bleeding and saved his life. But, on August 16, 1915, eight cars carrying 25 men who called themselves the Knights of Mary Phagan showed up at the Georgia State Prison at Milledgeville around 10 P.M. They cut the telephone lines, surprised and disarmed the guards, and entered the barracks containing Leo Frank. They grabbed him and made their escape. Early the next morning, they reached the outskirts of Marietta. At Frey's Grove, near Mary Phagan's girlhood home, they lynched Leo Frank. Someone took a photograph. Subsequently someone turned it into a postcard, a grisly memento of a brutal murder.

The conviction and murder of Leo Frank galvanized the American Jewish community. This was the worst single episode of anti-Semitism in American history. Prominent Jews organized the Anti-Defamation League to combat prejudice and to succor its victims. Other ethnic, religious, and racial groups followed their example.

THE BIRTH OF A NATION, THE NAACP, AND THE STRUGGLE OVER THE MEANING OF THE CIVIL WAR

On February 8, 1915, *The Birth of a Nation* premiered in Los Angeles. It is the most important movie ever made and quite possibly the most pernicious.[22] Not only was it the first feature-length movie, with an unprecedented budget and a cast literally of thousands, but it also introduced an array of techniques that have continued to shape movie making to this day. D. W. Griffith, the director and producer, largely invented the visual language of film narrative—jump cuts, fade-outs, dissolves, close-ups, and the like. He also co-wrote the score for the movie and so helped establish the standard that what the viewer hears should reinforce the visual message. Further, the film dealt with the most dramatic events in American history, the Civil War and its aftermath. The year of the film's release, 1915, marked the fiftieth anniversary of Lee's surrender to Grant and of Lincoln's assassination. Millions of Americans could remember those events. Millions more had grown up hearing about them from parents and grandparents. Veterans of the Grand Army of the Republic still marched down uncounted Main Streets on May 31, Memorial Day, as did former Confederates on their own Memorial Day.

The scale of the movie, its technical wizardry, and its subject matter made it the most successful film in history until the release of *Gone with the Wind*, in

1939, a movie that also told the story of the war and Reconstruction from a white southern point of view. That Griffith was a white Southerner mattered. That he based the film upon the novels of Thomas Dixon, also a white Southerner, novels that glorified the exploits of the Ku Klux Klan, mattered even more. Dixon was a man with a mission. He wanted to displace *Uncle Tom's Cabin* in the American imagination.[23] White Southerners had always reviled Harriet Beecher Stowe's saga of the Christ-like slave, with its detailed descriptions of the horrors of slavery and the brutality of slaveholders. Not only had the novel sold millions of copies over the decades, but it had also been turned into a play—more accurately, into several plays—that continued to tour the country. When Northerners thought of the Civil War, they thought first of slavery as depicted by Stowe, and they blamed slaveowners for secession and for the carnage four years of conflict had produced.

Dixon set out to change that. He was not alone. A generation of white southern scholars also determined to "rescue" the history of the white South. U. B. Phillips, for example, wrote several important books on American slavery in which he contended that slaveholders on the whole were kind masters who treated blacks as wayward children who needed discipline. Indeed, Phillips argued, the plantation system was financially disadvantageous, in large measure because of the expenses that the planter went to so that the slaves would be treated well. Phillips presented slavery as a "school" in which blacks learned English, became Christians, and acquired the rudiments of white civilization.[24] William Dunning, another prominent white southern historian, explained Reconstruction as a disastrous attempt to give power to freedmen who, along with corrupt northern carpetbaggers, committed outrages upon innocent whites.[25]

Another member of this generation of southern white scholars was Woodrow Wilson. Dixon had been a classmate, and Wilson screened the film in the White House. It was the first movie ever shown there. It is not at all certain that Wilson praised it as "history written with lightning," although that statement is often attributed to him. But, whatever he actually said, his stamp of approval was clear.[26] Griffith used several quotations from Wilson's multivolume *A History of the American People* (1902), including one title card that introduced the second part of the film, that dealt with Reconstruction and that described the KKK as a necessary response to the excesses of black and carpetbagger government.

The Birth of a Nation follows two white families, one northern and one southern. Friends before the war, the menfolk fight valiantly on opposite sides and even meet on the battlefield when one is wounded. The Confederates, despite their heroic efforts, ultimately lose. The southern hero, nicknamed the "Little Colonel," returns to his family home. Soon he will be joined there by the northern heroine, who is the daughter of one of the leading "Radical Republicans." Loosely based on Thaddeus Stevens, this character is determined that blacks shall enjoy full equality with whites. His mulatto protégé becomes lieutenant governor of the Reconstruction government (presumably of South Carolina) and develops an infatuation with the daughter. She loves the "Little Colonel." Their musical theme is "The Perfect Love Song." But, she cannot marry him because

Scene from *The Birth of a Nation*, 1915. Courtesy of Photofest.

of his rejection of her father's politics. She does re-establish her friendship with members of his family, including his little sister.

Sister goes off into the woods to get some water. A lustful black soldier follows. Terrified, she runs blindly away until she is cornered on the top of a cliff. Choosing death before dishonor, she jumps. The "Little Colonel" decides to avenge his sister and to lead the struggle against Reconstruction by forming the Ku Klux Klan. White vigilantes hunt the black soldier down, try him before a kangaroo court, and hang him. Meanwhile, black legislators, shown as drinking and ogling white women in the visitors' gallery, pass a law permitting racial intermarriage. This enables the villainous lieutenant governor to propose to the heroine. She is outraged at his impudence and threatens to have him horsewhipped. He, however, has no intention of being denied. She faints into his arms. He orders his underlings to arrange the marriage, and they carry her off. Just then, his mentor, her father, arrives on the scene: "I intend to marry a white woman." The congressman readily approves. "The woman I intend to marry is your daughter." The congressman absolutely forbids it. It is not your decision, the congressman is told. Then, just in the nick of time, the "Little Colonel" and a troop of hooded Klansmen arrive, rout the blacks, and rescue the daughter. The congressman learns his lesson. His daughter and the "Little Colonel" marry, symbolizing the birth of the new America, one founded on the principle of white supremacy.

As history, *The Birth of a Nation* is almost entirely misleading. But leading historians vouched for its accuracy. Only W.E.B. Du Bois, founder of the NAACP, tried to tell the true history of Reconstruction.[27] And he was largely ignored for his pains. As a portrayal of blacks, the movie is vicious. They are depicted as dishonest, drunken, lazy, and rapists. In addition, the film endorses the standard white defense of lynching, that it was necessary in order to protect white womanhood. As a portrayal of the KKK, *The Birth of a Nation* creates a myth of noble white men valiantly resisting oppression and protecting their women. Unsurprisingly, a new Ku Klux Klan was organized in 1915 in the wake of the movie's success. By the mid-1920s, it would have more than 4 million members.[28]

Du Bois and other NAACP activists did everything they could to prevent the film's success.[29] At the time, there was no motion picture production code to appeal to. Instead, individual towns, cities, counties, and states had (or did not have) their own censorship boards. As a result, the NAACP had to mount individual campaigns wherever their membership was large enough to offer some promise of success. Their first efforts were in Los Angeles, the home of the film industry. City authorities turned them down flat. Film was rapidly becoming one of the biggest industries in the country, not only in terms of revenue but also in number of jobs. *The Birth of a Nation* was the biggest picture ever made, one that promised to bring even greater prosperity to the city.

Next the NAACP turned to New York. It pursued two tracks. One was an appeal to the mayor, the progressive reformer John Purroy Mitchel, to censor the most objectionable scenes. The other was a call to boycott the Liberty Theatre in Times Square, where the film was to open. Mitchel, according to the NAACP official Mary Childs Nerney, initially agreed to cut the suicide of the little sister and forced marriage scenes. If so, he soon changed his mind.

The boycott proved equally unsuccessful. Griffith and his associates developed an ingenious series of countermeasures. One was advance ticket sales and reserved seating. Customers did not need to stand on line outside the box office surrounded by picket signs and protesters. They did not even have to arrange their own transportation in many instances. The producers hired special trains from New Jersey and Connecticut. Men in full Klan regalia on horseback stood between moviegoers and protesters. Just going to the movie became a dramatic but safe adventure.

The NAACP sought an injunction against the film on the grounds that its portrayal of blacks might lead to public disorder and violence. In the event, however, there was no violence. And people all over the country flocked to see the movie. So popular did it prove that it was re-released several times between 1917 and 1930. Each time, it proved a success at the box office. Each time, the NAACP launched new protests, sought new injunctions, and called for the worst scenes to be censored. Only in Kansas, which banned the film, did they succeed. Elsewhere, local authorities occasionally made minor cuts. But the key scenes that glorified lynching and Klan violence remained intact.

For Griffith, the issue was artistic freedom. He had made what he sincerely believed was an historically accurate film. Leading scholars affirmed his contention. President Wilson himself supplied judgments Griffith used. Students at Columbia University who attended William Dunning's lectures on Reconstruction heard a similar, if less melodramatic, version of events.

For Thomas Dixon, and for the white southern scholars who sentimentalized plantation slavery and caricatured black rule, the stakes were the meanings of the Civil War and Reconstruction. Abraham Lincoln had cast the war as a struggle to see whether a nation dedicated to the ideal of equality "could long endure." Dixon, Phillips, Dunning, and Woodrow Wilson all believed that Reconstruction had proved that racial equality was not an ideal but a nightmare. True, the Confederacy was "the Lost Cause," but the real meaning of equality was the equality of free white men. To read their books today is to be struck by the highly selective way they assembled their evidence. All historians have to assess the reliability of their sources. Dunning and the others discounted evidence of white racism and violence, such as the race riots in New Orleans and Memphis in 1866. They ignored the achievements of the Reconstruction governments, starting with the creation of the first public school systems in the South. They overemphasized the extent of corruption. In short, they read the evidence in the light of their own loyalties to a white-dominated South. Du Bois's *Black Reconstruction* effectively challenged their claims. Other historians, however, paid no attention to his work.

White supremacy, symbolized in the film by the marriage of the southern groom and the northern bride, made the "new nation" possible. The symbolism was fraught with meaning. Northern cartoonists, during and after the War, exploited the fact that the names of many southern states were female. Caroline and her sisters were routinely shown defying the authority of "Brother Jonathan," the predecessor of Uncle Sam. Reconstruction cartoons showed the southern bride promising to love, honor, and *obey* her northern husband.[30] Dixon's novels and Griffith's film reversed these gender roles. It was the southern hero who established the terms of the new union. It was the northern bride who submitted to his better judgment.

For Du Bois and the NAACP, the battle over the film was one of many they waged against the pervasive racism and discrimination encountered by people of color in virtually every aspect of their lives. It was a particularly important battle because of the power of the new medium. Americans, regardless of color, had fallen in love with the movies. A decade before *The Birth of a Nation*, movies rarely lasted more than 10 or 15 minutes, were shown in small and not necessarily very clean storefronts, and cost a nickel to see. Within a few years, large studios had begun to organize production and distribution. Specially constructed theaters were being built everywhere. The star system was born. One of the first stars was Lillian Gish, who played the heroine of *The Birth of a Nation*. How blacks, and other groups, were depicted on film would help determine how they thought about themselves, as well as how others imagined them.[31] Stereotypes would shape expectations and justify discrimination.

The struggle over *The Birth of a Nation* was a woefully unequal contest. Du Bois had historical accuracy and the principles of the Declaration of Independence on his side. He had the support of a handful of enlightened progressive reformers, such as Jane Addams. Griffith had the historians, if not history, on his side. He also had white racism.

IMMIGRATION RESTRICTION AND THE GREAT WAR

World War I added still another concern to Americans' catalogue of reasons to fear immigrants, namely that the newcomers and their children might prove loyal to Germany, the Austro-Hungarian empire, or Ireland, rather than to the United States. They were "hyphenated Americans." And, as President Wilson informed an audience of newly naturalized citizens in 1915, American did "not consist of groups." Furthermore, anyone who still thought of himself as belonging to a group, a German-American or Italian-American, say, was not a real American.[32] Theodore Roosevelt was even more emphatic on this point. He announced he did not want the support of anyone during his 1916 run for the Republican nomination who was not "prepared to say that every citizen of this country has to be pro-United States first, last, and all the time, and not pro-anything else at all."[33] Not to be outdone, the Democratic platform, over which President Wilson had full control, declared that "the indivisibility and coherent strength of the nation" to be the "supreme issue." There were, it alleged, "conspiracies" to further "the interests of foreign countries," and it condemned "as subversive" any "organization that has for its object the advancement of the interest of a foreign Power . . . by intimidating the Government, a political party, or representatives of the people."[34]

Immigrants supposedly brought un-American ideologies such as socialism and anarchism to their new homes. The Haymarket Bombing came to symbolize the new menace. On May 4, 1886, police marched in formation into Haymarket Square, in Chicago, to break up a rally in support of striking workers at the McCormick Reaper Works. Why the police decided to act when they did remains a mystery. The rally was ending as they arrived. Only a few hundred remained out of the original gathering of thousands. And the rally had been entirely peaceful. Nonetheless, the police arrived in force. Some unknown person threw a bomb into their ranks. The explosion killed several officers. Several others died or were wounded when their colleagues began firing wildly.

Although the police never determined who threw the bomb, blame immediately fell upon those who organized the rally. Several were immigrants, although Albert Parsons, was from Texas. All were either socialists or anarchists. The image of the bomb-throwing alien burned in the popular imagination.

Hyphens did not immediately cease political efforts on behalf of Ireland or Germany. Instead, they pursued a strategy of calling upon Wilson to be true to his own policy of neutrality. In October 1916, Jeremiah A. O'Leary of the American Truth Society charged the president with being "pro-British," "truckling to the British Empire," and creating a "dictatorship over Congress." Wilson replied, "I would feel deeply mortified to have you or anyone like you vote for me. Since you have access to many disloyal Americans and I have not, I will ask you to convey this message to them."[35]

What Roosevelt and Wilson demanded was the impossible. America *did* consist of multiple ethnic and religious groups, as the president's audience in 1915 could have explained to him had he wished to listen. The chances in life of members of these groups depended in large measure on the public standing of their ethnic and/or religious group. They were judged by their names, their accents, and their religions. They experienced stereotyping and discrimination. Now they had to prove their loyalty.

German-Americans encountered the most suspicion. Schools stopped teaching the German language. German-American societies lost members. German-language newspapers lost readers. People anglicized their names, so that Ochs, for example, became Oakes.

Other ethnics faced similar problems. Those from Poland, Hungary, and other portions of the German and Austro-Hungarian empires were legally enemy aliens, citizens of countries with which the United States was at war as of April 1917. Virtually all of them felt no love for the empires that had conquered and annexed their homelands. Their personal loyalties did not affect their legal status, however. As a result of their citizenship, they were not eligible for the military draft. International law forbade governments from impressing citizens of enemy nations into their armed forces. This exclusion led self-styled real Americans to complain that immigrants were getting a free ride. In fact, many immigrants voluntarily joined the Army or the Navy.

This led to another legal issue. If any of these sailors and soldiers were captured, they would not be treated as prisoners of war, because they were not American citizens.[36] Instead, they would be tried and probably executed as traitors. The solution was legislation that exempted these immigrants from the required waiting time for naturalization. Thousands at a time became citizens in special ceremonies at training camps around the country.

Despite this display of patriotism, suspicion did not dissipate. The Committee on Public Information (CPI), created to manage government propaganda—its own word—campaigns, established the Foreign Language Information Service (FLIS), which took over editorial control of the foreign-language press. All news stories, editorials, and advertisements had to be cleared by Washington. FLIS staff also wrote stories and editorials that the foreign-language press dutifully printed.[37]

The freedom of movement and employment opportunities of immigrants from Germany and Austro-Hungary were restricted. On April 16, 1917, just two weeks after asking for the declaration of war, President Wilson issued regulations limiting the rights of alien enemies. They could not own firearms, aircraft, or radio equipment. They could not publish an "attack" upon any branch of the U.S. government. They could not live in areas listed as prohibited by the president. They could be removed by presidential order to relocation camps. Alien enemies could not leave the country without permission, and they had to carry a registration card. On November 16, 1917, additional regulations limited alien enemies' access to docks, railroads, and warehouses.

The "war to make the world safe for democracy" fueled the hysteria, hatred, and fear that characterized nativism. The national Council of National Defense that oversaw the mobilization of the economy set up state councils. During Liberty Loan drives, men from the councils, according to George Creel, who headed the Committee on Public Information, would demand from the foreign-born "a statement of earnings, expenditures, savings, etc." and then stipulate the contribution "dazed victims were expected to make." Anyone who insisted on deciding the matter for himself faced "expulsion from the community, personal ill treatment, or a pleasant little attention like painting the house yellow."[38]

Nativist zeal, in turn, led to calls for immigration restriction. The Immigration Act of 1917, passed over President Wilson's objections, excluded "aliens over sixteen years of age, physically capable of reading, who cannot read the English language, or some other language or dialect, including Hebrew or Yiddish." Foes of immigration had called for this literacy test for decades. Grover Cleveland had vetoed it in 1891; William Howard Taft had done the same in 1913. Henry Cabot Lodge, a Republican senator from Massachusetts, spelled out the case for the test. The sources of immigration had shifted from northern and western Europe to southern and eastern nations like Italy, Poland, Hungary, and Russia. These so-called new immigrants posed two threats. One was that they lowered "the quality of our citizenship." The other was that they undersold the native-born American in the labor market and thereby lowered wages for all. The literacy test would meet both dangers, Lodge maintained, because immigrants from Great Britain, Canada, Scandinavia, and Germany were overwhelmingly literate. Their migration would continue. Restrictionists like Lodge believed that the test would bar the so-called new immigrants. The facts proved otherwise.

Immigration during 1917 and 1918 was effectively restricted by the war and the difficulties it imposed upon travel. As a result, 1919 and 1920 were the first years in which the literacy test came into play. The numbers of people seeking to immigrate quickly reached prewar levels. And the proportion of immigrants coming from eastern and southern Europe remained the same. What did change because of the 1917 law was the number of immigrants from Asia. That fell to zero because the law created an "Asiatic Barred Zone."

Despite the failure of the literacy test to limit the immigration of those deemed undesirable, restrictionists did not question their stereotyping of immigrants from southern and eastern Europe as ignorant. Nor did they rethink the whole question of the alleged immigrant menace. Instead, they looked to a more reliable way of reducing the number of newcomers in the Emergency Immigration Restriction Act of 1921. That law established quotas for each group based upon its proportion of the population. Since German-Americans, Irish-Americans, Canadian-Americans, and Anglo-Americans outnumbered Italian-Americans, Polish-Americans, and Greek-Americans, their home countries got the largest quotas. The restriction act of 1924 made the quota system permanent and used the Census of 1890 to determine quotas, since the influx from eastern and southern Europe largely came after that date. Both the 1921 and 1924 measures retained the "Asiatic Barred Zone." One can imagine members of those groups excluded or whose quotas were minuscule mocking President Wilson's statement of 1915: "America does not consist of groups."

THE PALMER RAIDS AND THE FIRST RED SCARE, 1919–1920

The bomb-throwing anarchist haunted the nativist imagination at least since the Haymarket Bombing in Chicago in 1886.[39] By 1919, he had a new, even more menacing ideology to espouse—Bolshevism. Communism joined anarchy and socialism to form an unholy trinity of un-American creeds. Its source was Russia, recently renamed the Union of Soviet Socialist Republics (USSR), also called the Soviet Union.

In February 1917, exhausted by years of unsuccessful war with Germany, Russian workers overthrew the tsar in the first Russian Revolution. A provisional government, led by the socialist Alexander Kerensky, however, decided to continue the war with Germany. (Russia's allies, France and England, exerted considerable pressure on the new regime to do so lest Germany be able to concentrate all of its resources against them.) The decision was deeply unpopular among the Russian people and opened the way for a second, communist-led revolution in October 1917. The Bolsheviks quickly gained control of St. Petersburg and Moscow. It would take them years of civil war to consolidate their hold over the entire country. The new government promised "Peace, Land, and Bread" and quickly delivered on the first. In March 1918, the Soviet Union signed a separate peace with Germany.

For three and a half years, Germany had fought a two-front war. Now all was quiet on the eastern front. Germany put all its military might into the campaign in the west. Most Americans saw the Soviet Union's treaty with the Kaiser as an act of betrayal that cost tens of thousands of British, French, and American lives. Some, however, saw the Bolshevik Revolution as heralding a new age in which working people would overthrow their capitalist oppressors. These radicals were further encouraged by the postwar tumult in Germany, especially by the communist uprising in Berlin. In Hungary, too, in the wake of the collapse of the Austro-Hungarian Empire, a Bolshevik-style movement emerged and briefly seized power. Radicals dreamed of a similar revolution in the United States. For the great majority of Americans, in contrast, such a prospect was a nightmare.

Might there be a communist revolution in the United States in 1919? There were worrisome signs that it could happen, and there were ambitious and opportunistic politicians eager to stoke such fears. Among the signs was a series of terrorist bombings. In April, the Post Office discovered 38 bombs that had been mailed to leading American politicians and capitalists. Then an Italian anarchist set off a bomb outside Attorney General A. Mitchell Palmer's home. The house itself was partially destroyed and the bomber killed. Palmer and his family were unharmed. The most terrifying and deadly attack came on September 16, 1919, at one minute past noon outside the J. P. Morgan bank on Wall Street. A man drove a horse and wagon up to the building, dismounted, and sped away. Then came the explosion—100 pounds of dynamite, rigged to a timer and wrapped with small pieces of iron. The blast killed 31 people and injured hundreds more, most of them office workers thronging the sidewalks as they hurried to get lunch.

Another sign was a series of bitterly contested strikes. On September 9, 1919, the Boston police struck for higher wages, leaving public safety to the improvised efforts of volunteers. Massachusetts governor Calvin Coolidge became a national figure by breaking the strike. In Pittsburgh, Gary (Indiana), Cleveland, Birmingham, Chicago, and other steel-making centers, workers shut down the entire industry. The leader of the strike, William Z. Foster, ran for president in 1920 as the candidate of the newly formed Communist Party of the United States of America (CPUSA). Most frightening of all, in Seattle, workers shut down the entire city with a general strike. This was a tactic the Bolsheviks had used. Further, the Seattle workers copied the soviet system (*soviet* is the Russian word for committee) by organizing a series of workers' committees. One oversaw electrical power and made sure that hospitals and other essential agencies did not lose electricity. Another guaranteed that there was an adequate supply of milk for children and nursing mothers. Still others organized food pantries, staffed ambulances and firehouses, and provided other basic services. There was no violence.

It was not a revolution. Anna Louise Strong, one of the strike's organizers and then its historian, was insistent on that. But, she added, it did demonstrate that the workers had learned how to make a revolution. "An editorial in the *Union Record*, two weeks after the strike, discusses the workers' government just arising in Belfast, and draws comparison with the Seattle general strike." The editorial pointed to the "quiet mass action" of both, of the "tying up of industry," and of the assumption of day-to-day authority for the well-being of the population by the strike committee. There had been "no revolution" in Seattle. But, should there be another strike, as more and more control "slips gradually" into the hands of the strike committee, matters might turn "suddenly to violence" in a "test of force" that would indeed be a revolution.[40]

The bombings stopped after September's horrific blast in New York. The strikes failed. The Red Scare, however, increased in intensity. In part, this happened because influential political leaders wanted it to happen. The most important of these was A. Mitchell Palmer, the Attorney General and one of those targeted during the wave of terrorist bombings.

Palmer had his eye on the presidency in 1920. But no one had ever moved from the Justice Department to the White House. The most common path to nomination by a major party was to first serve as the governor of a large state. As a result, Palmer had to find a way to turn himself into plausible candidate. His genuine fear of alien radicals plus his political ambitions led him to launch a campaign to eradicate a largely imaginary Red menace. "Like a prairie-fire," he wrote in 1920,

> the blaze of revolution was sweeping over every American institution of law and order a year ago. It was eating its way into the homes of the American workmen, its sharp tongues of revolutionary heat were licking the altars of the churches, leaping into the belfry of the school bell, crawling into the sacred corners of American homes, seeking to replace marriage vows with libertine laws, burning up the foundations of society.

The government was in jeopardy, Palmer claimed. Justice Department sources reported a conspiracy organized "by the organization known as the Communist Party of America, with headquarters in Chicago," in accord with the "manifesto planned at Moscow last March by Trotzky, Lenin and others addressed 'To the Proletariats of All Countries.'"

Palmer concluded "that communism in this country was an organization of thousands of aliens who were direct allies of Trotzky [one of the organizers of the Bolshevik Revolution]." "Aliens of the same misshapen caste of mind and indecencies of character," he continued, " were making the same glittering promises of lawlessness, of criminal autocracy to Americans, that they had made to the Russian peasants." There were "upwards of 60,000 of these organized agitators of the Trotzky doctrine in the United States."[41]

What the Justice Department did to sweep the nation clean began with the "Palmer Raids." They were organized by Palmer's special assistant, J. Edgar Hoover, who would subsequently become the director of the Federal Bureau of Investigation (FBI). On November 7, 1919, the second anniversary of the Bolshevik Revolution, the first set of raids netted 10,000 suspected communists and anarchists. The evidence against them was so weak that the vast majority were ultimately released without charges. They were suspects because their names ended in "ski" or "sky." Or they subscribed to a socialist newspaper[42] or belonged to the Industrial Workers of the World or some other organization Palmer and Hoover deemed subversive. On January 2, 1920, a second series of raids led to another 6,000 arrests. As with the first set of alleged Bolsheviks, those seized were not formally charged and were held without trial.[43]

Palmer and Hoover planned to deport all of these people without so much as a hearing to determine their fitness to remain in the United States. Palmer proclaimed his "own determination to drive from our midst the agents of Bolshevism with increasing vigor and with greater speed, until there are no more of them left among us."

The S.S. *Buford*, popularly known as the "Soviet Ark," set sail from New York on December 21, 1919, headed for Russia. On board were 249 radicals. A few, such as Emma Goldman, were well known. Goldman was an anarchist, feminist, and advocate of contraception. She was not a communist and ultimately went into exile in France with her long-time collaborator Alexander Berkman. Neither posed any danger to the United States.[44] Nor did any of the others on the *Buford*.

Standing in the way of further deportations was a bureaucrat, an Assistant Secretary of Labor named Louis F. Post, who oversaw the Immigration and Naturalization Service. He began a systematic review of all 16,000 detainees, one by one. In the overwhelming majority of cases, he found no evidence of any intent to overthrow the government of the United States or to engage in any other unlawful act. Palmer and his allies raged, and Post found himself threatened with impeachment.[45] He resisted the pressure, however, by demonstrating to Congress that a great many of the alleged Bolsheviks had no connection to the Communist Party or to any other subversive group.[46]

Palmer inadvertently came to Post's aid by proclaiming that the "Reds" intended to launch their revolution on May Day, May 1, 1920. Fear peaked as the dreaded day approached. But nothing happened on May Day or on any day thereafter. Palmer's fantasies of tens of thousands of followers of Trotsky taking over America suddenly appeared to be the ravings of a fanatic. The Red Scare petered out. The Democrats did not nominate Palmer. And the successful Republican candidate, Warren G. Harding, campaigned on the slogan that the United States needed "normalcy, not nostrums."

Nonetheless, the Red Scare took a lasting toll by effectively narrowing the political spectrum. Organizations attacked as un-American, from the IWW to the Socialist Party, no longer had a place in politics or in the union movement.[47] The new Communist Party never gained such a place. Suspicions of immigrant disloyalty helped the movement to restrict immigration succeed in the 1920s. And politicians like A. Mitchell Palmer would have successors in the post–World War II Second Red Scare. Senator Joseph McCarthy did not invent the techniques he used in his own campaign against an equally imaginary Red Menace.

THE CHICAGO RACE RIOT OF 1919

Between 1915, when Henry Ford began to hire African Americans as a way of heading off unionism—many unions refused to enroll blacks—and 1920, approximately half a million southern blacks moved north. This was the beginning of what became known as the "Great Migration." The *Chicago Defender* and other so-called race papers played a key role in promoting the migration. They advertised jobs and encouraged employers to turn to black workers as the American entry into World War I created labor shortages.[48] Because southern blacks were often desperately poor, employers sent to the South agents who recruited workers and arranged for their railroad fares. Southern whites deeply resented competition from Northerners offering significantly higher wages.

If better pay drew African Americans, Jim Crow policies in the South also motivated the migration north. Surely things could not be this bad in the North, many migrants thought.[49]

But, northern whites also resented blacks who competed with them for housing, jobs, and even space on the beaches fronting Lake Michigan. These whites, often immigrants or their children, believed that the meatpacking plants, steel mills, and other big employers wanted black employees because they were less likely to strike. They also had learned the racial rules of American society, including all of the prejudices and stereotypes. The war made matters worse. The switchover to wartime production meant, amid much else, that no new civilian housing was constructed. As more and more black families came north, they bid up the rents on available apartments and tenements, typically by 50 percent on Chicago's South Side, adding to white ethnic resentment. When blacks moved into formerly all-white neighborhoods, unknown persons set off some 24 bombs between July 1, 1917, and July 27, 1919, the first day of the riot; the bombs targeted black families and black and white real estate agents with black clients. No one was even arrested, much less convicted in any of the bombings.[50]

Black political strength also angered whites. The Democrats were the party of slavery and Jim Crow in the minds of most African Americans. The Republicans were the party of Abraham Lincoln. In April 1919, the Republican mayor was re-elected by a margin of just over 21,000 out of almost 700,000 votes cast. The mayor carried the largest black-majority ward by more than 12,000 votes, enough to determine the outcome.

Throughout the spring and early summer of 1919, white gangs, particularly the Irish-American "Ragen's Colts," attacked blacks. Several blacks were murdered, others severely beaten. Blacks were especially at risk in public spaces such as parks, beaches, and playgrounds. The message was clear: these areas were for whites only, no matter what the law said. As with the bombings, the police made no arrests.[51]

On Sunday, July 27, these episodic assaults escalated into a full-scale race riot that raged for seven days and sputtered on in isolated incidents for another six, claimed 38 lives (15 whites and 23 blacks), seriously injured another 537 (178 whites, 342 blacks, and 17 of unknown race), and left about 1,000 (overwhelmingly Lithuanians) homeless.[52] Unlike the race riot in Washington, DC, that same summer, there were no accusations that blacks had attacked white women or committed any other crimes. Instead, the precipitating incident involved a black teenage boy who was floating in Lake Michigan at the Twenty-ninth Street beach. The beach had been the scene of earlier racial tensions, which the police attempted to allay by proclaiming an invisible line running down to the water and out across the lake. On one side of the line, by Twenty-ninth Street, only whites could swim. On the other, toward Twenty-seventh, was the black beach. That afternoon, a teenage African American boy tried to enter the water at

Twenty-ninth. The white bathers drove him off. A little while later, several more black teenagers appeared on the white beach. Whites began to throw stones. The blacks beat a tactical retreat and then returned fire. White women and children took whatever shelter they could find as the males of both races continued the skirmish.

Meanwhile, 17-year-old Eugene Williams, who had entered the water back on Twenty-seventh, was swimming toward Twenty-ninth. When the rocks started flying, he grabbed hold of a floating railroad tie to try to protect himself. As a white man swam toward him, he let go and drowned. Blacks assumed he had been hit in the head by one of the stones and demanded that the police arrest the white man they claimed had been hurling rocks at Williams. The policeman refused.

Both blacks and whites dived in a series of unsuccessful attempts to find Williams's body. Meanwhile, a growing crowd of African American men and boys gathered. When the same white policeman arrested one of their number on the complaint of a white man, they attacked the officer. The riot began.

The tragedy at the beach set the pattern. White and black men squared off against each other. None of the 38 dead were women or children. Only 10 of the 537 injured were women or girls. But newspapers incorrectly reported that both black and white gangs targeted women. The *Chicago Defender,* on August 2, 1919, provided a particularly inflammatory, and entirely inaccurate, example. It reported that a young woman and her baby had been killed by a white mob. The "baby's brains," it alleged, were beaten "against a telegraph pole." Then "one rioter severed [the woman's] breasts."

The newspapers reported many other imaginary atrocities and thereby contributed to the mob fever that gripped both white and black communities.

On the Monday morning after Williams's death, July 28, tensions ran high, but there were few incidents. That changed in the late afternoon and early evening as black and white workers streamed home. White mobs, led by teenage gang members, apparently started the trouble. They gathered at street corners where trolley lines intersected and where black riders would get off one car to board another. The mob attacked any black man they could get their hands on. Soon the violence escalated, as whites shook stopped trolley cars, knocked them off the wires above so that they had no power, and then dragged black passengers off the cars and beat them. Blacks soon retaliated. Bands of young black males piled into cars and set off to find potential white victims.

The transit authorities shut down the trolley lines in the hope of curtailing the violence. Instead, by forcing whites and blacks to walk to work through each other's turf, they made even more conflict inevitable. Although they appeared chaotic, there was a pattern to the riots. Young males, if white organized in gangs, if black brought together by the desire for revenge, would assault someone who happened to be in the wrong place at the wrong time. A crowd of supporters would collect and, frequently, join in. The police would arrive, often too late to do more than summon an ambulance. If the remnants of the mob were still on the scene, they would almost never identify any of the ringleaders. Word of the latest atrocity, usually exaggerated, would make it back to the white or black community, members of which would then retaliate.

Thousands of state militia finally brought order. The mass arson of Saturday, August 2, that left nearly 1,000 homeless, was the last major episode.

A coroner's jury immediately convened, followed quickly by a grand jury. Both came to similar conclusions. One was that the Chicago police had performed poorly. They had been completely ineffective in dealing with any of the violent attacks on blacks that had led up to the riot. This had led the black community to the conclusion that it had to protect itself, that the police would not enforce the law impartially. Once the riot began, the police arrested far more blacks than whites, even though there were many more white than black rioters. Further, both juries concluded that the police force was undermanned, that the city needed at least another 1,000 officers. Another conclusion both shared was that newspapers made the riot worse by publishing exaggerated or imaginary stories that inflamed members of both the white and the black communities. Each report also singled out the role of white gangs, such as Ragen's Colts. These were sponsored by local politicians who paid the rent on a storefront clubhouse where young men gathered. Often, the members turned to petty crime, secure in the knowledge that their patron would protect them should they be arrested. Neither report called for the elimination of these "athletic clubs." They did call for their reform. And both hoped that the young men would turn away from them and toward more wholesome alternatives such as the YMCA.

Both reports also emphasized the causal role of the housing shortage and of the substandard housing blacks in particular had to make do with. The city was urged to encourage the building of additional affordable housing and to improve existing housing stock in the so-called Black Belt. If there was enough good housing available for blacks, both the grand and the coroner's juries believed, a form of voluntary segregation would take place. That, in turn, would bring the turf battles to an end. Racial hostilities would cool.

Neither report called for any other form of segregation of the races. Both accepted that the stockyards, steel mills, and other blue-collar employers would provide jobs for both blacks and whites. Both indeed called upon employers and unions to accept blacks on an equal basis. So, too, for public spaces and conveyances. Blacks should have equal access to Grant and Jackson Parks, sites of pre-riot violence against African Americans. They should have equal access to the beaches along Lake Michigan. The attempt to create black and white beaches had failed disastrously. But the white members of the coroner's and grand juries did believe that blacks would voluntarily stay out of white neighborhoods if only there were enough good housing in the black portions of the city. In actuality, the races would continue to contest housing space. Housing segregation would later be reinforced by federal housing programs that built high-rise "projects" on the South Side that quickly turned into black slums.

Analyses of the riot by African Americans shared many of these conclusions. Walter White summarized their views for *The Crisis*, the official publication of the National Association for the Advancement of Colored People, but placed primary emphasis on racial prejudice.

The coroner's and grand jury reports skirted around the edges of racism as a causal factor, perhaps because they hoped to influence both white and black Chicagoans. And they placed more importance on the housing shortages and less upon the economic competition than White. But of all of the factors White cited, substantive differences emerged only on two. In addition to ignoring racial prejudice, the juries did not discuss the impact of returning soldiers and sailors. Walter White, in contrast, called attention to what would soon be called the "New Negro," one who had fought in "the war to make the world safe for democracy" and who was determined to enjoy a measure of that democracy in his own life.

VOICES OF THE DECADE

JAMES OPPENHEIM AND ARTURO GIOVANNETTI

The Lawrence strike of 1912 has traditionally been known as the "Bread and Roses" strike after the poem by James Oppenheim published before the strike in the *American Magazine* (December 1911) and dedicated to "the women in the West." In 1916, the novelist and social activist Upton Sinclair published *The Cry for Justice: An Anthology of the Literature of Social Protest*. This apparently was the first work to connect the strike with the poem. An unfortunate side effect of the linking of strike and poem is that it has led to the relative neglect of another poem, "The Walker," written by Arturo Giovannetti while in jail awaiting trial on the trumped-up charge of accessory to murder. Giovannetti and Joe Ettor, the strike organizer, were found innocent despite the efforts of the judge to persuade the jury to return a guilty verdict. Oppenheim's poem became associated with the strike because it captured the vision of a more equitable society that animated the strikers. Giovannetti's poem has long been neglected. It expresses the agony of the idealist imprisoned for his beliefs.

Bread and Roses

As we go marching, marching, in the beauty of the day,
A million darkened kitchens, a thousand mill lofts gray,
Are touched with all the radiance that a sudden sun discloses,
For the people hear us singing: Bread and Roses! Bread and Roses!

As we go marching, marching, we battle too for men,
For they are women's children, and we mother them again.
Our lives shall not be sweated from birth until life closes;
Hearts starve as well as bodies; give us bread, but give us roses.

As we go marching, marching, unnumbered women dead
Go crying through our singing their ancient call for bread.
Small art and love and beauty their drudging spirits knew.
Yes, it is bread we fight for, but we fight for roses too.

As we go marching, marching, we bring the greater days,
The rising of the women means the rising of the race.
No more the drudge and idler, ten that toil where one reposes,
But a sharing of life's glories: Bread and roses, bread and roses.

Our lives shall not be sweated from birth until life closes;
Hearts starve as well as bodies; bread and roses, bread and roses.

The Walker

I hear footsteps over my head all night.
They come and they go. Again they come and they go all night.
They come one eternity in four paces and they go one eternity in four
    paces, and between the coming and the going there is silence and the
    Night and the Infinite.
For infinite are the nine feet of a prison cell, endless is the march
    of him who walks between the yellow brick wall and the red
    iron gate, thinking things that cannot be chained and cannot
    be locked, but that wander far away in the sunlit world, each
    in a wild pilgrimage after a destined goal.

Throughout the restless night I hear the footsteps over my head,
Who walks? I know not. It is the phantom of the jail, the sleepless
    brain, a man, the man, the Walker.
One-two-three-four: four paces and the wall.
One-two-three-four: four paces and the iron gate.
He has measured his pace, he has measured it accurately, scrupulously,
    minutely, as the hangman measures the rope and the
    gravedigger the coffin—so many feet, so many inches so
    many fractions of an inch for each of the four paces.
One-two-three-four. Each step sounds heavy and hollow over my
    head, and the echo of each step sounds hollow within my head
    as I count them in suspense and in dread that once, perhaps, in
    the endless walk, there may be five steps instead of four
    between the yellow brick wall and the red iron gate.

But he has measured the space so
   accurately, so scrupulously, so minutely that nothing breaks the grave
   rhythm of the slow, fantastic march.

When all are asleep, (and who knows but I when all sleep?) three
   things are still awake in the night. The Walker, my heart
   and the old clock which has the soul of a fiend—for never,
   since a coarse hand with red hair on its fingers swung for
   the first time the pendulum in the jail, has the old clock tick-
   tocked a full hour of joy.

Yet the old clock which marks everything and records everything,
   and to everything tolls the death knell, the wise old
   clock that knows everything, does not know the number of
   the footsteps of the Walker nor the throbs of my heart.
For not for the Walker, nor for my heart is there a second, a
   minute, an hour or anything that is in the old clock—there
   is nothing but the night, the sleepless night, the watchful
   night, and footsteps that go, and footsteps that come and the
   wild, tumultuous beatings that trail after them forever.

All the sounds of the living beings and inanimate things, and all
   the voices and all the noises of the night I have heard in my
   wistful vigil.
I have heard the moans of him who bewails a thing that is dead
   and the sighs of him who tries to smother a thing that will
   not die;
I have heard the stifled sobs of the one who weeps with his head
   under the coarse blankets, and the whisperings of the one
   who prays with his forehead on the hard, cold stone of the floor;
I have heard him who laughs the shrill sinister laugh of folly at
   the horror rampant on the yellow wall and at the red eyes
   of the nightmare glaring through the iron bars;
I have heard in the sudden icy silence him who coughs a dry
   ringing cough and wished madly that his throat would not
   rattle so and that he would not spit on the floor, for no sound
   was more atrocious than that of his sputum upon the floor;
I have heard him who swears fearsome oaths which I listen to in
   reverence and awe, for they are holier than the virgin's
   prayer;
And I have heard, most terrible of all, the silence of two hundred
   brains all possessed by one single, relentless, unforgiving
   desperate thought.
All this have I heard in the watchful night,
   And the murmur of the wind beyond the walls,

And the tolls of a distant bell,
And the woeful dirge of the rain
And the remotest echoes of the sorrowful city
And the terrible beatings, wild beatings, mad beatings of the One
   Heart which is nearest to my heart.

All this have I heard in the still night;
But nothing is louder, harder, drearier, mightier or more awful than
   the footsteps I hear over my head all night.
Yet fearsome and terrible are all the footsteps of men upon this
   earth, for they either descend or climb.
They descend from little mounds and high peaks and lofty altitudes
   through wide roads and narrow paths, down noble marble
   stairs and creaky stairs of wood—and some go down to the
   cellar, and some to the grave, and some down to the pits
   of shame and infamy, and still come to the glory of an unfathom-
   able abyss where there is nothing but the staring white, stony
   eyeballs of Destiny.
And again other footsteps climb. They climb to life and to love,
   to fame, to power, to vanity, to truth, to glory and to the
   scaffold—to everything but Freedom and the Ideal.
And they all climb the same roads and the same stairs others go
   down; for never, since man began to think how to overcome
   and overpass man, have other roads and other stairs been
   found.
They descend and they climb, the fearful footsteps of men,
   and some limp, some drag, some speed, some trot, some run—
   they are quiet, slow, noisy, brisk, quick, feverish, mad, and most
   awful is their cadence to the ears of the one who stands still.
But of all the footsteps of men that either descend or climb, no
   footsteps are so fearsome and terrible as those that go straight
   on the dead level of a prison floor, from a yellow stone wall
   to a red iron gate.

All through the night he walks and he thinks. Is it more frightful
   because he walks and his footsteps sound hollow over my
   head, or because he thinks and speaks not his thoughts?
But does he think? Why should he think? Do I think? I only hear
   the footsteps and count them. Four steps and the wall. Four
   steps and the gate. But beyond? Beyond? Where goes he
   beyond the gate and the wall?

He goes not beyond. His thought breaks there on the iron gate
   Perhaps it breaks like a wave of rage, perhaps like a sudden
   flood of hope, but it always returns to beat the wall like a
   billow of helplessness and despair.

He walks to and fro within the narrow whirlpit of this ever storming
   and furious thought. Only one thought—constant, fixed
   immovable, sinister without power and without voice.
A thought of madness, frenzy, agony and despair, a hellbrewed
   thought, for it is a natural thought. All things natural are
   things impossible while there are jails in the world—bread,
   work, happiness, peace, love.
But he thinks not of this. As he walks he thinks of the most superhuman,
   the most unattainable, the most impossible thing in the world:
He thinks of a small brass key that turns just half around and
   throws open the red iron gate.

That is all the Walker thinks, as he walks throughout the night.
And that is what two hundred minds drowned in the darkness and
   the silence of the night think, and that is also what I think.
Wonderful is the supreme wisdom of the jail that makes all think
   the same thought. Marvelous is the providence of the law
   that equalizes all, even, in mind and sentiment. Fallen is the
   last barrier of privilege, the aristocracy of the intellect.
The democracy of reason has leveled all the two hundred minds
   to the common surface of the same thought.
I, who have never killed, think like the murderer;
I, who have never stolen, reason like the thief;
I think, reason, wish, hope, doubt, wait like the hired assassin
   the embezzler, the forger, the counterfeiter, the incestuous,
   the raper, the drunkard, the prostitute, the pimp, I, I who
   used to think of love and life and flowers and song and
   beauty and the ideal.
A little key, a little key as little as my little finger, a little key of
   shining brass.
All my ideas, my thoughts, my dreams are congealed in a little
   key of shiny brass.
All my brain, all my soul, all that suddenly surging latent power
   of my deepest life are in the pocket of a white-haired man
   dressed in blue.

He is great, powerful, formidable, the man with the white hair,
   for he has in his pocket the mighty talisman which makes
   one man cry, and one man pray, and one laugh, and one
   cough, and one walk, and all keep awake and listen and think
   the same maddening thought.
Greater than all men is the man with the white hair and the small
   brass key, for no other man in the world could compel two
   hundred men to think for so long the same thought. Surely
   when the light breaks I will write a hymn unto him which
   shall hail him greater than Mohammed and Arbues and Tor-

quemada and Mesmer, and all the other masters of other
men's thoughts. I shall call him Almighty, for he holds everything of all and of me in a little brass key in his pocket.
Everything of me he holds but the branding iron of contempt and
the claymore of hatred for the monstrous cabala that can
make the apostle and the murderer, the poet and the procurer,
think of the same gate, the same key and the same
exit on the different sunlit highways of life.

My brother, do not walk any more.
It is wrong to walk on a grave. It is a sacrilege to walk four
steps from the headstone to the foot and four steps from the
foot to the headstone.
If you stop walking, my brother, no longer will this be a grave,
—for you will give me back my mind that is chained to your
feet and the right to think my own thoughts.
I implore you, my brother, for I am weary of the long vigil, weary
of counting your steps, and heavy with sleep.
Stop, rest, sleep, my brother, for the dawn is well nigh and it is
not the key alone that can throw open the gate.

From *The Collected Poems of Arturo Giovannitti*, Arturo M. Giovannitti (New York: Arno Press, 1975), 147–149.

MADISON GRANT

Madison Grant was a zoologist who became a spokesperson for the eugenics movement in the early twentieth century. Eugenics (from the Greek for good genes) taught that different ethnic, religious, and racial groups constituted competing "stocks." Those groups with the superior heredity would forge ahead of those that, in the words of another advocate of these ideas, "evolution had always left behind." Grant made it clear that the "great race" was the Anglo-Saxon. Blacks, Mexicans, Jews, Asians, and eastern and southern Europeans were all biologically inferior. But, there was a paradox captured in the title of Grant's best-selling book. The "great race" was losing out to inferior races. How could that be? Did not evolution guarantee the survival of the fittest? Fitness, in turn, was a matter of reproducing. The fittest had the most offspring. The birthrate of Grant's great race, however, had been declining for decades and lagged behind that of the supposedly lesser races. His book was a call to arms. The best people, people like him, should have more children. The genetically inferior should be sterilized. In the 1920s and 1930s, most states adopted Grant's program and began to sterilize the mentally handicapped, women who bore children outside marriage, and others deemed unfit. Eugenics also influenced the immigration restriction legislation of 1921 and 1924.

There exists to-day a widespread and fatuous belief in the power of environment, as well as of education and opportunity to alter heredity, which arises from the dogma of the brotherhood of man, derived in turn from the loose thinkers of the French Revolution and their American mimics. Such beliefs have done much damage in the past, and if allowed to go uncontradicted, may do much more serious damage in the future. Thus the view that the negro slave was an unfortunate cousin of the white man, deeply tanned by the tropic sun, and denied the blessings of Christianity and civilization, played no small part with the sentimentalists of the Civil War period, and it has taken us fifty years to learn that speaking English, wearing good clothes, and going to school and to church, does not transform a negro into a white man. Nor was a Syrian or Egyptian freedman transformed into a Roman by wearing a toga, and applauding his favorite gladiator in the amphitheatre. We shall have a similar experience with the Polish Jew, whose dwarf stature, peculiar mentality, and ruthless concentration on self-interest are being engrafted upon the stock of the nation.

Recent attempts have been made in the interest of inferior races among our immigrants to show that the shape of the skull does change, not merely in a century, but in a single generation.

In 1910, the report of the anthropological expert of the Congressional Immigration Commission, gravely declared that a round skull Jew on his way across the Atlantic might and did have a round skull child, but that a few years later, in response to the subtle elixir of American institutions, as exemplified in an East Side tenement, might and did have a child whose skull was appreciably longer; and that a long skull south Italian, breeding freely, would have precisely the same experience in the reverse direction. In other words, the Melting Pot was acting instantly under the influence of a changed environment.

What the Melting Pot actually does in practice, can be seen in Mexico, where the absorption of the blood of the original Spanish conquerors by the native Indian population has produced the racial mixture which we call Mexican, and which is now engaged in demonstrating its incapacity for self-government [a reference to the Mexican Revolution]. The world has seen many such mixtures of races, and the character of a mongrel race is only just beginning to be understood at its true value.

It must be borne in mind that the specializations which characterize the higher races are of relatively recent development, are highly unstable and when mixed with generalized or primitive characters, tend to disappear. Whether we like to admit it or not, the result of the mixture of two races, in the long run, gives us a race reverting to the more ancient, generalized and lower type. The cross between a white man and an Indian is an Indian; the cross between a white man and a negro is a negro; the cross between a white man and a Hindu is a Hindu; and the cross between any of the three European races [Nordic or Aryan, Alpine, and Mediterranean] and a Jew is a Jew.

From "The Physical Basis of Race." In *The Passing of the Great Race: Or, the Racial Basis of European History* (New York: Scribner's, 1916).

JOE HILL

Both Joe Hill, a Swedish-born IWW organizer, and Elizabeth Gurley Flynn, an Irish-American labor activist to whom he dedicated his most famous song "The Rebel Girl," became legendary figures during the 1910s. Hill was arrested in Salt Lake City in 1914, accused of murdering a grocer and his son. Hill denied the charge but refused to provide an alibi. The honor of a woman was at stake, he claimed. Historians remain unsure whether Hill was guilty or not. They agree that he did not receive a fair trial. That fact, the popularity of his many songs, and his cool courage while awaiting execution by firing squad all helped turn him into a martyr. In a farewell letter he wrote: "Don't mourn. Organize!" Flynn, the "Rebel Girl," was arrested for the first time in 1906, when she was 16. From then on, she participated in one strike after another, often winding up in jail on charges ranging from vagrancy to inciting to riot.

> There are women of many descriptions
> In this queer world, as everyone knows.
> Some are living in beautiful mansions,
> And are wearing the finest of clothes.
> There are blue blooded queens and princesses,
> Who have charms made of diamonds and pearl;
> But the only and thoroughbred lady
> Is the Rebel Girl.
>
> **Chorus:**
>
> That's the Rebel Girl, that's the Rebel Girl!
> To the working class she's a precious pearl.
> She brings courage, pride and joy
> To the fighting Rebel Boy.
> We've had girls before, but we need some more
> In the Industrial Workers of the World.
> For it's great to fight for freedom
> With a Rebel Girl.
>
> Yes, her hands may be hardened from labor,
> And her dress may not be very fine;
> But a heart in her bosom is beating
> That is true to her class and her kind.
> And the grafters in terror are trembling
> When her spite and defiance she'll hurl;
> For the only and thoroughbred lady
> Is the Rebel Girl.
>
> **Repeat chorus**

From "Joe Hill Memorial Edition" of the Industrial Worker *Little Red Songbook* (London: Printed and Sold by W. Oliver, No 12, Bartholomew-Close, 1916), p. 36.

WOODROW WILSON

This speech, delivered in 1915 to an audience of newly naturalized citizens in Philadelphia, is usually remembered for the phrase "too proud to fight," President Wilson's explanation of his policy of neutrality in the World War. But he made the reference to neutrality in passing. The central preoccupation of the speech is what it means to be an American. In welcoming these newly minted citizens, Wilson made it clear that they were not to promote the interests of their native lands. You must devote yourselves to your new land, he told them, by becoming "thorough Americans." You must not think of yourself as belonging to a particular nationality group if you are to be "worthy" to "live under the Stars and Stripes." Immigrants and their children, in Theodore Roosevelt's phrase, must be "100 Per Cent. Pro-American." Events would show that Wilson and T.R. both assumed that anyone who criticized their policies was "no worthy son to live under the Stars and Stripes."

> It warms my heart that you should give me such a reception, but it is not of myself that I wish to think to-night, but of those who have just become citizens of the United States. This is the only country in the world which experiences this constant and repeated rebirth. Other countries depend upon the multiplication of their own native people. This country is constantly drinking strength out of new sources by the voluntary association with it of great bodies of strong men and forward-looking women. And so by the gift of the free will of independent people it is constantly being renewed from generation to generation by the same process by which it was originally created. It is as if humanity had determined to see to it that this great nation, founded for the benefit of humanity, should not lack for the allegiance of the people of the world.
>
> You have just taken an oath of allegiance to the United States. Of allegiance to whom? Of allegiance to no one, unless it be God. Certainly not of allegiance to those who temporarily represent this great Government. You have taken an oath of allegiance to a great ideal, to a great body of principles, to a great hope of the human race. You have said, "We are going to America," not only to earn a living, not only to seek the things which it was more difficult to obtain where you were born, but to help forward the great enterprises of the human spirit—to let man know that everywhere in the world there are men who will cross strange oceans and go where a speech is spoken which is alien to them, knowing that, whatever the speech, there is but one longing and utterance of the human heart, and that is for liberty and justice.
>
> And while you bring all countries with you, you come with a purpose of leaving all other countries behind you—bringing what is best of their spirit, but not looking over your shoulders and seeking to perpetuate what you intended to leave in them. I certainly would not be one even to suggest that a man ceases to love the home of his birth and the nation of his origin—these things are very sacred and ought not to be put out of our hearts—but it is one thing to love the place where you were born and it is another thing to dedicate yourself to the

place to which you go. You cannot dedicate yourself to America unless you become in every respect and with every purpose of your will thorough Americans. You cannot become thorough Americans if you think of yourselves in groups. America does not consist of groups. A man who thinks of himself as belonging to a particular national group in America, has not yet become an American, and the man who goes among you to trade upon your nationality is no worthy son to live under the Stars and Stripes.

My urgent advice to you would be not only always to think first of America, but always, also, to think first of humanity. You do not love humanity if you seek to divide humanity into jealous camps. Humanity can be welded together only by love, by sympathy, by justice, not by jealousy and hatred. I am sorry for the man who seeks to make personal capital out of the passions of his fellow men. He has lost the touch and ideal of America, for America was created to unite mankind by those passions which lift and not by the passions which separate and debase.

We came to America, either ourselves or in the persons of our ancestors, to better the ideals of men, to make them see finer things than they had seen before, to get rid of things that divide, and to make sure of the things that unite. It was but an historical accident no doubt that this great country was called the "United States," and yet I am very thankful that it has the word "united" in its title; and the man who seeks to divide man from man, group from group, interest from interest, in the United States is striking at its very heart.

It is a very interesting circumstance to me, in thinking of those of you who have just sworn allegiance to this great Government, that you were drawn across the ocean by some beckoning finger of hope, by some belief, by some vision of a new kind of justice, by some expectation of a better kind of life.

No doubt you have been disappointed in some of us; some of us are very disappointing. No doubt you have found that justice in the United States goes only with a pure heart and a right purpose, as it does everywhere else in the world. No doubt what you found here didn't seem touched for you, after all, with the complete beauty of the ideal which you had conceived beforehand.

But remember this, if we had grown at all poor in the ideal, you brought some of it with you. A man does not go out to seek the thing that is not in him. A man does not hope for the thing that he does not believe in; and if some of us have forgotten what America believed in, you, at any rate, imported in your own hearts a renewal of the belief. That is the reason that I, for one, make you welcome.

If I have in any degree forgotten what America was intended for, I will thank God if you will remind me.

I was born in America. You dreamed dreams of what America was to be, and I hope you brought the dreams with you. No man that does not see visions will ever realize any high hope or undertake any high enterprise.

Just because you brought dreams with you, America is more likely to realize the dreams such as you brought. You are enriching us if you came expecting us to be better than we are.

See, my friends, what that means. It means that America must have a consciousness different from the consciousness of every other nation in the world. I am not saying this with even the slightest thought of criticism of other nations. You know how it is with a family. A family gets centered on itself if it is not careful and is less interested in the neighbors than it is in its own members.

So a nation that is not constantly renewed out of new sources is apt to have the narrowness and prejudice of a family. Whereas, America must have this consciousness, that on all sides it touches elbows and touches hearts with all the nations of mankind.

The example of America must be a special example. The example of America must be the example not merely of peace because it will not fight, but of peace because peace is the healing and elevating influence of the world and strife is not.

There is such a thing as a man being too proud to fight. There is such a thing as a nation being so right that it does not need to convince others by force that it is right.

So, if you come into this great nation as you have come, voluntarily seeking something that we have to give, all that we have to give is this: We cannot exempt you from work. No man is exempt from work anywhere in the world. I sometimes think he is fortunate if he has to work only with his hands and not with his head. It is very easy to do what other people give you to do, but it is very difficult to give other people things to do. We cannot exempt you from work; we cannot exempt you from the strife and the heartbreaking burden of the struggle of the day—that is common to mankind everywhere. We cannot exempt you from the loads you must carry; we can only make them light by the spirit in which they are carried. That is the spirit of hope, it is the spirit of liberty, it is the spirit of justice.

When I was asked, therefore, by the Mayor and the committee that accompanied him to come up from Washington to meet this great company of newly admitted citizens I could not decline the invitation. I ought not to be away from Washington, and yet I feel that it has renewed my spirit as an American.

In Washington men tell you so many things every day that are not so, and I like to come and stand in the presence of a great body of my fellow-citizens, whether they have been my fellow-citizens a long time or a short time, and drink, as it were, out of the common fountains with them and go back feeling that you have so generously given me the sense of your support and of the living vitality in your hearts, of its great ideals which made America the hope of the world.

From "Americanism and the Foreign-Born," May 10, 1915, as reprinted in *American Ideals*, edited by Norman Foerster and William Whatley Pierson (Boston: Houghton Mifflin, 1917), pp. 178–182.

GEORGE M. COHAN AND IRVING BERLIN

One of the ironies of American patriotism during World War I, a patriotism that extolled "100 Per Cent. Americanism" and castigated "hyphenated" Americans, is that the two most popular songs of the era were written by hyphens. George M. Cohan, an Irish-American, grew up in vaudeville performing in his family's act. He then wrote, produced, and starred in a series of Broadway shows. His songs were nostalgic ("Mary"), patriotic ("I'm a Yankee Doodle Dandy"), and proudly Irish-American ("Harrigan"). "Over There" was the patriotic anthem of the war years. Irving Berlin was a Jewish immigrant, born in Russia and raised on New York's Lower East Side. He got his start writing Yiddish-language parodies of popular songs and in 1911 had his first hit song, "Alexander's Ragtime Band." Berlin wrote so many popular songs over the next 50 years that his fellow composer Jerome Kern said of him: Irving Berlin has no place in American music; he *is* American music. In the 1920s, the industrialist Henry Ford would rail against Berlin's influence on American popular music as part of his anti-Semitic campaign. Although plagued with poor eyesight, Berlin volunteered for military service and wrote a popular musical show to raise money for the war effort. "Oh! How I Hate to Get Up in the Morning" was the comic hit of the show. He also wrote a patriotic hymn for the show but decided not to use it. It was "God Bless America," which became the American anthem of World War II and for which Berlin never accepted royalties.

"Over There"

Johnnie, get your gun,
Get your gun, get your gun,
Take it on the run,
On the run, on the run.
Hear them calling, you and me,
Every son of liberty.
Hurry right away,
No delay, go today,
Make your daddy glad
To have had such a lad.
Tell your sweetheart not to pine,
To be proud her boy's in line.

Chorus sung twice

Over there, over there,
Send the word, send the word over there—
That the Yanks are coming,
The Yanks are coming,
The drums rum-tumming
Ev'rywhere.
So prepare, say a pray'r,

Send the word, send the word to beware.
We'll be over, we're coming over,
And we won't come back till it's over
Over there.

Johnnie, get your gun,
Get your gun, get your gun,
Johnnie show the Hun
Who's a son of a gun.
Hoist the flag and let her fly,
Yankee Doodle do or die.
Pack your little kit,
Show your grit, do your bit.
Yankee to the ranks,
From the towns and the tanks.
Make your mother proud of you,
And the old Red, White and Blue.

Chorus sung twice

"Oh! How I Hate to Get Up in the Morning"

The other day I chanced to meet a soldier friend of mine,
He'd been in camp for sev'ral weeks and he was looking fine;
His muscles had developed and his cheeks were rosy red,
I asked him how he liked the life, and this is what he said:

First chorus:

"Oh! how I hate to get up in the morning,
Oh! how I'd love to remain in bed;
For the hardest blow of all, is to hear the bugler call;
You've got to get up, you've got to get up
You've got to get up this morning!
Some day I'm going to murder the bugler,
Some day they're going to find him dead;
I'll amputate his reveille, and step upon it heavily,
And spend the rest of my life in bed."

Second chorus:

"Oh! how I hate to get up in the morning,
Oh! how I'd love to remain in bed;
For the hardest blow of all, is to hear the bugler call;
You've got to get up, you've got to get up
You've got to get up this morning!
Oh! boy the minute the battle is over,
Oh! boy the minute the foe is dead;

I'll put my uniform away, and move to Philadelphia,
And spend the rest of my life in bed."

Second verse:

A bugler in the army is the luckiest of men,
He wakes the boys at five and then goes back to bed again;
He doesn't have to blow again until the afternoon,
If ev'ry thing goes well with me I'll be a bugler soon.

Repeat Chorus One

Repeat Chorus Two

"Over There" (1917) by George M. Cohan and "Oh! How I Hate to Get Up in the Morning" (1918) by Irving Berlin

WALTER WHITE

Walter White was a young civil rights worker for the National Association for the Advancement of Colored People (NAACP) when he wrote this analysis of the Chicago race riot in 1919. He would spend his adult life working with the NAACP, ultimately serving as its general secretary. His identification with African Americans, he emphasized, was a choice. As he wrote in his autobiography, his skin was white, his eyes were blue, his hair color was blond: "The traits of my race are nowhere visible upon me."

Four weeks spent in studying the situation in Chicago, immediately following the outbreaks, seem to show at least eight general causes for the riots, and the same conditions, to a greater or less degree, can be found in almost every large city with an appreciable Negro population. These causes, taken after a careful study in order of their prominence, are:

1　Race Prejudice.
2　Economic Competition.
3　Political Corruption and Exploitation of Negro Voters.
4　Police Inefficiency.
5　Newspaper Lies about Negro Crime.
6　Unpunished Crimes Against Negroes.
7　Housing.
8　Reaction of Whites and Negroes from War.

Some of these can be grouped under the same headings, but due to the prominence of each they are listed as separate causes.

Prior to 1915, Chicago had been famous for its remarkably fair attitude toward colored citizens. Since that time, when the migratory movement from the South assumed large proportions, the situation has steadily grown more and more tense. This was due in part to the introduction of many Negroes who were unfamiliar with city ways and could not, naturally, adapt themselves immediately to their new environment. Outside of a few sporadic attempts, little was done to teach them the rudimentary principles of sanitation, of conduct or of their new status as citizens under a system different from that in the South. During their period of absorption into the new life, their care-free, at times irresponsible and sometimes even boisterous, conduct caused complications difficult to adjust. But equally important, though seldom considered, is the fact that many Southern whites have also come into the North, many of them to Chicago, drawn by the same economic advantages that attracted the colored workman. The exact figure is unknown, but it is estimated by men who should know that fully 20,000 of them are in Chicago. These have spread the virus of race hatred and evidences of it can be seen in Chicago on every hand. This same cause underlies each of the other seven causes.

With regard to economic competition, the age-long dispute between capital and labor enters. Large numbers of Negroes were brought from the South by the packers and there is little doubt that this was done in part so that the Negro might be used as a club over the heads of the unions. John Fitzpatrick and Ed Nockels, president and secretary, respectively, of the Chicago Federation of Labor, and William Buck, editor of the New Majority, a labor organ, openly charge that the packers subsidized colored ministers, politicians and Y.M.C.A. secretaries to prevent the colored workmen at the stockyards from entering the unions. On the other hand, the Negro workman is not at all sure as to the sincerity of the unions themselves. The Negro in Chicago yet remembers the waiters' strike some years ago, when colored union workers walked out at the command of the unions and when the strike was settled, the unions did not insist that Negro waiters be given their jobs back along with whites, and, as a result, colored men have never been able to get back into some of the hotels even to the present day. The Negro is between "the devil and the deep blue sea." He feels that if he goes into the unions, he will lose the friendship of the employers. He knows that if he does not, he is going to be met with the bitter antagonism of the unions. With the exception of statements made by organizers, who cannot be held to accountability because of their minor official connection, no statements have been made by the local union leaders, outside of high sounding, but meaningless, protestations of friendship for the Negro worker. He feels that he has been given promises too long already. In fact, he is "fed up" on them. What he wants are binding statements and guarantees that cannot be broken at will.

With the possible exception of Philadelphia, there is probably no city in America with more of political trickery, chicanery and exploitation than Chicago. Against the united and bitter opposition of every daily newspaper in Chicago, William Hale Thompson was elected again as mayor, due, as was claimed, to the Negro and German vote. While it is not possible to state that the anti-Thompson element deliberately brought on the riots, yet it is safe to say that they were not averse to its coming. The possibility of such a clash was seen many months before it actually occurred, yet no steps were taken to prevent it. The purpose of this was to secure a twofold result. First, it would alienate the Negro set from Thompson through a belief that was expected to grow among the colored vote when it was seen that the police force under the direction of the mayor was unable or unwilling to protect the colored people from assault by mobs. Secondly, it would discourage the Negroes from registering and voting and thus eliminate the powerful Negro vote in Chicago. Whether or not this results remains to be seen. In talking with a prominent colored citizen of Chicago, asking why the Negroes supported Thompson so unitedly, his very significant reply was:

> The Negro in Chicago, as in every other part of America, is fighting for the fundamental rights of citizenship. If a candidate for office is wrong on every other public question except this, the Negroes are going to vote for that man, for that is their only way of securing the things they want and that are denied them.

The value of the Negro vote to Thompson can be seen in a glance at the recent election figures. His plurality was 28,000 votes. In the second ward it was 14,000 and in the third, 10,000. The second and third wards constitute most of what is known as the "Black Belt."

The fourth contributing cause was the woeful inefficiency and criminal negligence of the police authorities of Chicago, both prior to and during the riots. Prostitution, gambling and the illicit sale of whisky flourish openly and apparently without any fear whatever of police interference. In a most dangerous statement, State's Attorney Maclay Hoyne, on August 25, declared that the riots were due solely to vice in the second ward. He seemed either to forget or to ignore the flagrant disregard of law and order and even of the common principles of decency in city management existing in many other sections of the city.

All of this tended to contribute to open disregard for law and almost contempt for it. Due either to political "pull" or to reciprocal arrangements, many notorious dives run and policemen are afraid to arrest the proprietors.

During the riots the conduct of the police force as a whole was equally open to criticism. State's Attorney Hoyne openly charged the police with arresting colored rioters and with an unwillingness to arrest white rioters. Those who were arrested were at once released. In one case a colored man who was fair enough to appear to be white was arrested for carrying concealed weapons, together with five white men and a number of colored men. All were taken to a police station; the light colored man and the five whites being put into one cell and the other colored men in another. In a few minutes the light colored man and the five whites were released and their ammunition given back to them with the remark, "You'll probably need this before the night is over."

Fifth on the list is the effect of newspaper publicity concerning Negro crime. With the exception of the Daily News, all of the papers of Chicago have played up in prominent style with glaring, prejudice-breeding headlines every crime or suspected crime committed by Negroes. Headlines such as "NEGRO BRUTALLY MURDERS PROMINENT CITIZEN," "NEGRO ROBS HOUSE" and the like have appeared with alarming frequency and the news articles beneath such headlines have been of the same sort. During the rioting such headlines as "NEGRO BANDITS TERRORIZE TOWN," "RIOTERS BURN 100 HOMES—NEGROES SUSPECTED OF HAVING PLOTTED BLAZE" appeared. In the latter case a story was told of witnesses seeing Negroes in automobiles applying torches and fleeing. This was the story given to the press by Fire Attorney John R. McCabe after a casual and hasty survey. Later the office of State Fire Marshal Gamber proved conclusively that the fires were not caused by Negroes, but by whites. As can easily be seen such newspaper accounts did not tend to lessen the bitterness of feeling between the conflicting groups. Further, many wild and unfounded rumors were published in the press-incendiary and inflammatory to the highest degree, a few of them being given below in order to show their nature. Some are:

Over 1,000 Negroes had been slain and their bodies thrown in "Bubbly Creek" and the Chicago River.
A Negro had been lynched and hanged from a "Loop" building overlooking Madison Street.
A white woman had been attacked and mutilated by a Negro on State Street.
A Negro woman had been slain, her breasts cut off and her infant had been killed by having its brains dashed out against a wall.
A white child had been outraged by a colored man.
A white child had been kidnapped by a band of colored men and its body later found, badly mutilated and dismembered.

Immediately following the riots, a white woman was murdered in Evanston, Ill. Immediately the crime was laid at the door of a colored man with whom the woman had been intimate a number of years. Pitiful stories were told of the woman waiting for hours on street corners for "just one look at her Billiken-like, mulatto lover," played up under headlines such as "CONFESSION EXPECTED TODAY FROM NEGRO SUSPECT," "NEGRO SUSPECT RAPIDLY WEAKENING" and the like which clearly led one to believe that the colored man was guilty. A few days later, in an obscure item on an inside page, a short account was given of the release of the colored suspect "because insufficient evidence to hold him" existed. A long period of such publicity had inflamed the minds of many people against Negroes who otherwise would have been unprejudiced. Much of the blame for the riots can be laid to such sources.

For a long period prior to the riots, organized gangs of white hoodlums had been perpetrating crimes against Negroes for which no arrests had been made. These gangs in many instances masqueraded under the name of "Athletic and Social Clubs" and later direct connection was shown between them and incendiary fires started during the riots. Colored men, women and children had been beaten in the parks, most of them in Jackson and Lincoln Parks. In one case a young colored girl was beaten and thrown into a lagoon. In other cases Negroes were beaten so severely that they had to be taken to hospitals. All of these cases had caused many colored people to wonder if they could expect any protection whatever from the authorities. Particularly vicious in their attacks was an organization known locally as Ragen's Colts."

Much has been written and said concerning the housing situation in Chicago and its effect on the racial situation. The problem is a simple one. Since 1915 the colored population of Chicago has more than doubled, increasing in four years from a little over 50,000 to what is now estimated to be between

125,000 and 150,000. Most of them lived in the area bounded by the railroad on the west, 30th Street on the north, 40th Street on the south and Ellis Avenue on east. Already overcrowded, this so-called "Black Belt" could not possibly hold the doubled colored population. One cannot put ten gallons of water in a five-gallon pail. Although many Negroes had been living in "white" neighborhoods, the increased exodus from the old areas created an hysterical group of persons who formed "Property Owners' Associations" for the purpose of keeping intact white neighborhoods. Prominent among these was the Kenwood-Hyde Park Property Owners' Improvement Association, as well as the Park Manor Improvement Association. Early in June the writer, while in Chicago, attended a private meeting of the first named at the Kenwood Club House, at Lake Park Avenue and 47th Street. Various plans were discussed for keeping the Negroes in "their part of the town," such as securing the discharge of colored persons from positions they held when they attempted to move into "white" neighborhoods, purchasing mortgages of Negroes buying homes and ejecting them when mortgage notes fell due and were unpaid, and many more of the same calibre. The language of many speakers was vicious and strongly prejudicial and had the distinct effect of creating race bitterness.

In a number of cases during the period from January, 1918, to August, 1919, there were bombings of colored homes and houses occupied by Negroes outside of the "Black Belt." During this period no less than twenty bombings took place, yet only two persons have been arrested and neither of the two has been convicted, both cases being continued.

Finally, the new spirit aroused in Negroes by their war experiences enters into the problem. From Local Board No. 4, embracing the neighborhood in the vicinity of State and 35th Streets, containing over 30,000 inhabitants of which fully ninety per cent are colored, over 9,000 men registered and 1,850 went to camp. These men, with their new outlook on life, injected the same spirit of independence into their companions, a thing that is true of many other sections in America. One of the greatest surprises to many of those who came down to "clean out the niggers" is that these same "niggers" fought back. Colored men saw their own kind being killed, heard of many more and believed that their lives and liberty were at stake. In such a spirit most of the fighting was done.

From "The Causes of the Chicago Race Riot," *The Crisis* 18 (October 1919), p. 25.

RACE RELATIONS BY GROUP

AFRICAN AMERICANS

January 1, 1913, was the 50th anniversary of the Emancipation Proclamation. Later in the year, President Woodrow Wilson embarked upon the segregation of the federal government. The conjunction of these events illustrates the triumphs and trials experienced by black Americans in the 1910s. Fifty years of freedom witnessed the development of strong religious and educational institutions, the growth of a professional class of ministers, doctors, lawyers, and teachers, the emergence of a middle class, and an efflorescence of artistic achievement. Most blacks remained in the South, although that would start to change in a big way in the second half of decade. In the South, they endured segregation, discrimination, violence, and poverty. Wilson's election meant that a white Southerner and a committed white supremacist would bring segregation to the one remaining area of relatively equal opportunity. Blacks had traditionally found the federal government a source of employment, and the Washington, DC, area had a vibrant middle-class black community.

Birth of a Nation opened to national and then international acclaim in 1915. The National Association for the Advancement of Colored People (NAACP) tried to get local and state authorities to ban the film or, at least, censor the most inflammatory scenes. Based on the novels of Thomas Dixon, a college classmate of Woodrow Wilson, the film tells the story of two white families, one northern and one southern, their valiant service in the Civil War, and their opposing views of Reconstruction. Dixon glorified the Ku Klux Klan, castigated opponents of white supremacy, and portrayed African Americans as "reverting" to savagery. The NAACP especially objected to two scenes that showed blacks seeking to force themselves upon innocent white women. *Birth of a Nation* was shown, uncut, all across the country. Its premiere was in the White House. It became the most successful film in history, a title it held until 1939, when *Gone with the Wind*, another glorification of white Southerners in the wake of the Civil War, made even more money.

The year 1915 also marked the start of the "Great Migration," the movement of hundreds of thousands and then millions of African Americans to the industrial centers of the North and the Mid-West. As with migration generally, there were both push and pull factors. Pushing blacks out of the rural South were poverty, segregation, the uncounted humiliations of Jim Crow, and lynching. Pulling them north were jobs, first and foremost. The World War meant that European immigration was greatly reduced, opening opportunities in basic industries like steel and automotives. A new labor militancy among European immigrants, evidenced in the strikes in Lawrence, Massachusetts, and Paterson, New Jersey, also led employers to look south. They had historically pursued a policy of divide-and-conquer by deliberately hiring workers from diverse backgrounds. Hiring African Americans seemed a logical next step in this strategy.

Other attractions included the absence of legal segregation, the right to vote and serve on juries, and the promise of holding one's head high without fear. The urban North, the newcomers soon discovered, was not the Promised Land. They encountered discrimination in housing and employment. Whites there could be as violent as any in the South. But, wages were higher. Schools were better. There was an African American press unafraid to speak out. Most important, there were emerging black population centers like Harlem and Chicago's South Side, where a vibrant music and arts scene could flourish and where blacks could build political bases.

The race riot in East St. Louis, Illinois, in 1917, epitomizes the racial problems that arose in the North. Blacks had historically been but a small portion of the city's population. But employers looking to weaken the power of unions began hiring African Americans by the hundreds. White workers, most of them immigrants or their children, called protest meetings and then turned to violence. So severe was the destruction that a congressional investigation could not even determine the number killed. The estimate was between 40 and 200. About 6,000 people were left homeless.

In July, the NAACP organized a march in New York City. A pamphlet published for the occasion explained the protest: "Why We March: Thirty Years of Lynching." The march set a precedent. Blacks would increasingly turn to this form of protest as a way of demonstrating their discontent and determination.

In 1916, Marcus Garvey established the Universal Negro Improvement Association (UNIA). Garvey wanted to see Africans and African Americans working together. His "Back to Africa" campaign drew immediate criticism from the NAACP. Garvey would get into legal troubles in the 1920s, and the UNIA would

Marcus Garvey, c. 1920. Courtesy of Library of Congress.

founder. But his message of "Black Power" would endure. It combined the impatience of African Americans for the realization of racial equality and a radicalized version of Booker T. Washington's argument that the Negro would have to pull himself up by his own bootstraps.

East St. Louis was the first of a long list of race riots that would mar the war and the immediate postwar years. The one in Houston in August 1917 demonstrated that racial antipathy could prove more powerful than patriotism. Some 370,000 blacks served in the military during the war. One company was sent to Houston to guard a new fort under construction. Black military police had a number of run-ins with white Houston police, who insisted that African American soldiers adopt the servile attitude demanded of all blacks. Some soldiers, particularly new recruits from the North, refused. On the night of August 23, more than 100 black soldiers took their rifles and moved off the post and toward Houston. In the resulting firefight, 13 persons died, 12 of them white. Nineteen were wounded, 14 of them white. It was the first time black soldiers had shot white Southerners since Reconstruction. The Army moved immediately to discipline the soldiers. Eighteen were hanged, others sentenced to the brig. But a new note of black refusal to accept discriminatory treatment had been sounded. There would be a "New Negro" in the 1920s when black soldiers returned to civilian life.

Race riots continued throughout 1918 and reached a terrible peak in 1919, when there were 26. The worst was in Chicago. But the others were bad enough. Most were triggered by accusations, usually false, of rape. That was the case in Washington, DC, when white servicemen attacked black neighborhoods. Whatever touched them off, however, the riots shared underlying causes. Most basic was white racism. America was supposed to be a "white man's country." When blacks took jobs previously held only by whites, moved into neighborhoods that had previously been all-white, or even tried to swim in Lake Michigan, enraged whites decided to put them in their place.

There were other causes, as well. One was the housing shortage of the war years. With materials being commandeered for the war effort, few new houses were built. This meant that blacks competed with working-class whites for space. Landlords and real estate agents quickly learned that they could charge blacks more than whites had previously paid. Whites blamed blacks for the spike in rents. Another source of bad feeling was the competition for jobs. The war meant labor shortages, as millions of men served in the military. Peace, however, brought demobilization. It also brought an end to war contracts. The number of jobs shrank just as millions of soldiers, sailors, and marines re-entered the labor market.

Contributing to the racial tensions was often incompetent and/or racist police work. Blacks in Chicago had been killed in public parks in the months leading up to the riot, for example. But the police had not apprehended anyone for the crimes. This led blacks to decide that they had to look out for themselves and whites to believe that they could attack African Americans without concern about being arrested. The press, too, helped make the bad situation worse.

Newspapers, both white and black, routinely printed wildly exaggerated stories that further inflamed racial animosities.

EUROPEAN AMERICANS

A total of 5,735,811 immigrants came to the United States during the 1910s, more than 2 million of them from Italy. The vast majority of the others also came from Europe. Had war not broken out in August 1914, the totals might easily have doubled. Old-stock Americans, that is, white Protestants of northern and western European ancestry, thought of themselves as the "real" Americans and viewed these "huddled masses yearning to breathe free," as Emma Lazarus described them, with alarm. As they could learn from reading about the 42-volume report of the Dillingham Commission, immigrants from Italy and elsewhere in southern and eastern Europe were inferior to the "old" immigration from Great Britain, Germany, and Scandinavia. Few read the report itself. Even journalists contented themselves with the two summary volumes. These, as Oscar Handlin later demonstrated, systematically distorted the actual findings. Immigrants did not lower wages; they did not commit more crime; they did not suffer from higher levels of mental illness. Those findings were buried in the volumes no one got around to reading. Meanwhile, the distortions became the wisdom of the day.

Nativists had several ready explanations for the immigrants' alleged defects. One, increasingly more popular, drew upon eugenics. Madison Grant's *The Passing of the Great Race* (1916) became a bestseller. In it, he explained that, despite their inferior intelligence, the "new" immigrants were out-breeding "real" Americans. They could do this because of their willingness to submit to horrible living and working conditions. As the University of Wisconsin sociologist E. A. Ross phrased in it another bestseller, *The Old World in the New* (1914), "a Slav can stand dirt that would kill a white man." Poles, Lithuanians, and Hungarians were not white in Ross's estimation. He, Grant, and other advocates of eugenics wanted to reserve that distinction for people like themselves.

World War I heightened anti-immigrant sentiment. Initially, Woodrow Wilson pledged that the United States would be completely neutral, a stance hailed by German-Americans, Irish-Americans, Swedish-Americans, and Jewish Americans. German-Americans did not want to see their new country at war with their old Fatherland. Irish Americans opposed an alliance between the United States and England, their historic oppressor. Swedish-Americans distrusted Russia, Sweden's long-time enemy, and an ally of Great Britain and France. American Jews hated Russia. Its record of anti-Semitism was the worst in the world. Germany, on the other hand, had one of the best records—difficult as that may be to credit, given the events of the 1930s and 1940s. As the Wilson administration came more and more to support Great Britain, France, and Russia, these groups made their dissatisfaction plain. This raised the issue of "the hyphen" in the presidential politics of 1916.

Italian immigrant family at Ellis Island, c. 1910. Courtesy of Library of Congress.

Theodore Roosevelt again sought the Republican nomination. However, after splitting the party in 1912 with his third-party candidacy, party regulars were determined to punish him by denying him the nomination. Roosevelt hoped to generate so much popular support that the Republican leadership would be forced to accept him. He found two hot-button issues: preparedness and "100 Per Cent. Americanism." The first was a critique of Wilson's reluctance to put the United States on a war footing. Sooner or later, he argued, America would have to enter the war, and it needed to be prepared. The second issue targeted immigrants. The real patriot, Roosevelt thundered, must be pro-American first, last, and always and not pro anywhere else at all. T.R. did not get the nomination; he did determine the issues over which the election would be fought.

Woodrow Wilson countered the first issue by running on the slogan "He Kept Us Out of War." He eagerly embraced the second. He, too, could demand "100 Percent Americanism." Challenging the loyalty of his critics proved good politics. It also set the stage for the federal government's draconian wartime measures against enemy aliens and the Wilson administration's encouragement of vigilante nativism.

America's entry into the war, barely one month after Wilson's second inauguration, turned millions of un-naturalized Poles, Hungarians, and others from the

German, Austro-Hungarian, and Ottoman empires into enemy aliens. Technically, Poles were citizens of Germany, Austria-Hungary, or Russia. There was no Poland. It had been partitioned by the three empires. Poles in America had no love for any of the three. In 1914, 23,000 volunteered for service with the French Army to help defeat Germany and Austria-Hungary and to reconstitute their homeland as an independent nation. Similarly, Hungarians had no love for an empire that treated them as second-class citizens. They dreamed of an independent Hungary.

Nonetheless, the administration treated all immigrants from these countries as potential saboteurs and spies. It banned them from defense work, from the District of Columbia, and from flying in a plane, even as a passenger. Congress passed the Espionage Act, which made criticism of the war a crime. The Wilson administration used it to crush the Industrial Workers of the World and to cripple the Socialist Party. Both had large numbers of immigrant members, further proof in the eyes of "real" Americans that these newcomers could never be trusted.

One of the first new wartime agencies was the Committee on Public Information (CPI). Its task, as its chairman, George Creel, candidly remarked, was pro-war propaganda (his word). The suppression of criticism was the other side of the coin. One of the CPI's earliest acts was to take editorial control over the foreign-language press. All stories about the war or politics had to be cleared with its agents. Newspapers had to print CPI-drafted editorials. The agency also organized patriotic demonstrations such as "I Am an American Day," July 4, 1918. The CPI insisted that nationality groups march in ethnic costume and wave American flags. The latter was to prove their loyalty; the former was to identify them as "hyphens." How could you know that Polish-Americans loved their new land if they did not march in a body with visible symbols of their ethnic identity? If everyone mixed together, you could not be sure which groups were represented or how strongly.

Other federal agencies also acted. One was the national Council of Defense, created to coordinate wartime planning. It, in turn, created state councils. And these often moved aggressively to demand that immigrants prove their patriotism by purchasing a specific amount in war bonds. Protesting that they did not have enough money availed not at all. Those who did not pay up often found their houses painted yellow.

The Immigration and Naturalization Bureau increased its efforts to Americanize immigrants. It created textbooks for adult education, and it worked with local governments to get the books into the schools. Immigration and Naturalization had a rival, the Bureau of Education, which claimed that educational Americanization was part of its jurisdiction. Both agencies faced a common problem. Americanization classes for adults depended upon the immigrants' willingness to participate. Immigrants stayed away in droves. One reason is that teachers often used the same readings that they employed with small children. Another is that most educators believed that the classes should be entirely in English. Leonard Covello, in his memoir *The Heart Is the Teacher*, recalled his experience with a group of fellow Italian immigrants he attempted to teach as part of the Americanization campaign. He was a student at Columbia at the time and followed the all-English rule religiously. The class was proving a disaster. Attendance was declining. The remaining pupils maintained a sullen silence. Finally, Covello lost patience and began to complain, loudly and in Italian, about their unwillingness to cooperate. When he finished his tirade, one man raised his hand: "Why didn't you tell us you speak Italian?" he asked. After his outburst, Covello's class made rapid progress. They could ask questions in their own language, then learn how to ask and answer in English. Covello's was the exceptional class that tested the rule. Educational Americanization largely failed. Meanwhile, suspicion of and hostility to immigrants continued to increase.

Anti-German feeling became especially virulent. Symphony orchestras could not play Beethoven's symphonies or those of Brahms. Opera companies stopped performing Wagner. Restaurants changed their menus: the hamburger became Salisbury steak, the frankfurter became the hot dog, and sauerkraut became liberty cabbage. German-Americans dropped their subscriptions to German-language papers, stopped attending the meetings of ethnic clubs, and started Anglicizing family names.

In addition to the Espionage Act, Congress also moved in 1917 to restrict immigration by imposing a literacy requirement. The timing is significant. The war itself was restricting immigration. Yet, Congress still acted. The inadequacy of the literacy test did not become apparent until the latter half of 1919, when transatlantic travel reached prewar levels. Then, nativists discovered that the test had no discernible impact upon either the numbers or the sources of immigrants.

Anti-immigrant militancy continued to grow in the immediate postwar period. This was the time of the Great Red Scare. A strike, led by the Communist William Z. Foster, shut down the steel industry. Another shut down the city of Seattle. A strike committee oversaw the distribution of milk and medicine and the provision of essential services. Its leaders drew parallels with the strikes that had toppled the Russian tsar in 1917. Prominent public officials, including Attorney General A. Mitchell Palmer, received bombs in the mail. A huge explosion rocked Wall Street. Tens of thousands of Bolsheviks in America, Palmer warned, were intent upon revolution. Eager to stop them, or at least to claim credit for doing so, were an array of political opportunists. Palmer wanted the Democratic presidential nomination in 1920. Seattle's mayor Ole Hanson, who claimed credit for breaking his city's general strike, wanted the Republican nod. New York State senator Clayton Riley Lusk chaired a joint legislative committee and divided his time between issuing alarmist press bulletins and staging raids on radical organizations. A bribery scandal ended his political career before he could seek higher office.

In 1920, the New York State Assembly, despite the opposition of Governor Al Smith, voted to expel five Socialist members, all from New York City and all Jewish. There was no question, Smith argued, that they were duly elected and that their constituents were free to choose whomever they wished to represent them. The majority of the Assembly disagreed. Membership in the Socialist Party was sufficient proof of anti-Americanism for them. The New York legislators were following the lead of the U.S. Congress. In 1919, the House of Representatives refused to seat Socialist Victor Berger from Milwaukee for the very same reason.

All of this combined with traditional concerns about immigrants and with anti-Semitism and anti-Catholicism, both of which grew notably worse over the course of the decade. The arrest of Leo Frank in Atlanta in 1913 for the murder of 13-year-old Mary Phagan touched off a wave of Jew-baiting previously unknown to America. Frank's trial was so unfair that the presiding judge wrote Georgia's governor indicating his own doubts about Frank's guilt. When the governor commuted Frank's death sentence to life in prison, the Knights of Mary Phagan kidnapped him from prison and lynched him in her hometown. The Knights were guests of honor at the founding of the second Ku Klux Klan in 1915 in the wake of the success of *Birth of a Nation*. In response, American Jews founded B'nai Brith to defend both individual Jews and the group as a whole.

There was no similarly horrific instance of anti-Catholicism. But it continued to gain momentum. One straw in the wind was the praise heaped upon Mayor John Purroy Mitchel of New York, himself a Catholic, for his attacks upon the Archdiocese of New York. Under New York State law, religious orphanages received public funding. Mitchel wanted to end what he saw as a violation of the separation of church and state. Instead of pursuing this line of argument, however, he brought up old claims that the Catholic orphanages of the city mistreated the children under their care. Unsurprisingly, the Church defended itself, aided by Hebrew orphanages that also received state funding. Mitchel, sure that there was a conspiracy against him, resorted to tapping the phones of several priests. This outraged Catholics, but it made Mitchel a hero among Progressive reformers such as Theodore Roosevelt, who praised his courage in taking on the Church.

Despite spiking nativism, European ethnics continued to make their way in American society. In 1916, Woodrow Wilson appointed Louis Brandeis to the Supreme Court; he was the first Jewish justice.

NATIVE AMERICANS

In 1913, Joseph K. Dixon published *The Vanishing Race* about North American Indians. It was part of large-scale project, funded by the department store magnate John Wanamaker and his son, to "document" Indian ways of life before they disappeared. Dixon was no ethnologist; he did not speak any native languages. He was, however, a gifted photographer and an even better salesman. He staged elaborate pageants for schoolchildren in Philadelphia and New York that supposedly taught them about Native Americans. Dixon was hardly the first to exploit the public interest in "real" Indians. For decades, William "Buffalo Bill" Cody toured the United States and Europe with his "Wild West Show." Buffalo Bill always hired "real" Indians. One year, Sitting Bull re-enacted the Battle of

Little Big Horn. But Buffalo Bill offered hokum, not history. Indians whooped, wore war paint, and rode their ponies bareback. But the cavalry always arrived in the nick of time, in the early years led by Buffalo Bill himself, to save the wagon train or stagecoach. Buffalo Bill catered to fantasies about a West that existed only in the overheated imaginations of readers of dime novels. Dixon did not rely on sensational tales of derring-do. He turned instead to Henry Wadsworth Longfellow's epic poem "Hiawatha." But, it was no more true to life than Buffalo Bill's "Wild West Show."

Cody finally retired, after 30 years on the road, too old to continue galloping to the rescue. Dixon finished his movie version of "Hiawatha" and his other Wanamaker projects. The movies picked up where they left off. The western became a Hollywood staple. And studios often followed Buffalo Bill's practice of hiring "real" Indians to play fictional ones on the screen, where bands of renegades still stalked wagon trains, still rustled cattle, still menaced the beautiful white heroine. The hero, also white, invariably thwarted their evil purposes.

Back on the reservations, the Bureau of Indian Affairs conducted its own Americanization program, designed to get individual Native Americans to adopt English, including an English name, give up tribal ways, and assimilate. An unknown number did. Life on the reservation offered little hope. Poverty, alcoholism, and suicide were common. So was unemployment. As a result, some individuals took the bureau's advice. Those who did not found that the federal government continued to police their lives. In 1913, the Supreme Court ruled, in *U.S. v. Sandoval*, that the federal law that limited the sale of alcohol on reservations also applied to Pueblo lands, even though these had never been considered reservations. The court held that previous U.S. government actions had "attributed to the United States as a superior and civilized nation the power and duty of exercising a fostering care and protection over all dependent Indian communities within its borders." White Americans formed a "superior" nation and had the "duty" of protecting "dependent Indian communities." It was the same logic that William McKinley had invoked to justify the "benevolent assimilation" of our "little brown brother," the Filipino.

More than 17,000 Native Americans served in the military during World War I. Some Indians, however, became draft resisters. They were not citizens, they protested. They could not vote. Why should they be subject to conscription? Congress's belated answer came in 1919. It made all Native American veterans eligible for citizenship.

ASIAN AMERICANS

As was the case with Native Americans, Congress made Asian veterans eligible for citizenship. They, too, had been subject to the draft. Other governmental actions were uniformly hostile. In 1913, California passed a new Alien Land Law that barred Chinese, Japanese, and Korean nationals (all were barred from becoming citizens) from owning real estate and from leasing several types of property. In 1920, the state again tightened restrictions on Asians' ability to own property. Another 10 states adopted versions of the same measures. The U.S. Congress, as part of its 1917 immigration restriction legislation, by setting up an "Asiatic Barred Zone," prohibited immigration from Asia, with the exception of Japan, which was covered by the Gentlemen's Agreement, and from the Pacific Islands, with the exception of the Philippines, since the islands were an American possession.

By the end of the 1910s, however, such measures were largely too late. Thanks to "picture brides," a second generation of Chinese, Japanese, and Korean Americans was coming of age. They were citizens by birth. Everyone born in the United States is by that fact an American citizen. The Alien Land laws did not apply to them. As a result, their parents began to acquire property by the simple expedient of putting their children's names on the deeds. Japanese families purchased farmland and fishing boats and opened small business such as restaurants. Chinese families were more concentrated in cities. They sought to own buildings in the Chinatowns of San Francisco, Los Angeles, Seattle, New York, and other urban areas. They operated shops of various kinds and opened restaurants and, stereotypically, laundries.

Those of the second generation had more education than their parents, despite the segregated schools San Francisco and some other city authorities had made them attend. And, like their African American and European immigrant counterparts, they staffed a middle class of professionals and businessmen. Chinese-Americans sought out Chinese lawyers, doctors, and bankers. The Japanese and Koreans likewise patronized their own. Restrictions, in short, held down the number of Asian Americans in the United States. They could not prevent them from building viable and prosperous communities.

Popular stereotypes—the bane of every race, religious group, and nationality—continued to plague Asian Americans. Most focused upon the Chinese. They were the largest Asian group and had been in the United States the longest. In dime novels, they were gamblers, opium fiends, members of murderous secret societies called tongs, and, needless to say, always eager to ravish white women. Sax Rohmer, a British novelist, created the most memorable Chinese villain, Fu Man Chu. Rohmer based the character on Professor Moriarty, the criminal mastermind created by Arthur Conan Doyle to provide a suitable antagonist for Sherlock Holmes. Like the Professor, Fu Man Chu had studied at the leading European universities. Like him, too, he headed a criminal organization that spanned continents. Fu was, Rohmer maintained, the embodiment of the "Yellow Peril." Americans avidly read of Fu's evil doing, a fact not lost upon the movie studios. Soon, played by a white actor, he was frightening audiences who had never heard of Sax Rohmer.

D. W. Griffith attempted to move beyond stereotype in *Broken Blossom*, a film about an abused young girl (played by Lillian Gish, the heroine of *Birth of a Nation*) briefly rescued from her brutal father by a Chinese immigrant. Film historians cite it as one of Griffith's greatest achievements. Contemporary audiences did not agree. They wanted their Chinese to be sinister. *Broken Blossoms* lost money.

LATINOS

In 1910, the Mexican Revolution broke out. The turmoil lasted for years, until Victoriano Huerta was elected president in 1914. Among those most alarmed were Americans who had invested in Mexican oil fields, which Huerta promised to nationalize. The revolution had also turned against the Catholic Church, which had vigorously opposed it. This was enough for Woodrow Wilson to decide to dispatch American troops to Vera Cruz with the avowed intent of deposing Huerta. The United States, the president announced, was going to teach the Mexicans "to elect good men." Huerta obligingly resigned. The American forces withdrew—but only for two years. In 1916, Pancho Villa, a rebel opposed to the new Mexican government, led a raid on the border town of Columbus, New Mexico. President Wilson ordered General John "Black Jack" Pershing to capture Villa. For almost a year, Villa led Pershing a merry chase. "Black Jack" never caught up with him, although Hollywood did. During the pursuit, Villa appeared as himself in a movie!

The following year, the United States entered the war, and Congress passed a law that made residents of Puerto Rico, seized from Spain in the War of 1898, American citizens. The immediate effect was to make male Puerto Ricans eligible for the draft. The long-term effects were largely unforeseen. No one imagined a great migration from the island to the mainland. That was decades in the future. But citizenship meant that Puerto Ricans, when they did begin to arrive in large numbers, would not be immigrants. They would be identified as Latinos, a new category of American. In the past, Spanish-speaking Americans had been Mexicans. In the future, they would be Puerto Ricans, Central Americans, and Cubans, as well.

Any type of American short of a "real" American could expect discrimination and mistreatment. The year 1917 witnessed an especially egregious case in point. The copper mining town of Bisbee, Arizona, was home to numerous Mexican-Americans and European immigrants who worked in the mines. The copper companies prospered as the war increased demand. Higher prices meant higher profits. The miners, however, wanted their share. Wartime shortages were driving up the prices they paid for food, rent, and clothing. They wanted their wages to keep pace. They also wanted safer working conditions. The companies counted on the diversity of the work force to prevent the miners from organizing. But, as it had in Lawrence, Massachusetts, and in Paterson, New Jersey, the Industrial Workers of the World (IWW) succeeded in getting more than a thousand miners to join the "One Big Union."

It was a dangerous time for both the companies and the workers. Cooper was essential to the war effort. Any strike could be easily labeled unpatriotic. The

IWW opposed the American entry into the war. This would make the charge of anti-Americanism all the more convincing. On the other hand, the companies could not afford a work stoppage. There was too much money to be lost. So there was a strong argument in favor of striking. The companies did not want a strike, but it also did not want to negotiate a settlement. Not only would that cut into present profits, but it would also hamper the company's control of the workplace.

Company officials hit upon a bold plan. They would recruit a vigilante force, round up the miners, and deport all who would not agree to repudiate the IWW and the strike. Armed volunteers went door to door. They marched those who defied the companies down to a sports field, lined them up, and then forced them onto railroad boxcars. The trains took the men across the state line to New Mexico. Armed guards patrolled the roads leading to Bisbee to prevent anyone from returning.

The Bisbee Deportation, as the event came to be known, was a flagrant violation of the rights of the deported workers. For many Mexican-Americans, it amounted to a second dispossession. The United States had seized Arizona in the Mexican War. Many Mexicans had lost their property in the process. Now their grandchildren were being forcibly ejected from that same land. The Justice Department mounted an investigation. The deportation was clearly illegal. However, the report held, the laws violated were those of Arizona, not those of the United States. Arizona brought one person to trial. An all-white jury found him not guilty, and the state dropped the other cases.

Bisbee showed all too clearly how little Mexican-Americans and European immigrants could depend upon the rule of law. It was a lesson Native Americans and African Americans had already learned.

LAW AND GOVERNMENT

Entry into World War I marked a turning point in American policy toward immigrants from Asia and Europe. Congress passed, for the third time, a literacy test bill that required all prospective newcomers to demonstrate that they could read 40 words in any language they chose. As his predecessors had done, Woodrow Wilson vetoed the measure. This time, however, advocates for restriction mustered the necessary two-thirds majorities to make the bill a law. There was no pressing need for immigration restriction in 1917. The war made transatlantic passenger travel virtually impossible. Immigration from China, Japan (which had occupied Korea), and the Pacific Islands (excluding the Philippines) was already barred. But the 1916 presidential campaign, which had emphasized the danger of the "hyphen," that is, immigrant disloyalty, gave those who had been pressing for restriction the impetus they needed. In addition to the literacy test, the law created an "Asiatic Barred Zone," a pure exercise in redundancy since it barred only those whose immigration Congress had already prohibited.

The Espionage Act of 1917 had actual immediate consequences. It outlawed any action that a court might construe as hindering the war effort. The Wilson administration took it as a license to go after any person or group who opposed the war or its handling of the war. Among the first targets were the Industrial Workers of the World and the Socialist Party. Both had condemned American entry into the war. They had done so on the Marxist principle that workers' first loyalty should be to their fellow workers. In the words of the *Communist Manifesto*, "workers of the world unite! You have nothing to lose but your chains!" Socialist parties across Europe had ignored this injunction. Each had patriotically endorsed its country's policies. The IWW and the American Socialist Party, however, remained true to the Marxist faith. The Espionage Act made them easy targets. The Justice Department, in a series of raids in September 1917, arrested IWW and Socialist leaders. European immigrants provided much of the electoral strength of the Socialists.[53] When the government treated the Socialist Party as if it were undermining the war effort, it also impugned the loyalty of the party's immigrant supporters.

The IWW had enjoyed some success in organizing immigrant workers in the immediate prewar years—in Lawrence, Massachusetts, in 1912, in Paterson, New Jersey, in 1913—and it had carried that over into Bisbee, Arizona, in 1917. The Wilson administration's response to the ensuing Bisbee Deportation showed its determination to crush the "One Big Union." The deportation, the Justice Department ruled, violated state but not federal law. Therefore, it was up to Arizona authorities to protect the civil rights of Mexican-Americans and European immigrants, not to mention native-born union activists. Arizona put one person on trial. When he was found not guilty, the state abandoned further prosecutions. Not so the Wilson administration. It prosecuted the head of the American Socialist Party, Eugene V. Debs, for encouraging resistance to the draft. He would run for president in 1920 from prison. The Justice Department also successfully prosecuted William "Big Bill" Haywood and other IWW officials.

Also in 1917, the newly created Committee on Public Information (CPI) took control of the foreign-language press through its Foreign Language Information Service (FLIS). FLIS agents translated CPI-approved editorials and news stories into dozens of languages and screened editorials written by the papers' own editors. It also translated popular American songs on the grounds that singing of the beautiful blue Danube in German, while politically harmless, aroused in the immigrant a nostalgic longing for his homeland. Better he should sing "Yankee Doodle" in German. Other federal agencies also took it upon themselves to promote immigrant loyalty. The Immigration and Naturalization Service in the Labor Department and the Bureau of Education in the Department of the Interior launched competing educational Americanization programs. Each sought to work with school systems to enroll immigrants in night school classes in English and Civics.

Much of this activity proved ineffectual. FLIS's songbooks did not inspire multilingual renditions of American songs. Immigrants voted with their feet against Americanization classes. But FLIS censorship did shut down independent commentary in the foreign-language press. And the CPI's "I Am an American Day" (July 4, 1918) required hundreds of thousands of European ethnics to march in a public display of loyalty to the United States. The overall impact of these state-sponsored Americanization programs probably did not significantly increase patriotism among immigrants. These programs undoubtedly did lead to a decline in the number of foreign-language newspapers, particularly among German papers, to a significant decline in the readership of the surviving papers, and to a drop in the membership in ethnic organizations.

The restrictions placed upon enemy aliens, that is, those who were legally citizens of the German, Austro-Hungarian, and Ottoman empires, bore down heavily. They could not work in war-related industries. Given the mobilization the war required, this seriously limited their employment opportunities. Barring them from traveling to the District of Columbia was largely symbolic. It lent credence to the stereotype of the alien anarchist, bomb in hand, seeking to destroy the American government. The same is true of the prohibition forbidding enemy aliens from flying in planes, even as passengers. It guarded against a danger that did not yet exist.

Another set of congressional actions had to do with the draft. Enemy aliens were not eligible. This was not based upon fears about their potential disloyalty. Enemy aliens could, and did, volunteer for military service. The problem lay with the fact that, should they be captured, they would not be prisoners of war. Because they were citizens of the country they were fighting, they could be tried for treason before military tribunals. The solution was for the United States to naturalize all enemy aliens who volunteered. Not only did they become citizens, but so did their wives and foreign-born children.

Some Native Americans, such as those living in Oklahoma, were citizens. Others were not. All were eligible for the draft, however, as were Asian immigrants, none of whom were citizens. Some Indians resisted conscription. Why should they fight for a country that had taken their land, penned them up on reservations, and denied them the right to vote? Most, however, served in the war. In 1919, Congress belatedly made them and Asian veterans eligible for citizenship. Puerto Ricans became citizens by an act of Congress in 1917, which also made them eligible for the draft.

The fact that European and Asian immigrants, Mexican-Americans, Puerto Ricans, Native Americans, and African Americans all fought for their country in the Great War did not lead to first-class citizenship for any of them. Some, as noted, did become eligible for citizenship. This did not lessen the discrimination each group experienced. Their plight actually worsened in the immediate postwar period. The year 1919 was a year of race riots. It was also was the beginning of the Great Red Scare.

The "white-hot patriotism" the government encouraged rested upon fear, fear of the "Hun," as Germany was called, fear of alien spies and saboteurs, fear of disloyal "hyphens." The Bolshevik Revolution in Russia in October 1917 added a new fear. Attorney General A. Mitchell Palmer warned that there were tens of thousands of Bolsheviki, virtually all of them unnaturalized immigrants from eastern Europe, awaiting a signal from Moscow to rise up against the American government. There was a new American Communist Party, created by those in Socialist Party who believed the Russian Revolution was a turning point in history. The American journalist and Soviet sympathizer John Reed called his account of the revolution *Ten Days That Shook the World*. His older counterpart Lincoln Steffens returned from a visit to the new Soviet Union proclaiming, "I have seen the future." But Palmer's estimate of American revolutionaries was wildly exaggerated.

Many believed him, however. William Z. Foster, an avowed Marxist, led the strike that closed down the steel industry for months. A general strike in Seattle reminded many of the labor stoppages that had brought down the tsar. Among the many strikes of 1919, perhaps the most alarming was staged by the Boston police. The city's residents panicked. Harvard students volunteered to walk patrols, as did many others. Massachusetts governor Calvin Coolidge stoutly declared that there could be no right to strike against the public safety, a stand that won him the Republican vice presidential nomination the following year. In addition to strikes, there were waves of bombings. One enormous blast struck Wall Street and killed dozens. Smaller explosives were sent through the mail to prominent public figures, including Attorney General Palmer. His dire predictions of an imminent Red menace seemed only too likely to many.

Palmer's response was to round up the usual suspects—members of the Socialist and Communist parties, IWW loyalists, subscribers to radical newspapers. The Palmer Raids of 1919 and 1920 netted thousands, many of them unnaturalized immigrants. Palmer's plan was to use the Espionage Act to deport as many as possible. Standing in his way was a midlevel government official, Louis Post, who had to determine if there was sufficient evidence to justify deportation. Post decided that, in almost all cases, there was not. Palmer raged. Congress investigated. But Post stood his ground. Meanwhile, May Day, May 1, 1920, approached. May Day was the day, Palmer said, when the Bolsheviks in America would stage their insurrection. It arrived. Nothing happened. And the Red Scare fizzled out. In the fall, the Republican nominee, Warren Harding, obliquely referred to the hysteria in promising "normalcy, not nostrums." Nativism did not disappear, however.

In the middle of 1919, transatlantic passenger service approached prewar levels. Members of the Immigration Restriction League soon discovered that the literacy test on which they had placed such hopes was not working. Eastern and southern Europeans were pouring into the country, each able to read 40 words in his or her own language. Congress would act in 1921. In the meantime, the last wave of "new" immigrants came ashore.

Immigrants and their children discovered a new hero. Al Smith, son of a German father and an Irish mother, became governor of New York in 1918. He narrowly lost his bid for re-election in 1920, a victim of the Harding landslide, but won easily in 1922, 1924, and 1926. New York was the most populous state, and its governor automatically was talked about as a presidential possibility. Smith embodied much of what nativists most feared and hated. He was a Roman Catholic. He was a product of Tammany Hall, the most notorious political machine in the nation. He was an outspoken opponent of Prohibition and of the Red Scare. He vetoed the bills proposed by New York state senator Clayton Riley Lusk to combat "Reds." He not only defended the loyalty of immigrants, he identified with them. Smith had grown up on the Lower East Side of Manhattan, had gone to work as a boy at the Fulton Fish Market, and continued to live in his old neighborhood. Ethnic New Yorkers saw him as one of them. He talked like them. He dressed like them. And he was proof they were as good as anyone.

CULTURAL SCENE

Immigration meant more Catholics and Jews, especially in northern cities. Some Protestant churches reached out to the newcomers, hoping both to protect them from confidence artists and to convert them. The Catholic Church was quite concerned about these efforts and launched its own programs for immigrants. It distrusted settlement houses, as well, even though most had no formal denominational connection. The Church saw them as preaching a generic Protestantism. It viewed the Young Men's and Young Women's Christian Associations in the same light. The Catholic Youth Organization (CYO) was its answer. Like the Ys, it offered athletic programs, organized dances, and sponsored musical and dramatic societies, all in the name of keeping Catholic youth Catholic. The CYO and other ethnic and racial organizations, however, could not keep young people away from movies.

Movies became a national passion. Americans went to the movies twice or more a week. And the most successful film, *Birth of a Nation*, represented a major victory for white supremacy. Based on the novels of Thomas Dixon, especially *The Clansman*, D. W. Griffith's blockbuster put the theory of racial regression on the screen. The theory, widely espoused by academics and scientists as well as by white racists, held that African Americans would revert to their natural savage state because the benign institution of slavery was no longer holding them in check. Dixon wanted his novels to displace Harriet Beecher Stowe's *Uncle Tom's Cabin*. Tom was a Christ-like figure, generous and brave, sacrificed by evil slaveholders. Dixon wanted to replace him with blacks who menaced innocent white women. And he wanted to convince white Northerners that white supremacy was the only basis for the newly reunited United States. The wedding of the northern heroine and her Southerner savior symbolized this "birth of a nation." The brilliance of Griffith's movie—he is the father of much of the basic narrative language of film—brought Dixon's message home to millions.

Movies reflected the racism of the day, but not the nativism. The heads of the major studios were typically immigrants themselves or the children of immigrants. Many of the stars, such as Charlie Chaplin, who wrote, produced, and starred in the sympathetic comedy *The Immigrant,* were also first- or second-generation European ethnics. Hollywood, the new home of the motion picture industry, made few similar films. But it welcomed talent regardless of ethnic background or religious affiliation. It did regard race. Not only did it deal in stereotypes, but it also refused to hire African American or, with few exceptions, Asian American actors. Uncle Tom, for example, was played by a white actor in blackface. Late in the decade, Oscar Micheaux began making films for black audiences starring black actors. But the movie studios did not follow the lead of the record companies. Victor had signed George Walker and Bert Williams in 1901. Thereafter, it and its competitors pressed "race" records, typically blues and jazz, marketed to African American consumers. The movie studios, in contrast, ignored the black audience.

Immigrants also flocked to the theater. In 1882, the teen-age Boris Thomashesky produced the first Yiddish language play in the United States, at Turn Hall in New York City. By 1900, the Yiddish theater was thriving in the city. The most important venues were the Thalia and the Windsor theaters, on opposite sides of the Bowery, on the Lower East Side. Translations of Shakespeare were very popular. So were Yiddish versions of Ibsen's plays. The first production of *Hedda Gabler* in the United States, for example, was given in Yiddish in New York. Thomashesky was a great star, as was Bertha Kalich, the heroine of uncounted tragedies. Many actors who later achieved fame in Hollywood, such as Paul Muni, started out in the Yiddish theater.

Other ethnic groups also organized theatrical productions, albeit not on the same scale. Italian immigrants patronized small music halls where they could listen to local tenors and sopranos sing operatic arias and popular favorites. Churches often sponsored dramatic societies. Churches and synagogues hosted many cultural activities, beginning with religious music but including talent shows and even orchestral performances. African Americans and immigrants and their children also shaped American popular music.

The music industry was the most open to talent irrespective of race, religion, or ethnic background. Italian and German singers dominated the operatic world. Polish and Russian pianists and violinists played to sold-out audiences. Popular music welcomed all comers, albeit not on equal terms. The most popular songwriter was Irving Berlin, a Jewish immigrant from Russia who composed hundreds of hit tunes. His first was "Alexander's Ragtime Band" (1911). Curiously, it is a march, not a rag. But it paid tribute to the ragtime craze still sweeping the nation. George Gershwin, who regarded Berlin as a model, wrote his first hit, "Swanee,"

Bert Williams. Courtesy of Library of Congress.

in 1918, at the age of twenty. It was introduced by the most popular entertainer of the day, Al Jolson. Like Gershwin, he was the son of Jewish immigrants. That Gershwin, born and raised in Brooklyn, and Jolson, born and raised on the Lower East Side of Manhattan, enjoyed success with a song about a black man's homesickness for "the folks back home" in the South says much about how American popular culture was coming to reflect, and refract, the diversity of the population.

Some historians have seen the use of blackface by Jolson and other Jewish performers, such as Eddie Cantor and Fanny Brice, as a form of racism. And, of course, it was. It drew upon the nineteenth-century minstrel shows and made use of many of the same stereotypes and canards. Racism, however, does not exhaust the subject. "Swanee" also appropriated the Southerner's love for Dixie, an experience Gershwin and Jolson knew no more about than they did about African American life. As a result, the song and Jolson's performance dealt with a more basic human experience, the longing for home felt by anyone living in a strange new land.

There is at least one additional dimension to the use of blackface. In the nineteenth century, it had been the comparatively simple matter of white male entertainers putting on cork makeup and, in some instances, dresses and mimicking Black English. They were not trying to fool the audience into thinking they actually were black or female. Instead, they were creating a cultural space in which they could tell jokes and sing songs that propriety would otherwise prohibit. They could say and do things in blackface that they could not do in their own skins. In the early decades of the twentieth century, the appropriation of racial, ethnic, and religious identities became more complex. Consider the Marx Brothers, who were in the midst of a successful vaudeville career in the 1910s. Everyone knew that they were second-generation Jewish Americans from New York City. But the character Groucho was a WASP. His brother Chico's character was an Italian immigrant. And Harpo's had no cultural identity. He was pure id, to put the matter in Freudian terms, that is, desire unregulated by any inhibitions. Their comedy explored and exploded stereotypes. Groucho's WASP engaged in losing battles of wits with Chico's Italian. Harpo created havoc. But, somehow, they cooperated in the end and triumphed.

Often these entertainers explored what one scholar has called their "Jewface." Fanny Brice, for example, did not have a Yiddish accent. Her parents spoke English as their first language and did not speak Yiddish at all. But she cultivated an accent for her act. When she sang of being "second-hand Rose from Second Avenue," she placed herself culturally on the Lower East Side. And when she sang "I'm an Indian, Too," her Yiddish-inflected accent drove home the comic absurdity of the song. Her biggest hit, however, was "My Man," a torch song translated from French, which she sang without any accent at all. Audiences knew that Groucho was not a WASP, that Chico was not Italian, that Jolson was not black, and that Brice, while Jewish, was not from the Yiddish-speaking Lower East Side. Unlike Brice, Eddie Cantor did his comic songs without the accent, even though he was from the Lower East Side. In his act, he was an American of indeterminate ethnicity. But his stage name, Cantor, reminded audiences that he was a Jew. It is the cantor who sings the sacred songs at temple services.

This putting on and taking off of ethnic, racial, and religious masks could be, and often was, hateful. It could also function as a form of cultural diffusion. When Fanny Brice sang in a Yiddish accent, her listeners often sang along. When Groucho and Chico engaged in comic banter, one in non-inflected standard English and the other in garbled English in an Italian accent, it was Chico who got the last laugh. And when George Gershwin wrote and Al Jolson sang "Swanee" and millions were moved, something other than simple racism was in play.

Serious books also had a significant impact on American culture. Most of the successful novels were written by white Anglo-Saxon Protestant males. But readers of the *Smart Set* were getting their reading lists from H. L. Mencken, who prided himself on discovering new talent. The Irish-American Eugene O'Neill was hailed by Mencken as the first important American playwright. The German-American Theodore Dreiser was, Mencken averred, the most important novelist. The citadels of culture were beginning to lower the drawbridges, at least for white ethnics, if not for African Americans or Latinos.

The same can be said about painting and sculpture. The most important innovators of the early twentieth century, the Eight (sometimes called the Ashcan School), were Yankees, as were the great majority of established artists. But, John Sloan, George Bellows, Robert Henri, and their colleagues turned to urban scenes, often set in immigrant neighborhoods, for their subjects. Their challenge to the academy-trained artistic establishment opened the way for others, including immigrants and African Americans. Perhaps the most important was the Italian-born Joseph Stella, whose work was shown in the celebrated Armory Show in New York City in 1913, as was that of the Russian immigrant Abraham Walkowitz. The Armory Show marked the moment when so-called modern art—expressionism, cubism, symbolism, and related movements—made its American debut.

MEDIA AND MASS COMMUNICATIONS

Newspapers and magazines remained the most powerful mediums of mass communication. Every city had at least one daily paper. Large cities such as Chicago or Philadelphia or Detroit had half a dozen or more. Many readers purchased two newspapers a day, one in the morning and the other in the evening, and read both from cover to cover. Men often turned first to the sports section, children to the comics or "funny pages," and women to the "women's pages," which featured stories about fashion, social events, and homemaking. Everyone checked the movie listings. Not everyone admitted to reading the gossip columns, with their stories of movie and vaudeville stars. But almost every paper published them.

Foreign-language papers suffered during and after World War I. Government censorship and public hostility to the open display of ethnic loyalties, such as reading a paper in German on a trolley car, combined to cut into readership. Black newspapers, in contrast, flourished. Some, like the *Pittsburgh Courier* and the *Chicago Defender*, had national followings.

Americans also devoured magazines. Some, like *Collier's*, published stories about the major events and developments of the day. Others, like *The Saturday Evening Post*, concentrated more on fiction. H. L. Mencken and George Jean Nathan edited the *Smart Set*, "a magazine of cleverness," as they described it. The appeal was to the would-be sophisticate. He or she would discover James Joyce, Edna St. Vincent Millay, Damon Runyon, and Eugene O'Neill, along with reviews of the newest novels and plays. Those seeking political enlightenment could turn to the *New Republic,* co-edited by Walter Lippmann, still in his twenties and already on his way toward becoming the most influential journalist of the first half of the twentieth century. Those whose political sympathies were further to the left had *The Masses,* edited by Max Eastman and featuring the artwork of John Sloan, a founder of the "Ashcan School" of social realism. African Americans in increasing numbers subscribed to *The Crisis,* the monthly published by the NAACP and edited by W.E.B. Du Bois.

So-called penny dreadfuls, magazines selling for a nickel or a dime and filled with improbable adventure stories, continued to attract both male and female readers. Covers often showed stereotypical villains, often Asian or Native American, menacing a beautiful young woman. Heroes were equally clichéd. They were WASPs, stout of heart, clear of conscience, and handsome.

INFLUENTIAL THEORIES AND VIEWS OF RACE RELATIONS

In 1911, the anthropologist Franz Boas published *The Mind of Primitive Man,* and modern anthropology began. Boas rejected racial theories that claimed that behavioral traits were hereditary. Behavior was cultural, Boas maintained. Each population group adapted to the particular environment it inhabited. One could not place the resulting cultures along a continuum with the so-called primitive at one end and the "advanced" at the other. Cultures differed. But, none were superior to any others.

Boas directly attacked theories of racial retrogression. African Americans could not "revert" to savagery. First, Africans were not savages. More important, black Americans were the products of American culture and their own subcultures. Boas rejected all other forms of neo-Lamarckianism, as well. Individuals did not, could not, inherit acquired characteristics, such as self-reliance. Instead, they grew up in communities that prized self-reliance and worked at developing this valued trait. This stance put Boas in direct opposition to supporters of eugenics. Social progress, he taught, could not come from selective breeding or involuntary sterilization. It could arise only out of cultural change. The same was true of social regression.

Boas trained two generations of cultural anthropologists at Columbia University. Over time, he and they, with help from scholars in other fields, especially genetics, succeeded in discrediting white supremacy, racial retrogression, and other theories used to justify discrimination and segregation. That victory did not come in the 1910s, however. It came in the 1940s and 1950s. In the 1910s, these racial theories became more influential than ever. The success of *Birth of a*

Nation was one sign of this. Madison Grant's best-selling *The Passing of the Great Race* was another.

Eugenics continued to command increasing support both from the scientific community and from legislators. By 1914, 12 states had involuntary sterilization laws aimed at preventing those with supposed hereditary defects from reproducing. Depending upon the state, the defective included the feebleminded, those suffering from epileptic seizures or forms of insanity, and those likely to become public charges, that is, the poor. The actual number of sterilizations, outside California, reached about 500 by 1924. In California, about five times that number were deprived of the right to reproduce.

The war, meanwhile, provided those who wanted to restrict immigration or segregate the races with another argument. The U.S. military administered Intelligence Quotient (I.Q.) tests to all its personnel. The results seemingly proved what the eugenicists had been claiming. Whites of northern and western European background had the highest scores, followed by whites from southern and eastern Europe. African Americans had the lowest scores. Two factors, unrecognized at the time, explain the results. One is cultural bias. The questions presumed an acquaintance with white middle-class practices. The second is now called the "Flynn Effect." I.Q. scores have consistently risen over time. Those who create the questions have had to make them more demanding so that the median score remains 100. Does this mean that today's children are markedly more intelligent than their grandparents? Since intelligence is presumed to be an inherited characteristic, that cannot be the case. So, why do scores rise? One explanation is that each generation grows up in a social environment that places more emphasis upon abstract reasoning. Since this is what the I.Q. test seeks to measure, each generation does better than its predecessor. Those charged with interpreting the World War I military scores, however, saw them as scientifically precise measures of intelligence. The higher the score, the smarter the individual. The greater the difference in average scores among racial and ethnic groups, the clearer the proof that some were genetically more gifted than others.

I.Q. test results became a standard argument in favor of eugenics. Here was proof positive of white supremacy and of the unfitness of the "new" immigrants from southern and eastern Europe. Eugenicists did more than cite I.Q. results in pushing for immigration restriction. Proponents successfully urged school systems to administer the tests and to place children in different "tracks" on the basis of their scores. Those with the highest I.Q.s should receive special attention. Putting them together in the same classes would enable them to learn more rapidly. They should be encouraged to go on to college and the professions. Those with middling scores should also be placed together and counseled to seek jobs as bookkeepers and secretaries; those with the lowest scores should be discouraged from taking demanding courses. Instead, they should be encouraged to pursue blue-collar jobs. In school systems with sufficiently large student populations, this became the new order.

RESOURCE GUIDE

SUGGESTED READING

The Triangle Fire, March 25, 1911

McClymer, John F. *The Triangle Strike and Fire*. Fort Worth: Harcourt Brace College Publishers, 1998.
Stein, Leon. *The Triangle Fire*. Philadelphia: Lippincott, 1962.
Von Drehle, David. *Triangle: The Fire That Changed America*. New York: Atlantic Monthly Press, 2003.

The "Bread and Roses" Strike, Lawrence, Massachusetts, 1912

Cameron, Ardis. *Radicals of the Worst Sort: Laboring Women in Lawrence, Massachusetts, 1860–1912*. Urbana: University of Illinois Press, 1993.
Watson, Bruce. *Bread and Roses: Mills, Migrants, and the Struggle for the American Dream*. New York: Viking, 2005.

The Lynching of Leo Frank, 1915

Dinnerstein, Leonard. *The Leo Frank Case*. New York: Columbia University Press, 1968.
MacLean, Nancy. "Gender, Sexuality, and the Politics of Lynching: The Leo Frank Case Revisited." In *Under Sentence of Death: Lynching in the South*, ed. W. Fitzhugh Brundage. Chapel Hill: University of North Carolina Press, 1997, 158–188.
Oney, Steve. *And the Dead Shall Rise: The Murder of Mary Phagan and the Lynching of Leo Frank*. New York: Pantheon, 2003.

The Birth of a Nation, the NAACP, and the Struggle over the Meaning of the Civil War

Cripps, Thomas. *Slow Fade to Black: The Negro in American Film, 1900–1942*. New York: Oxford University Press, 1977.
Griffith, D. W. *The Man Who Invented Hollywood: The Autobiography of D. W. Griffith, A Memoir and Some Notes*. Ed. and annotated by James Hart. Louisville, KY: Touchstone, 1972.
Henderson, Robert M. *D. W. Griffith: His Life and Work*. New York: Oxford University Press, 1972.
Lang, Robert, ed. *The Birth of a Nation*. New Brunswick, NJ: Rutgers University Press, 1994.
Rogin, Michael. "'The Sword Became a Flashing Vision': D. W. Griffith's *The Birth of a Nation*." In *The Birth of a Nation*, ed. Robert Lang. New Brunswick, NJ: Rutgers University Press, 1994, 250–293.
Schickel, Richard. *D. W. Griffith: An American Life*. New York: Simon & Schuster, 1984.
Sklar, Robert. *Movie Made America: A Cultural History of American Movies*. New York: Random House, 1975.

Immigration Restriction and the Great War

Daniels, Roger. *Guarding the Golden Door: American Immigration Policy and Immigrants since 1882*. New York: Hill and Wang, 2004.

Fuchs, Lawrence H. "Immigration Reform in 1911 and 1981: The Role of Select Commissions." *Journal of American Ethnic History* 3(1) (1983): 58–89.

Handlin, Oscar. "Old Immigrants and New." In Handlin, *Race and Nationality in American Life*. Boston: Little, Brown, 1957. The classic study of the Dillingham Commission.

Jenks, Jeremiah W., and W. Jett Lauck. *The Immigration Problem*. New York: Funk & Wagnalls, 1912). A one-volume summary of the major findings of the Dillingham Commission's 42-volume *Report* by two staff members.

King, Desmond. *Making Americans: Immigration, Race, and the Origins of the Diverse Democracy*. Cambridge, MA: Harvard University Press, 2000.

Zeidel, Robert F. *Immigrants, Progressives, and Exclusion Politics: The Dillingham Commission, 1900–1927*. DeKalb: Northern Illinois University Press, 2004.

The Palmer Raids and the First Red Scare, 1919–1920

Coben, Stanley. *A. Mitchell Palmer: Politician*. New York: Columbia University Press, 1963.

Coben, Stanley. *A Study in Nativism: The American Red Scare of 1919–20*. Indianapolis: Bobbs Merrill, 1964.

Finan, Christopher M. *From the Palmer Raids to the Patriot Act: A History of the Fight for Free Speech in America*. Boston: Beacon Press, 2007.

Murray, Robert K. *Red Scare: A Study in National Hysteria*. Minneapolis: University of Minnesota Press, 1955.

Nielsen, Kim E. *Un-American Womanhood: Antiradicalism, Antifeminism, and the First Red Scare*. Columbus: Ohio State University Press, 2001.

Pfannestiel, Todd J. *Rethinking the Red Scare: The Lusk Committee and New York's Crusade against Radicalism, 1919–1923*. New York: Routledge, 2003.

The Chicago Race Riot of 1919

Arnesen, Eric. *Black Protest and the Great Migration: A Brief History with Documents*. Boston: Bedford Books of St. Martin's Press, 2003.

Grossman, James R. *Land of Hope: Chicago, Black Southerners, and the Great Migration*. Chicago: University of Chicago Press, 1989.

Rudwick, Elliott. *Race Riot at East St. Louis, July 2, 1917*. Carbondale: University of Southern Illinois Press, 1964.

Spear, Allan H. *Black Chicago: The Making of a Negro Ghetto, 1890–1920*. Chicago: University of Chicago Press, 1967.

Tuttle, William M. Jr. *Race Riot: Chicago in the Red Summer of 1919*. New York: Atheneum, 1970.

Madison Grant

Bruinius, Harry. *Better for All the World: The Secret History of Forced Sterilization and America's Quest for Racial Purity*. New York: Knopf, 2006.

Guterl, Matthew Pratt. *The Color of Race in America, 1900–1940*. Cambridge, MA: Harvard University Press, 2001.

Kevles, Daniel J. *In the Name of Eugenics: Genetics and the Uses of Human Heredity.* New York: Knopf, 1985.

Woodrow Wilson

Blum, John Morton. *Woodrow Wilson and the Politics of Morality.* Boston: Little, Brown, 1956.
Link, Arthur. *Woodrow Wilson and the Progressive Era, 1910–1917.* New York: Harper, 1954.

George M. Cohan and Irving Berlin

Bergreen, Lawrence. *As Thousands Cheer: The Life of Irving Berlin.* New York: Viking, 1990.
Hamm, Charles. *Irving Berlin: Songs from the Melting Pot: The Formative Years, 1907–1914.* New York: Oxford University Press, 1997.
McCabe, John. *George M. Cohan: The Man Who Owned Broadway.* Garden City, NY: Doubleday, 1973.

Walter White

White, Walter. *A Man Called White: The Autobiography of Walter White.* New York: Viking Press, 1948.

African Americans

Anderson, Jervis. *This Was Harlem: A Cultural Portrait, 1900–1950.* New York: Farrar Straus & Giroux, 1982.
Dray, Philip. *At the Hands of Persons Unknown: The Lynching of Black America.* New York: Random House, 2002.
Kirby, Jack Temple. *Darkness at the Dawning: Race and Reform in the Progressive South.* Philadelphia: Lippincott, 1972.
Lewis, David Levering. *W.E.B. Du Bois: Biography of a Race, 1868–1919.* New York: Holt, 1993.
McPherson, James M. *The Abolitionist Legacy: From Reconstruction to the N.A.A.C.P.* Princeton: Princeton University Press, 1975.
Sundquist, Eric J., ed. *Oxford W.E.B. Du Bois Reader.* New York: Oxford University Press, 1996.
Williamson, Joel. *The Crucible of Race: Black-White Relations in the American South since Emancipation.* New York: Oxford University Press, 1984.

European Americans

Bayor, Ronald H. *Race and Ethnicity in America: A Concise History.* New York: Columbia University Press, 2003.
Gerstle, Gary. *American Crucible: Race and Nation in the Twentieth Century.* Princeton: Princeton University Press, 2001.
Higham, John. *Send These to Me: Jews and Other Immigrants to Urban America.* New York: Atheneum, 1975.

Higham, John. *Strangers in the Land: Patterns of American Nativism, 1860–1925*. New Brunswick, NJ: Rutgers University Press, 1955.
McClymer, John F. *War and Welfare: Social Engineering in America, 1890–1925*. Westport, CT: Greenwood Press, 1980.
Nordstrom, Justin. *Danger on the Doorstep: Anti-Catholicism and American Print Culture in the Progressive Era*. Notre Dame, IN: University of Notre Dame Press, 2006.

Native Americans

Debo, Angie. *A History of the Indians of the United States*. Norman: University of Oklahoma Press, 1970.
Deloria, Vine. *American Indian Policy in the Twentieth Century*. Norman: University of Oklahoma Press, 1985.

Asian Americans

Chan, Sucheng, ed. *Entry Denied: Exclusion and the Chinese Community in America, 1882–1943*. Philadelphia: Temple University Press, 1991.
Daniels, Roger. *Asian American: Chinese and Japanese in the United States since 1850*. Seattle: University of Washington Press, 1988.
Hosokawa, Bill. *Nisei, The Quiet Americans: The Story of a People*. New York: Morrow, 1969.
Okihiro, Gary Y. *Margins and Mainstreams: Asians in American History and Culture*. Seattle: University of Washington Press, 1994.
Patterson, Wayne. *The Ilse: First-Generation Korean Immigrants in Hawai'i, 1903–1973*. Honolulu: University of Hawaii Press, 2000.
Patterson, Wayne. *The Korean Frontier in America: Immigration to Hawai'i, 1896–1910*. Honolulu: University of Hawaii Press, 1988.
Takaki, Ronald T. *Strangers from a Different Shore: A History of Asian Americans*. Boston: Little, Brown, 1989.

Latinos

Acuna, Rodolfo. *Occupied America: A History of Chicanos*. New York: Harper & Row, 1988.
Camarillo, Albert. *Chicanos in a Changing Society: From Mexican Pueblos to Mexican Barrios in Santa Barbara and Southern California, 1848–1930*. Cambridge, MA: Harvard University Press, 1979.
Daniel, Cletus. *Bitter Harvest: A History of California Farm Workers, 1870–1941*. Ithaca, NY: Cornell University Press, 1981.
Kiser, George C., and Martha W. Kiser, eds. *Mexican Workers in the United States: Historical and Political Perspectives*. Albuquerque: University of New Mexico Press, 1979.
Sanchez, George J. *Becoming Mexican American: Ethnicity, Culture and Identity in Chicano Los Angeles, 1900–1940*. New York: Oxford University Press, 1993.

Law and Government

Hofstadter, Richard. *The Age of Reform: From Bryan to FDR*. New York: Knopf, 1955.
McGerr, Michael E. *A Fierce Discontent: The Rise and Fall of the Progressive Movement in America, 1870–1920*. New York: Free Press, 2003.
Wiebe, Robert. *The Search for Order, 1877–1920*. New York: Hill & Wang, 1967.

Media and Mass Communications

Kitch, Carolyn L. *The Girl on the Magazine Cover: The Origins of Visual Stereotypes in American Mass Media*. Chapel Hill: University of North Carolina Press, 2001.

Ohmann, Richard M. *Selling Culture: Magazines, Markets and Class at the Turn of the Century*. New York: Verso, 1996.

Starr, Paul. *The Creation of the Media: The Political Origins of Modern Communications*. New York: Basic Books, 2004.

Cultural Scene

Gates, Henry Lewis, and Cornel West. *The African-American Century: How Black Americans Have Shaped Our Country*. New York: Free Press, 2000.

May, Henry. *The End of American Innocence: A Study of the First Years of Our Own Time*. New York: Knopf, 1959.

Lears, T. J. Jackson. *No Place of Grace: Anti-Modernism and the Transformation of American Culture, 1880–1920*. New York: Pantheon Books, 1981.

Influential Theories and Views of Race Relations

George W. Stocking, ed. *The Shaping of American Anthropology, 1883–1911: A Franz Boas Reader*. New York: Basic Books 1974.

Williams, Vernon J. *Rethinking Race: Franz Boas and His Contemporaries*. Lexington: University Press of Kentucky, 1996.

FILMS

Fiction

The Birth of a Nation & the Civil War Films of D. W. Griffith (1915). This DVD contains the original film plus a 1930 sound introduction featuring Griffith, along with related materials, including "New York vs. *The Birth of a Nation*," an archive of information documenting the battles over the film's 1922 re-release, and excerpts from a 1915 souvenir book and several original programs.

Yankee Doodle Dandy (1943). Released by Warner Bros. Pictures; screenplay by Robert Buckner and Edmund Joseph; original story by Robert Buckner; directed by Michael Curtiz. Biography of George M. Cohan.

WEB SITES

The Bisbee Deportation of 1917, http://www.library.arizona.edu/exhibits/bisbee/index.html, at the University of Arizona Web site, is a very rich compendium of primary materials and links to useful secondary sources. Among these is James W. Byrkit, *Forging the Copper Collar: Arizona's Labor-Management War of 1901–1921* (Tucson: University of Arizona Press, 1982), the standard account.

The Center for Educational Telecommunications (CET), http://www.cetel.org/res.html, maintains a highly useful guide to "Asian American History Resources Online."

"Deaths, Disturbances, Disasters, and Disorders in Chicago," http://www.chipublib.org/cplbooksmovies/cplarchive/chidisasters/index.php, at the Chicago Public Library Web site, contains the Cook County Coroner's Report, *The Race Riots: Biennial Report 1918–1919 and Official Record of Inquests on the Victims of the Race Riots of July and August, 1919, Whereby Fifteen White Men and Twenty-three Colored Men Lost Their Lives and Several Hundred Were Injured.*

Dillingham Commission Reports, http://library.stanford.edu/depts/dlp/ebrary/dillingham/body.shtml, available at Stanford University. The Commission, organized in 1907 by Congress, submitted its *Report* in 42 volumes in 1912. These contributed mightily to the immigration restriction movement.

"Homicide in Chicago, 1870–1930," http://homicide.northwestern.edu/pubs/negrochicago/, at Northwestern University, has *The Negro in Chicago*, the 1922 Chicago Commission on Race Relations report.

"Image Archive of the American Eugenics Movement," http://www.eugenicsarchive.org/eugenics/, at the Web site of the Cold Spring Harbor Laboratory, contains a wealth of materials, as well as highly useful historical essays.

"The Joe Hill Project," http://www.joehill.org/, "created and maintained by Professor Ron Yengich and his students in Honors 3374—Trial Rights of the Accused at the University of Utah," contains information about Hill's life, his involvement with the Industrial Workers of the World (IWW), his songs, and his trial and execution.

"The Lawrence Strike of 1912," http://ocp.hul.harvard.edu/ww/events_lawrencestrike.html, at the Open Collections Program, Women Working, 1800–1930, at the Harvard University Library, contains a good brief overview and links to contemporary accounts.

"The Leo Frank Case," http://www.cviog.uga.edu/Projects/gainfo/leofrank.htm, at the Carl Vinson Center of the University of Georgia, is a detailed chronology compiled by Charles Pou.

One selection from "Letters of Negro Migrants of 1916–18," *Journal of Negro History* 4, no. 3 (July 1919), followed by six selections from "Additional Letters of Negro Migrants of 1916–1918," *Journal of Negro History* 4, no. 4 (October 1919), is available at DePaul University, http://condor.depaul.edu/%7Echicago/primary_sources/letters1.html.

"Poetry of James Oppenheim, 1882–1932," at Day Poems, http://www.daypoems.net/poets/440.html, includes "Bread and Roses," "The New God," and several other works.

"Red Scare, 1918–1921," http://newman.baruch.cuny.edu/digital/redscare/default.htm, is a database of editorial cartoons created by Leo Robert Klein.

Richard Jensen, "American Political History On-Line," http://tigger.uic.edu/~rjensen/polgl.htm, is an extremely useful gateway to relevant primary and secondary sources.

"The Triangle Factory Fire," http://www.ilr.cornell.edu/trianglefire/about.html. The Kheel Center at Cornell University maintains a very rich Web site on the fire that includes news accounts, photographs, excerpts from the New York Factory Safety Commission reports, and other resources.

"The Triangle Factory Fire Trial," http://www.law.umkc.edu/faculty/projects/ftrials/triangle/trianglefire.html, at the University of Missouri Kansas City School of Law site, contains excerpts of the trial of the factory owners for manslaughter, newspaper accounts, and an overview by Professor Douglas Linder.

NOTES

1. Information on the fire is drawn from John F. McClymer, *The Triangle Strike and Fire* (Houston: Harcourt, Brace, 1998). The classic account, which drew upon the accounts of still living survivors, is Leon Stein, *The Triangle Fire* (1962). An excellent, and highly readable, recent account is David Von Drehle, *Triangle: The Fire That Changed America* (2003). Less useful is Richard A. Greenwald, *The Triangle Fire, the Protocols of Peace, and Industrial Democracy in Progressive Era New York* (2005). The Kheel Center at Cornell University maintains a very rich Web site on the fire that includes news accounts, photographs, excerpts from the New York Factory Safety Commission reports, and other resources, http://www.ilr.cornell.edu/trianglefire/about.html.

2. Reprinted in McClymer, *The Triangle Strike and Fire*.

3. See, for example, "Scenes at the Morgue," *New York Times*, March 26, 1911.

4. "Faint in a Frenzy over Tales of Fire," *New York Times*, March 30, 1911.

5. Frances Perkins, *The Roosevelt I Knew* (1946), pp. 22–26.

6. See her autobiography, *All for One* (1967) and Nancy Schrom Dye, *As Equals and as Sisters: Feminism, the Labor Movement, and the Women's Trade Union League of New York* (1980).

7. "Mass Meeting Calls for New Fire Laws," *New York Times*, April 3, 1911.

8. Frances Perkins on the Triangle Fire: Lecture excerpt by former Secretary of Labor given in 1964 at Cornell University (20 min.) at the Kheel Center Web site, http://www.ilr.cornell.edu/trianglefire/audio/default.html.

9. Bruce Watson, *Bread and Roses: Mills, Migrants, and the Struggle for the American Dream* (New York: Viking, 2005) is a recent account. Ardis Cameron, *Radicals of the Worst Sort: Laboring Women in Lawrence, Massachusetts, 1860–1912* (Urbana: University of Illinois Press, 1993) also discusses the strike in detail. This essay draws heavily upon two contemporary accounts: Charles P. Neill, *Report on Strike of Textile Workers in Lawrence, Mass. in 1912* (1912), the report of the Commissioner of Labor; and Justin Ebert, *The Trial of a New Society*, published by the Industrial Workers of the World, the union that led the strike. Unless otherwise specified, factual information is taken from Neill, *Report on the Strike*.

10. Quoted in Neill, *Report on Strike of Textile Workers*, p.12.

11. There was no Communist Party in the United States until 1919. It was formed only after the October Revolution in Russia led to the creation of the Soviet Union.

12. According to the Commissioner of Labor's *Report on Strike of Textile Workers* (p. 11), this was the number of paid-up members. Several thousand more may have joined at some point but were no longer active.

13. Ibid., p. 26.

14. Cited in ibid., p. 27.

15. Ibid., p. 94. The average wage for women over 18 was 13.5 cents, or $7.19 per week (53 hours worked on average). Men over 18 earned an average of 14.7 cents per hour, or $7.93 (also for 53 hours).

16. It was impossible for contemporaries to assess this since publicly held companies did not have to disclose this information until the New Deal.

17. Quoted in Neill, *Report on Strike of Textile Workers*, p. 41.

18. Textile companies offered increased pay (the premium) if workers met specified production goals. Even though the premium permitted workers to earn more, virtually all hated the system. They saw it as a way employers could speed up the work pace.

19. Subsequently, a jury found both innocent. Forensic evidence suggested that Lo Pezzi was killed by a policeman's bullet.

20. The following account draws upon several sources: Leonard Dinnerstein, *The Leo Frank Case* (New York: Columbia University Press, 1968); Steve Oney, *And the Dead Shall Rise: The Murder of Mary Phagan and the Lynching of Leo Frank* (New York: Pantheon, 2003); Nancy MacLean, "Gender, Sexuality, and the Politics of Lynching: The Leo Frank Case Revisited," in *Under Sentence of Death: Lynching in the South*, ed. W. Fitzhugh Brundage (Chapel Hill: University of North Carolina Press, 1997), 158–188; an earlier version of MacLean's article, with fuller notes, is "The Leo Frank Case Reconsidered: Gender and Sexual Politics in the Making of Reactionary Populism," *Journal of American History* 77 (December 1991): 917–948. There is a detailed chronology at the Carl Vinson Institute of Government, University of Georgia, http://www.cviog.uga.edu/Projects/gainfo/leofrank.htm. All quotations come from this source.

21. See especially MacLean, "The Leo Frank Case Reconsidered: Gender and Sexual Politics in the Making of Reactionary Populism."

22. The DVD *The Birth of a Nation & The Civil War Films of D. W. Griffith* (1915) contains the original film plus a 1930 sound introduction featuring Griffith, as well as related materials, including "New York vs. *The Birth of a Nation*," an archive of information documenting the battles over the film's 1922 re-release and excerpts from a 1915 souvenir book and several original programs. It also contains the seven short films on the Civil War Griffith made before he directed *The Birth of a Nation*. Robert Lang, ed., *The Birth of a Nation* (New Brunswick, NJ: Rutgers University Press, 1994) is the best overall discussion of the film and includes the shooting script, contemporary reviews (almost all highly positive), and several scholarly essays.

23. Dixon's publisher, Doubleday, Page, and Company, emphasized this in its advertisements for his *The Leopard's Spots: A Romance of the White Man's Burden* (1902). One ad, which appeared in *The Dial* of March 16, 1902, claimed: "This novel is as remarkable in its way as 'Uncle Tom's Cabin.' . . . That book gave, in the form of fiction, a picture of the Negro's sufferings from the Northern point of view. Mr. Dixon's book gives the Southern point of view of the same question, and as a picture it is as graphic and as striking as Mrs. Stowe's book."

24. A classic critique is Richard Hofstadter, "U. B. Phillips and the Plantation Legend," *Journal of Negro History* 29(2) (April 1944): 109–124. Phillips's *American Negro Slavery* (New York, 1918) was required reading for history graduate students until the 1960s.

25. A judicious assessment is Philip R. Muller, "Look Back without Anger: A Reappraisal of William A. Dunning," *Journal of American History* 61(2) (September 1974): 325–338. See William Archibald Dunning, *Reconstruction, Political and Economic, 1865–1877* (New York, 1907). This, too, was required reading in history graduate programs for at least two generations.

26. Wilson's biographer Arthur Link, who also edited the 69-volume edition of the *Papers of Woodrow Wilson*, credits Thomas Dixon with the "bold scheme" of showing

the film at the White House and thereby gaining the president's "implied endorsement." Wilson fell into this "trap." His adviser Joseph Tumulty urged the president to write a public letter making it clear that he did not approve of the movie. Wilson told him that he would like to but that it would make it appear that he was seeking to placate "that unspeakable fellow Trotter." This was William Monroe Trotter, head of the Boston NAACP. Arthur Link, *Wilson: The New Freedom* (Princeton: Princeton University Press, 1956), pp. 253–254.

27. W.E.B. Du Bois, *Black Reconstruction: An Essay toward a History of the Part Which Black Folk Played in the Attempt to Reconstruct Democracy in America, 1860–1880* (New York, 1935). Du Bois's Marxian approach proved off-putting to many historians.

28. A standard account is Kenneth Jackson, *The Ku Klux Klan in the City, 1915–1930* (New York: Oxford University Press, 1967). See also Kathleen M. Blee, *Women of the Klan: Racism and Gender in the 1920s* (Berkeley, CA: University of California, 1991); Leonard J. Moore, *Citizen Klansmen: The Ku Klux Klan in Indiana, 1921–1928* (Chapel Hill: University of North Carolina, 1991); and William D. Jenkins, *Steel Valley Klan: The Ku Klux Klan in Ohio's Mahoning Valley* (Kent, OH: Kent State University, 1990).

29. This account follows Thomas Cripps, "The Year of *The Birth of a Nation*," in Cripps, *Slow Fade to Black: The Negro in American Film, 1900–1942* (New York: Oxford University Press, 1977), pp. 41–69.

30. See the "American Civil War Cartoons" collection at the American Antiquarian Society, Worcester, MA.

31. See Manthia Diawara, "Black Spectatorship: Problems of Identification and Resistance," in *Black American Cinema*, ed. Manthia Diawara (New York: Routledge, 1993), pp. 211–220.

32. Address of the President of the United States, Convention Hall, Philadelphia, Pennsylvania, May 10, 1915.

33. Quoted in "Roosevelt or Hughes?" *Literary Digest* 52 (April 15, 1916): 1043. In its June 3, 1916, issue, the *Literary Digest* sampled editorial reactions to "Colonel Roosevelt's New Crusade," and found broad support. *Literary Digest* 52 (June 3, 1916): 1618.

34. "Democratic Campaign Issues," *Literary Digest* 52 (July 1, 1916): 4.

35. "The President and the Hyphen," *Literary Digest* 52 (October 14, 1916): 935. The *Digest* cited an article in the *New York Herald Tribune* that quoted one leading Democrat as saying, "We are going to make the hyphen the big talking point of the campaign. There isn't any other issue."

36. Many had not been in the United States long enough to become naturalized.

37. Daniel E. Weinberg, "The Foreign Language Information Service and the Foreign Born, 1918–1939: A Case Study of Cultural Assimilation Viewed as a Problem in Social Technology" (Ph.D. dissertation, University of Minnesota, 1973), is a detailed account of FLIS.

38. George Creel, *How We Advertised America* (1920), 180–181.

39. For a brief description, see p. 161.

40. Anna Louise Strong, *The Seattle General Strike of 1919: An Account of What Happened in Seattle and Especially in the Seattle Labor Movement, During the General Strike, February 6 to 11, 1919*. Originally issued by the History Committee of the General Strike Committee, March 1919, p. 68.

41. A. Mitchell Palmer, "The Case against the 'Reds,'" *Forum* 63 (1920), pp. 173–185.

164   Race Relations in the United States, 1900–1920

42. The largest Yiddish-language newspaper, *The Forward*, for example, advocated socialism but not communism, a distinction lost upon the Attorney General.

43. Because those arrested were aliens, they did not have the legal protections enjoyed by citizens, such as the right to know the charges against them (habeas corpus), the right to an attorney, and the right to a speedy trial.

44. As a young man, Berkman had engaged in what anarchists called the "propaganda of the deed," what we now call terrorism. In 1892, during the Homestead Strike against the Carnegie Steel Company, he unsuccessfully attempted to kill Henry Clay Frick, Carnegie's partner, who was in charge of breaking the steel union. Convicted of attempted murder, Berkman spent more than a decade in prison. He emerged a pacifist. See Alexander Berkman, *Prison Memoirs of an Anarchist* (1912).

45. A headline in the *New York Times* for April 16, 1920, read, "TAKE STEP IN HOUSE TO IMPEACH POST; Hoch Offers Preliminary Resolution after Conference with Republican Leaders. CHARGES FAVORS TO REDS, Measure Directs Committee to Inquire on the Blocking of Deportations." Hoch was a Republican congressman from Kansas.

46. See Louis F. Post's autobiographical *Deportations Delirium of 1920* (1923).

47. Both organizations continue to exist. Neither ever regained its prewar importance.

48. Woodrow Wilson segregated the military and the rest of the federal government. The Army had been a traditional source of employment for African Americans since the Civil War. But Wilson drastically limited the roles they could play. An excellent contemporary analysis of the migration is *The Negro in Chicago*, the report of the 1922 Chicago Commission on Race Relations, ch. 3. (Chicago: University of Chicago Press, 1922).

49. The black population of Chicago grew from 44,103 in 1910 to 109,594 in 1920, an increase of 148 percent. According to *The Negro in Chicago*, the bulk of this growth occurred between 1916 and 1919.

50. Ibid.

51 This account of the riot draws upon *The Negro in Chicago*, ch. 1.

52. At 3:35 A.M. on Saturday, August 2, a series of fires broke out that destroyed 49 houses in an immigrant neighborhood west of the stockyards. A total of 948 people lived in these buildings, most of them Lithuanian immigrants and their children. No one was ever apprehended for setting these fires. However, the grand jury that investigated the riot suspected that the fires were set by white "athletic clubs," that is, gangs, to stir up racial hatred.

53. The New York City mayoralty race in 1917 is a case in point. The Democratic candidate, John Francis "Red Mike" Hylan—his nickname referred to his hair color, not his politics—won handily in a four-man contest. The incumbent, John Purroy Mitchel, running as an independent, barely nosed out the Socialist Morris Hilquit for second. Almost all of the Socialist vote came from Jewish and Italian wards.

Selected Bibliography

BOOKS

Anderson, Jervis. *This Was Harlem: A Cultural Portrait, 1900–1950*. New York: Farrar Straus & Giroux, 1982.

Arnesen, Eric. *Black Protest and the Great Migration: A Brief History with Documents*. Boston: Bedford Books of St. Martin's, 2003.

Bailey, Thomas A. *Theodore Roosevelt and the Japanese-American Crises*. Palo Alto, CA: Stanford University Press, 1934.

Board of Lady Managers. *Report to the Louisiana Purchase Exposition Commission*. Cambridge, MA: Riverside Press, Houghton, 1905.

Breitbart, Eric. *A World on Display: Photographs from the St. Louis World's Fair, 1904*. Albuquerque: University of New Mexico Press, 1997.

Bruinius, Harry. *Better for All the World: The Secret History of Forced Sterilization and America's Quest for Racial Purity*. New York: Knopf, 2006.

Camarillo, Albert. *Chicanos in a Changing Society: From Mexican Pueblos to Mexican Barrios in Santa Barbara and Southern California, 1848–1930*. Cambridge, MA: Harvard University Press, 1979.

Cameron, Ardis. *Radicals of the Worst Sort: Laboring Women in Lawrence, Massachusetts, 1860–1912*. Urbana: University of Illinois Press, 1993.

Chadwick, Bruce. *The Reel Civil War: Mythmaking in American Film*. New York: Knopf, 2001.

Chan, Sucheng, ed. *Entry Denied: Exclusion and the Chinese Community in America, 1882–1943*, Philadelphia: Temple University Press, 1991.

Coben, Stanley. *A. Mitchell Palmer: Politician*. New York: Columbia University Press, 1963.

Coben, Stanley. *A Study in Nativism: The American Red Scare of 1919–20*. Indianapolis: Bobbs Merrill, 1964.

Correspondence Relating to the War with Spain: Including the Insurrection in the Philippine Islands and the China Relief Expedition, April 15, 1898, to July 30, 1902. Washington, DC: Center of Military History, U.S. Army, 1993, 2002.

Cripps, Thomas. *Slow Fade to Black: The Negro in American Film, 1900–1942*. New York: Oxford University Press, 1977.

Curriden, Mark, and Leroy Phillips, Jr. *Contempt of Court: The Turn-of-the-Century Lynching That Launched 100 Years of Federalism*. New York: Faber & Faber, 1999.

Daniel, Cletus. *Bitter Harvest: A History of California Farm Workers, 1870–1941*. Ithaca, NY: Cornell University Press, 1981.

Daniels, Roger. *Asian American: Chinese and Japanese in the United States since 1850*. Seattle: University of Washington Press, 1988.

Daniels, Roger. *Coming to America: A History of Race and Ethnicity in American Life*, 2nd ed. New York: HarperCollins, 2002.

Daniels, Roger. *Guarding the Golden Door: American Immigration Policy and Immigrants since 1882*. New York: Hill and Wang, 2004.

Daniels, Roger. *Not Like Us: Immigrants and Minorities in America, 1890–1924*. Chicago: Ivan R. Dee, 1997.

Diner, Hasia R. *Erin's Daughters in America: Irish Immigrant Women in the Nineteenth Century*. Baltimore: Johns Hopkins University Press, 1983.

Dinnerstein, Leonard. *The Leo Frank Case*. New York: Columbia University Press, 1968.

Dixon, Thomas Jr. *The Clansman: An Historical Romance of the Ku Klux Klan*. New York: Doubleday, Page, 1905.

Dixon, Thomas Jr. *The Leopard's Spots: A Romance of the White Man's Burden—1865–1900*. New York: Doubleday, Page, 1902.

Dixon, Thomas Jr. *The Traitor: A Story of the Fall of the Invisible Empire*. New York: Doubleday, Page, 1907.

Drake, St. Clair and Horace Clayton. *Black Metropolis*. New York: Harcourt, Brace, 1945.

Dray, Philip. *At the Hands of Persons Unknown: The Lynching of Black America*. New York: Random House, 2002.

Edwards, Rebecca. *New Spirits: Americans in the Gilded Age, 1865–1905*. New York: Oxford University Press, 2006.

Finan, Christopher M. *From the Palmer Raids to the Patriot Act: A History of the Fight for Free Speech in America*. Boston: Beacon Press, 2007.

Gerstle, Gary. *American Crucible: Race and Nationality in Twentieth Century America*. Princeton: Princeton University Press 2001.

Gilmour, David. *The Long Recessional: The Imperial Life of Rudyard Kipling*. New York: Farrar Straus & Giroux, 2002.

Gitelman, H. M. *Legacy of the Ludlow Massacre: A Chapter in American Industrial Relations*. Philadelphia: University of Pennsylvania Press, 1988.

Gosnell, Harold F. *Negro Politicians*. Chicago: University of Chicago Press, 1935; reprinted with a new Introduction by James Q. Wilson, 1967.

Gould, Lewis L. *The Spanish-American War and President McKinley*. Lawrence: University Press of Kansas, 1982.

Grossman, James R. *Land of Hope: Chicago, Black Southerners, and the Great Migration*. Chicago: University of Chicago Press, 1989.

Guterl, Matthew Pratt. *The Color of Race in America, 1900–1940*. Cambridge, MA: Harvard University Press, 2001.

Henderson, Robert M. *D. W. Griffith: His Life and Work*. New York: Oxford University Press, 1972.

Hoganson, Kristin L. *Fighting for American Manhood: How Gender Politics Provoked the Spanish-American and Philippine-American Wars*. New Haven, CT: Yale University Press, 1998.

Holt, Glen E., and Dominic A. Pacyga. *Chicago: A Historical Guide to the Neighborhoods—The Loop and South Side*. Chicago: Chicago Historical Society, 1979.

Hosokawa, Bill. Nisei, *The Quiet Americans: The Story of a People*. New York: Morrow, 1969.

Howe, Irving. *World of Our Fathers: The Journey of the East European Jews to America and the Life They Found and Made*. New York: Harcourt Brace Jovanovich, 1976.

Jones, Jacqueline. *Labor of Love, Labor of Sorrow: Black Women, Work, and the Family from Slavery to the Present*. New York: Basic Books, 1985.

Kellogg, Charles Flint. *NAACP: A History of the National Association for the Advancement of Colored People, 1909–1920*. Baltimore: Johns Hopkins University Press, 1967.

Kevles, Daniel J. *In the Name of Eugenics: Genetics and the Uses of Human Heredity*. New York: Knopf, 1985.

King, Desmond. *Making Americans: Immigration, Race, and the Origins of the Diverse Democracy*. Cambridge, MA: Harvard University Press, 2000.

Kirby, Jack Temple. *Darkness at the Dawning: Race and Reform in the Progressive South*. Philadelphia: Lippincott, 1972.

Kiser, George C., and Martha W. Kiser, eds. *Mexican Workers in the United States: Historical and Political Perspectives*. Albuquerque: University of New Mexico Press, 1979.

Kraut, Alan M. *Silent Travelers: Germs, Genes, and the "Immigrant Menace."* New York: Basic Books, 1994.

Kusmer, Kenneth L. *A Ghetto Takes Shape: Black Cleveland, 1870–1930*. Urbana: University of Illinois Press, 1976.

Lane, Ann J. *The Brownsville Affair: National Crisis and Black Reaction*. Port Washington, NY: Kennikat Press, 1971.

Lang, Robert, ed. *The Birth of a Nation*. New Brunswick, NJ: Rutgers University Press, 1994.

Lewis, David Levering. *W.E.B. Du Bois: Biography of a Race, 1868–1919*. New York: Holt, 1993.

Lieberson, Stanley. *A Piece of the Pie: Blacks and White Immigrants since 1880*. Berkeley: University of California Press, 1980.

McClymer, John F. *The Triangle Strike and Fire*. Houston: Harcourt, Brace, 1998.

McClymer, John F. *War and Welfare: Social Engineering in America, 1890–1925*. Westport, CT: Greenwood Press, 1980.

McGovern, George S., and Leonard F. Guttridge. *The Great Coalfield War*. Boston: Houghton Mifflin, 1972.

McMurry, Linda O. *To Keep the Waters Troubled: The Life of Ida B. Wells*. New York: Oxford University Press, 1998.

McPherson, James M. *The Abolitionist Legacy: From Reconstruction to the N.A.A.C.P.* Princeton: Princeton University Press, 1975.

Meier, August. *Negro Thought in America, 1880–1915: Racial Ideologies in the Age of Booker T. Washington*. Ann Arbor: University of Michigan Press, 1963.

Morgan, H. Wayne. *America's Road to Empire: The War with Spain and Overseas Expansion*. New York: Wiley, 1965.

Murray, Robert K. *Red Scare: A Study in National Hysteria, 1919–1920*. Minneapolis: University of Minnesota Press, 1955.

Nee, Victor, and Brett de Bary Nee. *Longtime Californ': A Documentary Study of an American Chinatown*. New York: Pantheon, 1973.

Nielsen, Kim E. *Un-American Womanhood: Antiradicalism, Antifeminism, and the First Red Scare*. Columbus: Ohio State University Press, 2001.

Nordstrom, Justin. *Danger on the Doorstep: Anti-Catholicism and American Print Culture in the Progressive Era*. Notre Dame, IN: University of Notre Dame Press, 2006.

Okihiro, Gary Y. *Margins and Mainstreams: Asians in American History and Culture.* Seattle: University of Washington Press, 1994.

Oney, Steve. *And the Dead Shall Rise: The Murder of Mary Phagan and the Lynching of Leo Frank.* New York: Pantheon, 2003.

Papanikolas, Zeese. *Buried Unsung: Louis Tikas and the Ludlow Massacre.* Salt Lake City: University of Utah Press, 1982.

Patterson, Wayne. *The Ilse: First-Generation Korean Immigrants in Hawaii, 1903–1973.* Honolulu: University of Hawaii Press, Center for Korean Studies, University of Hawaii, 2000.

Patterson, Wayne. *The Korean Frontier in America: Immigration to Hawaii, 1896–1910.* Honolulu: University of Hawaii Press, 1988.

Pfannestiel, Todd J. *Rethinking the Red Scare: The Lusk Committee and New York's Crusade against Radicalism, 1919–1923.* New York: Routledge, 2003.

Rudwick, Elliott. *Race Riot at East St. Louis, July 2, 1917.* Carbondale: Southern Illinois University Press, 1964.

Sanchez, George J. *Becoming Mexican American: Ethnicity, Culture and Identity in Chicano Los Angeles, 1900–1940.* New York: Oxford University Press, 1993.

Schickel, Richard. *D. W. Griffith: An American Life.* New York: Simon & Schuster, 1984.

Schoonover, Thomas David. *Uncle Sam's War of 1898 and the Origins of Globalization.* Lexington: University of Kentucky Press, 2003.

Sklar, Robert. *Movie Made America: A Cultural History of American Movies.* New York: Vintage Books, 1994.

Spear, Allan H. *Black Chicago: The Making of a Negro Ghetto, 1890–1920.* Chicago: University of Chicago Press, 1967.

Sundquist, Eric J., ed. *Oxford W.E.B. Du Bois Reader.* New York: Oxford University Press, 1996.

Trachtenberg, Alan. *The Incorporation of America: Culture and Society in Gilded Age America.* New York: Hill & Wang, 1982.

Tuttle, William M. Jr. *Race Riot: Chicago in the Red Summer of 1919.* New York: Atheneum, 1970.

Watson, Bruce. *Bread and Roses: Mills, Migrants, and the Struggle for the American Dream.* New York: Viking, 2005.

Webb, Michael. "'God Bless You All—I Am Innocent': Sheriff Joseph F. Shipp, Chattanooga, and the Lynching of Ed Johnson." In *Trial and Triumph: Essays in Tennessee's African American History,* ed. Carroll Van West. Knoxville: University of Tennessee Press, 2002, 281–309.

Welch, Richard E. *Response to Imperialism: The United States and the Philippine-American War, 1899–1902.* Chapel Hill: University of North Carolina Press, 1979.

Wells, Ida B. *The Autobiography of Ida B. Wells,* ed. Alfreda M. Duster. Chicago: University of Chicago Press, 1970.

White, Walter. *A Man Called White: The Autobiography of Walter White.* New York: Viking Press, 1948.

Wilkerson, Marcus. *Public Opinion and the Spanish-American War: A Study in War Propaganda.* New York: Russell & Russell, 1932.

Williamson, Joel. *The Crucible of Race: Black-White Relations in the American South since Emancipation.* New York: Oxford University Press, 1984.

Zeidel, Robert F. *Immigrants, Progressives, and Exclusion Politics: The Dillingham Commission, 1900–1927.* DeKalb: Northern Illinois University Press, 2004.

WEB SITES

"Asiatic Coolie Invasion" (1906), Virtual Museum of San Francisco, http://www.sfmuseum.org/1906.2/invasion.html (along with other examples of anti-Japanese sentiment from 1906).

"Deaths, Disturbances, Disasters, and Disorders in Chicago," Chicago Public Library, http://www.chipublib.org/cplbooksmovies/cplarchive/chidisasters/index.php (contains the Cook County Coroner's Report, *The Race Riots: Biennial Report 1918–1919 and Official Record of Inquests on the Victims of the Race Riots of July and August, 1919, Whereby Fifteen White Men and Twenty-three Colored Men Lost Their Lives and Several Hundred Were Injured*, a key source for exactly who did what and when).

Dillingham Commission Reports, Stanford University, http://library.stanford.edu/depts/dlp/ebrary/dillingham/body.shtml. "The Bisbee Deportation of 1917," University of Arizona, http://www.library.arizona.edu/exhibits/bisbee/index.html (a very rich compendium of primary materials and links to useful secondary sources, including James W. Byrkit, *Forging the Copper Collar: Arizona's Labor-Management War of 1901–1921* [Tucson: University of Arizona Press, 1982], the standard account).

"Effects of the Press on Spanish-American Relations in 1898 by John Baker," Humbolt State University, http://www.humboldt.edu/%7Ejcb10/spanwar.shtml.

"Homicide in Chicago, 1870–1930," Northwestern University, has *The Negro in Chicago*, the 1922 Chicago Commission on Race Relations report, http://homicide.northwestern.edu/pubs/negrochicago/.

"Jazz Age Chicago," http://chicago.urban-history.org/scrapbks/raceriot/raceriot.htm (newspaper accounts of the 1919 Chicago Riot).

"The Spanish-American War in U.S. Media Culture," by James Castonguay, at George Mason University, http://chnm.gmu.edu/aq/war/index.html.

"The Trial of Sheriff Joseph Shipp," http://www.law.umkc.edu/faculty/projects/ftrials/shipp/shipp.html.

"A War in Perspective: 1898–1998," New York Public Library online exhibition on the War of 1898, http://www.nypl.org/research/chss/epo/spanexhib/.

"The World of 1898: The Spanish-American War," Library of Congress, American Memory site, http://www.loc.gov/rr/hispanic/1898/.

Index

Addams, Jane, 30, 105
African Americans, 7–8, 42–45, 56–57, 81–82, 86–87, 132–36; blackface, 21, 150–51; Chicago race riot of 1919, 111–15; influence on popular culture, 11, 62–64; theory of "racial regression," 66–67, 148, 153. *See also* Lynching; National Association for the Advancement of Colored People; Niagara Movement
Alien enemies (during World War I), 83, 86, 106, 137; U.S. wartime policy toward, 138, 146
Alien Land laws, 142
American Protective Association (APA), 10
Americanization of immigrants, 138–41, 145–46. *See also* Nativism
Anarchist Exclusion Act (1901), 52
Anti-Catholicism, 10, 51, 55–56, 81, 83, 91, 140
Anti-Defamation League. *See* Anti-Semitism
Anti-Semitism, 10–11, 51, 140; Leo Frank case and, 82, 99–100, 140
Antiquities Act (1906), 47, 58
Aquinaldo, Ernesto, 11

Arizona Orphan Abduction, 55–56
Asian Americans, 48–51, 58–59, 61, 141–43. *See also* Chinese Americans; Filipinos; Japanese Americans; Korean Americans
Asian Exclusion League, 49, 50
Asiatic Barred Zone, 107, 108, 142, 145
Assimilation. *See* Nativism
Atlanta Compromise, 8, 44
Azusa Street Revival, 45, 63

Berlin, Irving, 66, 87, 149–50; "Oh! How I Hate to Get Up in the Morning," 126, 127–28
Birth of a Nation, The, 81, 100–105, 133, 148–49. *See also* W.E.B. Du Bois; Lynching; National Association for the Advancement of Colored People; Reconstruction
Bisbee Deportation, 83, 143–44, 145
Boas, Franz, 68, 153–54
Bolsheviks, 108, 109, 110, 111, 139, 147. *See also* Red Scare; Russian Revolution
Brandeis, Louis, 55, 140
"Bread and Roses" (Oppenheim), 115–16. *See also* Lawrence, Massachusetts, textile strike

Brice, Fannie, 65, 150, 151
Broken Blossom, 142–43
Brownsville riot (1906), 43
Buck v. Bell (1927), 10
Bureau of Indian Affairs, 20, 46, 47, 141
Burke Act (1906), 47, 58

Cahan, Abraham, 65. *See also The Forward*
Canadian immigrants, 51, 55, 64, 92
Cantor, Eddie, 150, 151
Carlisle Indian Industrial School, 20, 46, 47
Catholics, 11, 14, 16, 55, 64, 87, 90, 91, 140, 148. *See also* Anti-Catholicism
Chicago Defender, 61, 111, 113, 152
Chicago race riot, 111–15; Walter White on, 128–32
Chinese Americans, 9, 48–52, 56, 58, 59, 141; stereotypes of, 49, 142, 149
Cody, William ("Buffalo Bill"), 23, 52, 61, 140–41
Cohan, George M., 64, 87; and "Over There," 126–27
Committee on Public Information (CPI), 82, 106–7, 138, 145
Conley, Jim, and the trial of Leo Frank, 96–99
Council of National Defense, 107
Covello, Leonard, 138–39
Creel, George, 82–83, 107, 138. *See also* Committee on Public Information
Crisis, The, 115, 153. *See also* National Association for the Advancement of Colored People
Curtis, Edward Sheriff, 20–23
Czolgosz, Leon, 59

Dawes Severalty Act (1886), 20, 47, 58
Debs, Eugene V., 84, 145
DeMille, Cecil B., 23

Dewey, George, 11, 48
Dillingham Commission on Immigration, 53, 60, 67, 136
Dixon, Joseph K., and *The Vanishing Race*, 19–23, 140
Dixon, Thomas, and *The Birth of a Nation*, 101, 104, 133, 148–49
Du Bois, W.E.B.: *The Birth of a Nation*, 100–105; *The Crisis*, 153; criticism of Booker T. Washington, 8, 44; National Association for the Advancement of Colored People (NAACP), 44; Niagara Movement, 44; Reconstruction, 103–4
Dunning, William, 101, 104

East St. Louis Race Riot, 86–87, 134
Eliot, Charles W., 11, 66–67
Emergency Immigration Act (1921), 85, 107–8
Espionage Act (1917), 138, 145, 147
Ettor, Joe, 93, 95, 115
Eugenics, 10, 44, 52–53, 60, 68, 86, 120–21, 136, 153, 154
European immigrants and ethnics, 51–55, 85–86, 136–40, 145, 146; and immigration restriction, 9–10; Madison Grant on, 120–21
Expatriation Act (1907), 53

Factory Investigating Commission (New York), in wake of Triangle Fire, 90–91
Filipinos, 11–16, 49, 58
Fletcher, Rebecca Latimer, advocacy of lynching, 68
Flynn, Elizabeth Gurley, inspiration for "The Rebel Girl," 122
Ford, Henry, 81, 126
Foreign Language Information Service (FLIS), 106, 145
Forward, The, 54, 65

Frank, Leo, lynching of, 82, 95–100, 140–43
Fu Man Chu, 50–51, 142

Garvey, Marcus, and the Universal Negro Improvement Association (UNIA), 134
Gentlemen's Agreement, 9, 50, 59, 142
Gershwin, George, 149–50, 151
Giovannetti, Arturo, and "The Walker," 115, 116–20
Grant, Madison, 86, 120–21, 136, 154
Great migration of blacks to North, 111–12, 133–34
Griffith, D. W., 142; and *The Birth of a Nation*, 100–105, 148–49

Haymarket bombing, 52, 105
Haywood, William ("Big Bill"), 95, 145
Hiawatha, 20–22, 141
Hill, Joe, composer of "The Rebel Girl," 122
Holmes, Oliver Wendell, 10, 19
Hoover, J. Edgar, and the Palmer Raids, 110
Houston Race Riot (1917), 135
Hyphen, the, 82, 105, 126, 136, 138, 144, 147

Immigration and Naturalization Bureau, 53, 60, 138, 145
Immigration Restriction Act (1917), 85, 105–108, 144
Immigration Restriction Act (1924), 108
Immigration Restriction League, 36, 53, 59–60, 147
Industrial Workers of the World (IWW), 83, 147; and Joe Hill, 122; role in Bisbee copper strike (1917), 143–44, 145; role in "Bread and Roses" strike (Lawrence, 1912), 91–95

Intelligence Quotient (IQ) tests, 86, 154; and "Flynn Effect," 154
Irish Americans, 10; George Washington Plunkitt on, 34; Henry Cabot Lodge on, 39, 51; influence on popular culture, 64, 65, 87, 126–27, 151–52; role in 1919 Chicago race riot, 112; and Woodrow Wilson, 136

Japanese Americans, 33–34, 48–50, 56, 58–59, 141, 142
Japanese and Korean Exclusion League, 33–34
Jeffries, Jim, 43, 61
Jews, 10, 11, 51, 54–55, 60, 62–63, 65, 82, 83, 87, 136, 139–40, 140, 149–50, 151; blackface and "Jewface," 150–51; Madison Grant on, 120; and Yiddish theater, 149. *See also* Frank, Leo
Jim Crow. *See* Segregation
Johnson, Ed, lynching of, 16–19
Johnson, Jack, 43, 61, 62
Jolson, Al, 150–51
Joplin, Scott, 45, 63, 64

Kipling, Rudyard, and "The White Man's Burden," 15–16, 23–27, 48
Kishinev Massacre, 51
Knights of Mary Phagan, 82; and the lynching of Leo Frank, 100, 140
Know-Nothings, 10
Korean Americans, 33–34, 49, 50, 56, 59, 141–42
Ku Klux Klan (KKK), 81, 82; and *The Birth of a Nation*, 100–105, 133; and the lynching of Leo Frank, 140

Latinos, 55–56, 83, 143–44; Madison Grant on, 121
Lawrence, Massachusetts, textile strike ("Bread and Roses" strike of 1912), 91–95

Literacy test, 36–41, 53, 59–60, 107, 139, 147
Lodge, Henry Cabot, and restriction of immigration, 36–41, 60, 67, 107
Lone Wolf v. Hickcock (1903), 47, 57, 58
Longfellow, Henry Wadsworth, 21
Lynching, 8; *The Birth of a Nation*, 103; Ed Johnson, lynching of 16–19; George H. White Bill, 42, 57; Ida B. Wells on, 16, 30–33; Leo Frank, lynching of, 82, 95–100; NAACP march against, 134; Rebecca Latimer Fletcher on, 68

Marx Brothers, 151
Melting Pot, The, 53–54; Madison Grant on, 121
Mencken, H. L., 11, 151–52
Mexican Americans. *See* Latinos
Mind of Primitive Man, The, 68, 153
Minstrelsy, 21, 149–50
Mitchel, John Purroy, 103, 140
Motion pictures, 21–22, 62, 81, 100–105, 133, 142–43, 148–49. *See also Birth of a Nation, The*

National Association for the Advancement of Colored People (NAACP), *The Birth of a Nation*, campaign against, 100–105, 133; blacks in military, equal treatment of, 86; *The Crisis*, official publication of, 115, 153; founding of, 42, 44; lynching, 1917 NYC march against, 134; Marcus Garvey, opposition to, 134
Native Americans, 19–23, 45–48, 57–58, 140–41, 146
Nativism, 9–10, 52, 82; Red Scare and, 84–85, 139–40, 147; World War I and, 82–84, 107, 136–39
Naturalization Act (1906), 53

Neo-Lamarckianism, theory of, 36, 67–68, 153
Niagara Movement, 42, 44. *See also* National Association for the Advancement of Colored People

"Oh! How I Hate to Get Up in the Morning," 126, 127–28
"100 Per Cent. Americanism," 82, 126, 137
"100 Per Cent. Pro-American," 123
Oppenheim, James, "Bread and Roses," 115–16
Organic Act (1900), 58–59
"Over There" anthem of World War I, 126–27

Palmer, A. Mitchell, 84–85; role in First Red Scare, 108–11, 139, 147
Palmer Raids. *See* Red Scare
Perkins, Frances, 90–91
Phagan, Mary, murder of, 82, 95–100, 140
Philippines, war against, 11, 24–27, 29, 48–49
Phillips, U. B., 101, 104
Plessy v. Ferguson (1896), 7–8, 56–57
Plunkitt, George Washington, 34
Post, Louis F., 85, 111
Puerto Ricans, 55, 143, 146. *See also* Latinos

Race riots, 44–45, 111–15, 128–32, 134, 135–36
"Race suicide," theory of, 66–67
Racial and ethnic stereotypes, 10, 21, 23, 49, 65, 99, 105, 111, 142, 149, 150–51
Racial retrogression, theory of, 148–49, 153–54
Reconstruction, 42; *The Birth of a Nation* depiction of, 100–105, 133
Red Scare, 84–85, 108–11, 139–40, 147–48

Rohmer, Sax, 50, 142. *See also* Fu Man Chu
Roosevelt, Theodore, 8, 9, 11, 27–30, 42–43, 44, 48–49, 50, 53, 59, 60, 67, 68, 82, 105–6, 137
Ross, E. A., 10, 86, 136
Russian Revolution (1917), 84, 108, 109, 139

Schneiderman, Rose, 90–91
Seattle general strike (1919), 109, 139, 147
Segregation, 7–8, 42–45, 56–57, 112, 114, 132–36, 153
Seymour, Rev. William J., 45, 63. *See also* Azusa Street Revival
Shaler, Nathaniel Southgate, and theory of "racial retrogression," 67–68
Shipp, Sheriff Joseph, 8, 16–19
Smith, Al, 90, 148
St. Louis World's Fair (1904), Philippine Reservation at, 11–16
Steel Strike (1919), 84, 139
Steffens, Lincoln, 147; and *The Shame of the Cities*, 34–35
Strong, Anna Louise, and the Seattle General Strike, 109
Sweetser, Col. E. Roy, 91–92

Tammany Hall, 34–35, 60, 90, 148
Taylor, Nevada, 16–17
Thorpe, Jim, 46, 47–48
Tillman, Sen. Benjamin ("Pitchfork Ben"), 25–27
Triangle Fire, 87–91

Universal Negro Improvement Association (UNIA), 134–35

"The Uprising of the Twenty Thousand" (shirtwaist strike of 1909–1910), 54–55, 89. *See also* Triangle Fire

Vanishing Race, The (1913), 19–23, 140
Vaudeville, 45, 62, 63, 64

Wagner, Robert, 90
"The Walker" (Giovannetti), 115, 116–20
Walker, Francis Amasa, and "race suicide," 66–67
Walker, George, 65, 149
Walker, Madame C. J., 64
Wanamaker, John, 20–22, 140
Washington, Booker T., and the Atlanta Compromise, 8; criticized by W.E.B. Du Bois, 8, 44; invited to White House, 8, 42–43
Watson, Tom, 68; role in trial and lynching of Leo Frank, 99
Wells-Barnett, Ida B., antilynching campaign, 16, 30–33, 42
White, Cong. George H. (Rep., N.C.), antilynching bill, 42, 57
White, Walter, 45, 115; on "The Causes of the Chicago Race Riot," 128–32
"White Man's Burden," 15–16, 23–27, 48
Williams, Bert, 65, 149–50
Wilson, Woodrow, 82–84, 86, 101, 104, 105–8, 132–33, 136–40, 143, 144–45; speech to naturalized citizens (1915), 123–25
Winters v. United States (1908), 47, 57
World War I, 82–84, 86, 105–8, 136–39, 144–46

About the Author

JOHN F. MCCLYMER is Professor of History at Assumption College, Worcester, Massachusetts.